COMPARED AND CONTRASTED

WEAPONS OF WORLD WAR II

COMPARED AND CONTRASTED

WEAPONS OF WORLD WAR II

TOP SPEED · ARMAMENT · CALIBER · RATE OF FIRE

MICHAEL E. HASKEW

CHARTWELL
BOOKS, INC.

This edition published in 2012 by

CHARTWELL BOOKS, INC.
A division of
BOOK SALES, INC.
276 Fifth Avenue Suite 206
New York, New York 10001
USA

ISBN: 978-0-7858-2925-6

Project Editor: Michael Spilling
Design: Colin Hawes/Andrew Easton
Picture Research: Terry Forshaw

Printed in China

Contents

Introduction

The weapons of World War II refined the art of warfare, further developing a division of labour among armaments that had become more and more apparent during the conflicts of the first half of the twentieth century. The combat efficiency of modern weapons such as the tank, machine gun and submarine were dramatically improved while purpose-built weapons were conceived, rapidly tested and deployed to the field.

Comparing and contrasting World War II weapons begins with the understanding that some weapons of World War I actually survived intact for the subsequent generation of military operations, while others were forward reaching and futuristic in scope, without precedent. Despite the recent horrors of trench warfare during World War I, the subsequent financial constraints of the inter-war years, and the impact of the Great Depression, nations were compelled to augment and modernize their armed forces as the spectre of renewed conflict loomed.

In the case of tanks and armoured vehicles, those intended for reconnaissance, tank-versus-tank combat and infantry support were distinguished from one another, while self-propelled assault guns, tank destroyers, armoured cars, halftracks, and other equipment were designed and constructed to carry out clearly defined roles. Often, these weapons were capable of fulfilling multiple battlefield tasks, however, and their relative weight, firepower, range, and speed are considered on these pages.

Multiple Roles

Aircraft emerged as key players in the strategic and tactical outcome of World War II battles, with fast and agile fighters vying for domination of the skies to allow medium and heavy bombers to attack high value targets on the ground. The sleek fighters pushed the limits of piston engine performance, and eventually the war entered the jet age. Fighters were armed with an array of machine guns, cannon, and rockets capable of destroying an opponent in seconds.

The bombers carried payloads of massive destructive capability and were capable of laying waste to military targets as well as civilian infrastructure. A variety of patrol, ant-submarine, and reconnaissance aircraft were utilised during the war. Aircraft performance is evaluated with an eye to the role each was expected to play.

Artillery remained the heaviest of ground weapons during World War II, and its deployment was decisive on numerous occasions. Lighter field artillery and heavy weapons were designed and constructed to provide cover for offensive operations, break up enemy attacks, bombard fixed fortifications, and to silence enemy artillery. The plunging fire of the howitzer and the flatter trajectory of the cannon were combined, depending on the firing mission at hand, and the range of each weapon was critical to its success. Calibre, range, weight and rate of fire were all measurements of potential effectiveness.

Despite treaty restrictions, the major powers constructed mammoth warships that exceeded tonnage limitations and put behemoth battleships to sea in anticipation of the last major ship-versus-ship combat in history. However, the aircraft carrier emerged as the decisive weapon, while ships of all types conducted operations from strategic control of the sealanes to commerce raiding, convoy escort, shore bombardment, the landing of troops on hostile shores, and the transport of supplies and materiel. Evaluations of firepower, tonnage, range, capacity and mission-specific capabilities provide insight into the naval war across the globe.

Feature 1
Compares a key aspect of weapons' capabilities (in this case, service ceiling).

Feature 2
Compares a similar aspect of weapons' capabilities (here, maximum speed).

Feature 3
Some spreads include a third set of data for more detailed comparisons.

Weapons Type
Features a number of similar weapons types to compare relevant data.

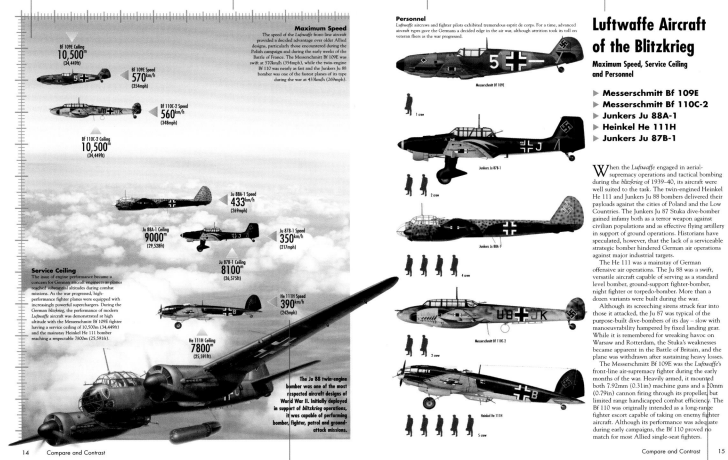

Within the image:

Maximum Speed
The speed of the *Luftwaffe* front-line aircraft provided a decided advantage over older Allied designs, particularly those encountered during the Polish campaign and during the early weeks of the Battle of France. The Messerschmitt Bf 109E was swift at 570km/h (354mph), while the twin-engine Bf 110 was nearly as fast and the Junkers Ju 88 bomber was one of the fastest planes of its type during the war at 433km/h (269mph).

Bf 109E Ceiling **10,500ᵐ** (34,449ft)

Bf 109E Speed **570**km/h (354mph)

Bf 110C-2 Speed **560**km/h (348mph)

Bf 110C-2 Ceiling **10,500ᵐ** (34,449ft)

Service Ceiling
The issue of engine performance became a concern for German aircraft engineers as planes reached substantial altitudes during combat missions. As the war progressed, high-performance fighter planes were equipped with increasingly powerful superchargers. During the German *blitzkrieg*, the performance of modern *Luftwaffe* aircraft was demonstrated at high altitude with the Messerschmitt Bf 109E fighter having a service ceiling of 10,500m (34,449ft) and the mainstay Heinkel He 111 bomber reaching a respectable 7800m (25,591ft).

Ju 88A-1 Speed **433**km/h (269mph)

Ju 88A-1 Ceiling **9000ᵐ** (29,528ft)

Ju 87B-1 Speed **350**km/h (217mph)

Ju 87B-1 Ceiling **8100ᵐ** (26,575ft)

He 111H Speed **390**km/h (242mph)

He 111H Ceiling **7800ᵐ** (25,591ft)

The Ju 88 twin-engine bomber was one of the most respected aircraft designs of World War II. Initially deployed in support of *blitzkrieg* operations, it was capable of performing bomber, fighter, patrol and ground-attack missions.

Personnel
Luftwaffe aircrews and fighter pilots exhibited tremendous esprit de corps. For a time, advanced aircraft types gave the Germans a decided edge in the air war, although attrition took its toll on veteran fliers as the war progressed.

Messerschmitt Bf 109E — 1 crew

Junkers Ju 87B-1 — 2 crew

Junkers Ju 88A-1 — 4 crew

Messerschmitt Bf 110C-2 — 2 crew

Heinkel He 111H — 5 crew

Luftwaffe Aircraft of the Blitzkrieg

Maximum Speed, Service Ceiling and Personnel

▶ **Messerschmitt Bf 109E**
▶ **Messerschmitt Bf 110C-2**
▶ **Junkers Ju 88A-1**
▶ **Heinkel He 111H**
▶ **Junkers Ju 87B-1**

When the *Luftwaffe* engaged in aerial-supremacy operations and tactical bombing during the *blitzkrieg* of 1939–40, its aircraft were well suited to the task. The twin-engined Heinkel He 111 and Junkers Ju 88 bombers delivered their payloads against the cities of Poland and the Low Countries. The Junkers Ju 87 Stuka dive-bomber gained infamy both as a terror weapon against civilian populations and as effective flying artillery in support of ground operations. Historians have speculated, however, that the lack of a serviceable strategic bomber hindered German air operations against major industrial targets.

The He 111 was a mainstay of German offensive air operations. The Ju 88 was a swift, versatile aircraft capable of serving as a standard level bomber, ground-support fighter-bomber, night fighter or torpedo-bomber. More than a dozen variants were built during the war.

Although its screeching sirens struck fear into those it attacked, the Ju 87 was typical of the purpose-built dive-bombers of its day – slow with manoeuvrability hampered by fixed landing gear. While it is remembered for wreaking havoc on Warsaw and Rotterdam, the Stuka's weaknesses became apparent in the Battle of Britain, and the plane was withdrawn after sustaining heavy losses.

The Messerschmitt Bf 109E was the *Luftwaffe's* front-line air-supremacy fighter during the early months of the war. Heavily armed, it mounted both 7.92mm (0.31in) machine guns and a 20mm (0.79in) cannon firing through its propeller, but limited range handicapped combat efficiency. The Bf 109 was originally intended as a long-range fighter escort capable of taking on enemy fighter aircraft. Although its performance was adequate during early campaigns, the Bf 110 proved no match for most Allied single-seat fighters.

Specifications
Includes specifications for precise comparison of data.

Analysis
Includes concise analysis to provide context for comparison.

Evolution

The evolution of small arms during the war is captured in the continuing issue of bolt action rifles to troops while the semi-automatic rifle, the submachine gun, the light and heavy machine gun, and eventually the world's first true assault rifles revolutionized the concept of warfare on the ground. The rate of fire, reliability, and magazine capacity of this type of weapon directly impacted on the combat efficiency of the individual soldier.

The weapons of World War II, therefore, present a diverse array of armaments, the tools that facilitated the momentous decisions made on the battlefield. Of course, determining the best of each weapons type is an exercise in subjectivity. For some, one strong attribute may outweigh a shortcoming in another area for a particular weapon. In the end, this book will answer some questions while raising others – encouraging the reader to look further into this fascinating field of study.

Air Power

The advent of air power transformed warfare in the twentieth century. Air supremacy became a prerequisite for other successful operations on the ground and at sea. During World War II, specialized aircraft types came into their own, with strategic and tactical applications. Heavy bombers conducted raids against enemy targets, both military and civilian. Fighters battled one another for mastery of the air. Medium and light bombers, patrol planes, ground-attack and reconnaissance aircraft and other types were produced in great numbers, while it became readily apparent that the development and deployment of air power were war-winning military endeavours.

Within this new sphere of modern warfare, the air forces of the major powers developed their own identities as independent services, growing steadily in strength, numbers and complexity. Technology advanced at a startling pace as the performance and firepower of propeller-driven aircraft increased substantially, ultimately ushering in the jet age.

LEFT: A North American P-51D Mustang fighter, named 'Ferocious Frankie' by its ground crew, carries out a patrol. This Mustang was regularly flown by Major Wallace Hopkins of the 374th Fighter Squadron, 361st Fighter Group.

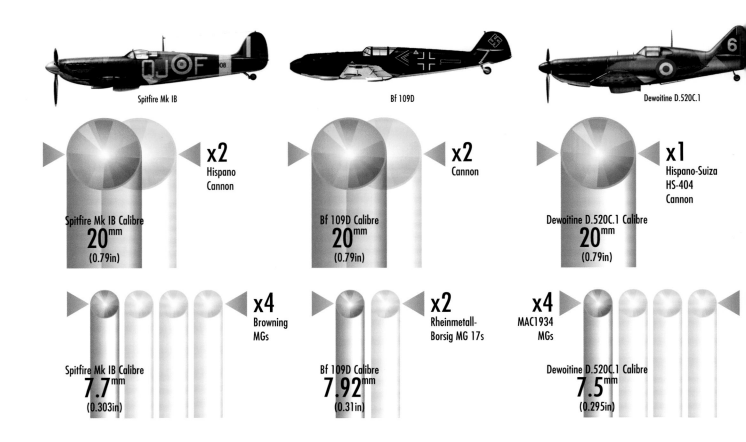

Spitfire Mk IB

Bf 109D

Dewoitine D.520C.1

x2 Hispano Cannon

Spitfire Mk IB Calibre
20mm
(0.79in)

x2 Cannon

Bf 109D Calibre
20mm
(0.79in)

x1 Hispano-Suiza HS-404 Cannon

Dewoitine D.520C.1 Calibre
20mm
(0.79in)

x4 Browning MGs

Spitfire Mk IB Calibre
7.7mm
(0.303in)

x2 Rheinmetall-Borsig MG 17s

Bf 109D Calibre
7.92mm
(0.31in)

x4 MAC1934 MGs

Dewoitine D.520C.1 Calibre
7.5mm
(0.295in)

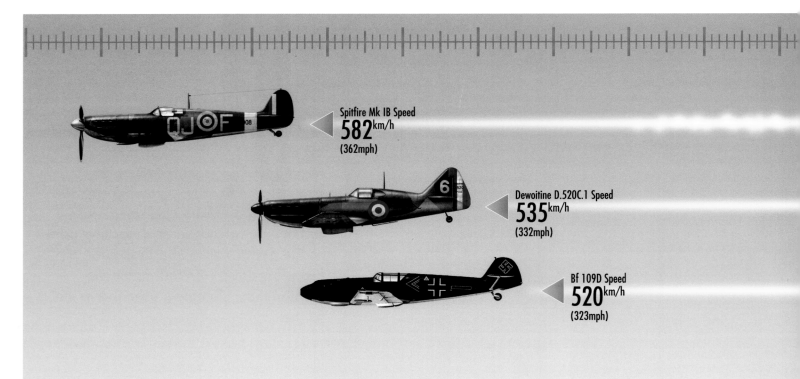

Spitfire Mk IB Speed
582km/h
(362mph)

Dewoitine D.520C.1 Speed
535km/h
(332mph)

Bf 109D Speed
520km/h
(323mph)

Maximum Speed

Outclassing the biplane designs of the interwar years, sleek monoplane fighters reached new blazing speeds as World War II approached. Soon enough, however, even these would be eclipsed by a new generation of late-war fighter aircraft. Among the fastest of the early wartime aircraft were the British Supermarine Spitfire Mk IB, the French Dewoitine D.520C.1 and the German Messerschmitt Bf 109D.

PZL P.11c

Gladiator Mk I

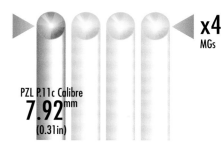

x4
MGs

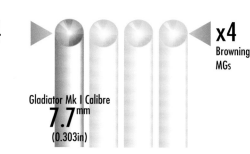

x4
Browning
MGs

PZL P.11c Calibre
7.92mm
(0.31in)

Gladiator Mk I Calibre
7.7mm
(0.303in)

Weapons Calibre
The most modern of early World War II fighters were not only faster than earlier biplane designs but also more heavily armed. British, French and German fighters regularly carried a combination of machine guns and 20mm (0.79in) cannon capable of downing an enemy aircraft with a single well-placed shot.

Fighters: European Theatre, 1939–40

Weapons Calibre and Maximum Speed

► **Supermarine Spitfire Mk IB**
► **Dewoitine D.520C.1**
► **Messerschmitt Bf 109D**
► **Gloster Gladiator Mk I**
► **PZL P.11c**

One of the heaviest weapons of World War II intended for true air-to-air combat was the 20mm (0.79in) cannon, and both the British Supermarine Spitfire Mk IB and some German Messerschmitt Bf 109Ds were equipped with the weapon to augment a complement of machine guns, 7.7mm (0.303in) and 7.92mm (0.31in) respectively. The earliest production models of the Bf 109D were armed with machine guns only, and the aircraft saw extensive action during the Spanish Civil War. By 1939, though, the improved Bf 109E was becoming available in larger numbers and the earlier version was withdrawn from service. The Spitfire Mk IB was equipped with a pair of wing-mounted 20mm (0.79in) cannon; however, these Hispano weapons were prone to jamming and the project was abandoned after only 30 examples of this Spitfire variant were produced for trials. Indeed in the case of both the Spitfire and the Bf 109, these early attempts to upgun machines that would become legend were largely failures.

The French Dewoitine D.520C.1 was comparable to its German adversary in many ways, even proving more manoeuvrable than the Bf 109E. However, a relative few reached the skies in defence of France since the aircraft was introduced in January 1940 and the Third Republic capitulated to the Germans six months later. The agile Spitfire was faster than its German or French counterparts with its 757.6kW (1030hp) Rolls-Royce Merlin engine.

Two biplane designs, already outclassed at the beginning of the war, the British Gloster Gladiator and the Polish PZL P.11c, were ponderously slow compared with new monoplanes developed in the 1930s. The PZL P.11c was armed with a scant pair of 7.92mm (0.31in) machine guns and retained the early open cockpit.

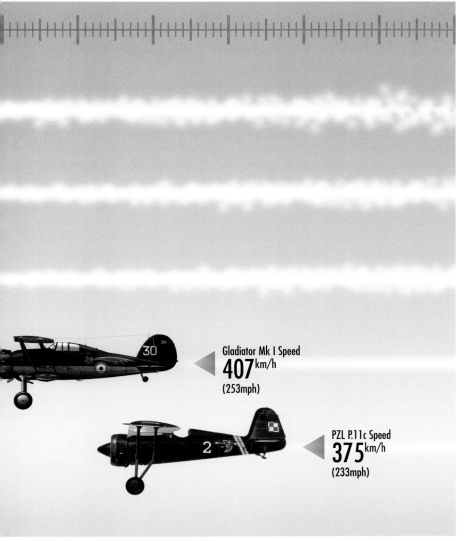

Gladiator Mk I Speed
407km/h
(253mph)

PZL P.11c Speed
375km/h
(233mph)

Flight Formations: Early 1940

Luftwaffe *Schwarm* versus RAF Flight; Maximum Speed

▶ **Messerschmitt Bf 109E-3**
▶ **Hawker Hurricane Mk I**

WING

LEADER

WING

Bf 109E-3 Speed
570 km/h
(354mph)

Practical experience gained during the Spanish Civil War validated the basic *Luftwaffe* flying formations of World War II, and for a time tipped the balance during air-to-air combat decidedly in favour of German pilots. The *Schwarm* was the brainchild of a pair of *Luftwaffe* fighter aces, Colonel Werner Mölders, the first pilot in history to reach 100 aerial victories, and Colonel Günther Lützow, who compiled 110 kills and more than 300 combat missions. Both achieved ace status in the skies over Spain.

The *Luftwaffe Schwarm* typically consisted of a pair of two-plane formations called *Rotten* (singular *Rotte*) flying in a loose formation similar to the fingers on an outstretched hand. In this formation, also referred to as the 'Finger Four', each pilot benefited from maximum visibility, while the aircraft were positioned for mutual support and quick reaction in combat situations. The *Schwarm* leader, or *Schwarmführer*, flew in the forward position with his wingman to the left, while the second *Rotte* took up station to his right.

In practice, the Finger Four proved vastly superior to the standard Royal Air Force (RAF) 'V' or 'Vic' formation, which required its three aircraft to remain in tight formation, with the leader slightly ahead and the two wingmen on each side. Due to the restrictive positioning in this formation, each pilot was required to pay close attention to the adjacent aircraft to avoid a mid-air collision. In the 'V' formation, only the leader was granted an advantageous field of vision.

Rapidly, Royal Air Force pilots recognized the deficiency of the Vic formation, and an attempt to remedy the situation with the rear Vic weaving to provide cover to three others in a larger formation was a dismal failure. In 1940, during the Battle of France and the subsequent Battle of Britain, RAF pilots adopted the Finger Four more frequently, particularly those under the command British ace Squadron Leader Douglas Bader.

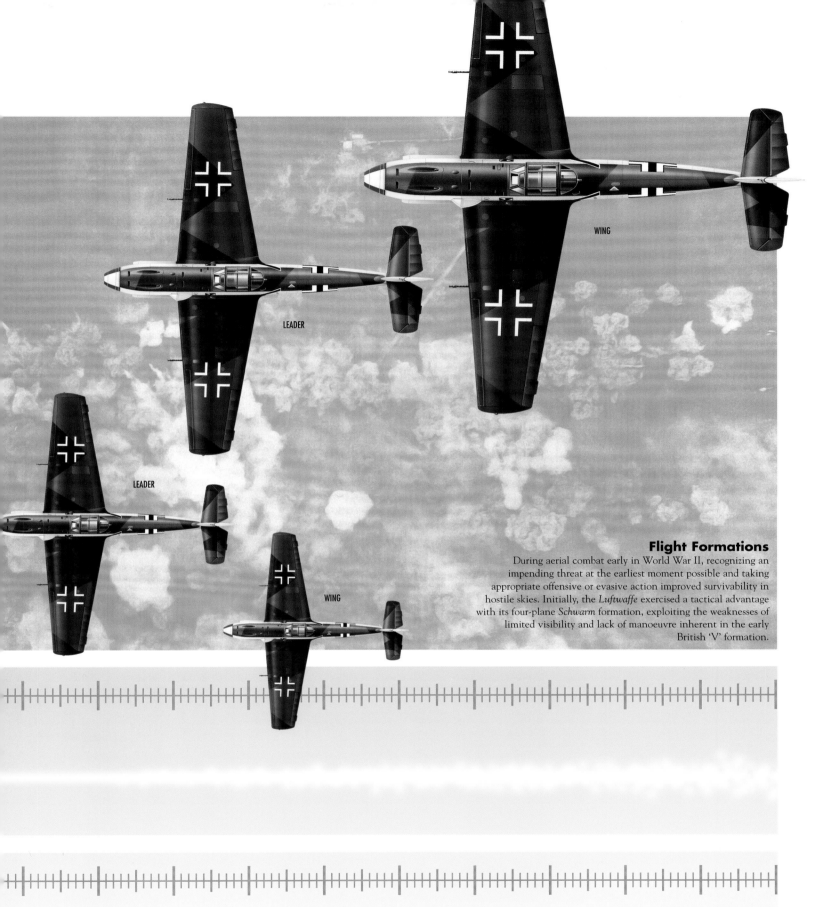

LEADER

WING

LEADER

WING

Flight Formations

During aerial combat early in World War II, recognizing an impending threat at the earliest moment possible and taking appropriate offensive or evasive action improved survivability in hostile skies. Initially, the *Luftwaffe* exercised a tactical advantage with its four-plane *Schwarm* formation, exploiting the weaknesses of limited visibility and lack of manoeuvre inherent in the early British 'V' formation.

Hurricane Mk I Speed
496 km/h
(308mph)

Maximum Speed

With its inverted V12 Daimler-Benz DB 601 engine, the German Bf 109E-3 fighter was substantially faster in the air than the most numerous modern fighter plane available to Britain's Royal Air Force, the Hawker Hurricane Mk I, powered by the 757.6kW (1030hp) Rolls-Royce Merlin Mk II or Mk III engine. The agile Bf 109E was capable of an airspeed of up to 570km/h (354mph), while the Hurricane could reach 496km/h (308mph).

Maximum Speed

The speed of the *Luftwaffe* front-line aircraft provided a decided advantage over older Allied designs, particularly those encountered during the Polish campaign and during the early weeks of the Battle of France. The Messerschmitt Bf 109E was swift at 570km/h (354mph), while the twin-engine Bf 110 was nearly as fast and the Junkers Ju 88 bomber was one of the fastest planes of its type during the war at 433km/h (269mph).

Bf 109E Ceiling
10,500ᵐ
(34,449ft)

Bf 109E Speed
570km/h
(354mph)

Bf 110C-2 Speed
560km/h
(348mph)

Bf 110C-2 Ceiling
10,500ᵐ
(34,449ft)

Ju 88A-1 Speed
433km/h
(269mph)

Ju 88A-1 Ceiling
9000ᵐ
(29,528ft)

Ju 87B-1 Speed
350km/h
(217mph)

Ju 87B-1 Ceiling
8100ᵐ
(26,575ft)

Service Ceiling

The issue of engine performance became a concern for German aircraft engineers as planes reached substantial altitudes during combat missions. As the war progressed, high-performance fighter planes were equipped with increasingly powerful superchargers. During the German *blitzkrieg*, the performance of modern *Luftwaffe* aircraft was demonstrated at high altitude with the Messerschmitt Bf 109E fighter having a service ceiling of 10,500m (34,449ft) and the mainstay Heinkel He 111 bomber reaching a respectable 7800m (25,591ft).

He 111H Speed
390km/h
(242mph)

He 111H Ceiling
7800ᵐ
(25,591ft)

LEFT: The Ju 88 twin-engine bomber was one of the most respected aircraft designs of World War II. Initially deployed in support of *blitzkrieg* operations, it was capable of performing bomber, fighter, patrol and ground-attack missions.

Personnel

Luftwaffe aircrews and fighter pilots exhibited tremendous esprit de corps. For a time, advanced aircraft types gave the Germans a decided edge in the air war, although attrition took its toll on veteran fliers as the war progressed.

Messerschmitt Bf 109E

1 crew

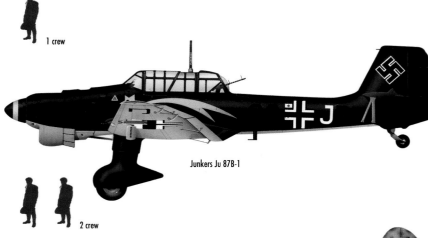

Junkers Ju 87B-1

2 crew

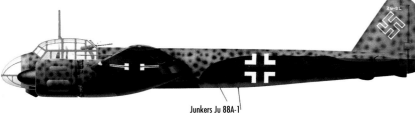

Junkers Ju 88A-1

4 crew

Messerschmitt Bf 110C-2

2 crew

Heinkel He 111H

5 crew

Luftwaffe Aircraft of the Blitzkrieg

Maximum Speed, Service Ceiling and Personnel

▶ **Messerschmitt Bf 109E**
▶ **Messerschmitt Bf 110C-2**
▶ **Junkers Ju 88A-1**
▶ **Heinkel He 111H**
▶ **Junkers Ju 87B-1**

When the *Luftwaffe* engaged in aerial-supremacy operations and tactical bombing during the *blitzkrieg* of 1939–40, its aircraft were well suited to the task. The twin-engined Heinkel He 111 and Junkers Ju 88 bombers delivered their payloads against the cities of Poland and the Low Countries. The Junkers Ju 87 Stuka dive-bomber gained infamy both as a terror weapon against civilian populations and as effective flying artillery in support of ground operations. Historians have speculated, however, that the lack of a serviceable strategic bomber hindered German air operations against major industrial targets.

The He 111 was a mainstay of German offensive air operations. The Ju 88 was a swift, versatile aircraft capable of serving as a standard level bomber, ground-support fighter-bomber, night fighter or torpedo-bomber. More than a dozen variants were built during the war.

Although its screeching sirens struck fear into those it attacked, the Ju 87 was typical of the purpose-built dive-bombers of its day – slow with manoeuvrability hampered by fixed landing gear. While it is remembered for wreaking havoc on Warsaw and Rotterdam, the Stuka's weaknesses became apparent in the Battle of Britain, and the plane was withdrawn after sustaining heavy losses.

The Messerschmitt Bf 109E was the *Luftwaffe*'s front-line air-supremacy fighter during the early months of the war. Heavily armed, it mounted both 7.92mm (0.31in) machine guns and a 20mm (0.79in) cannon firing through its propeller, but limited range handicapped combat efficiency. The Bf 110 was originally intended as a long-range fighter escort capable of taking on enemy fighter aircraft. Although its performance was adequate during early campaigns, the Bf 110 proved no match for most Allied single-seat fighters.

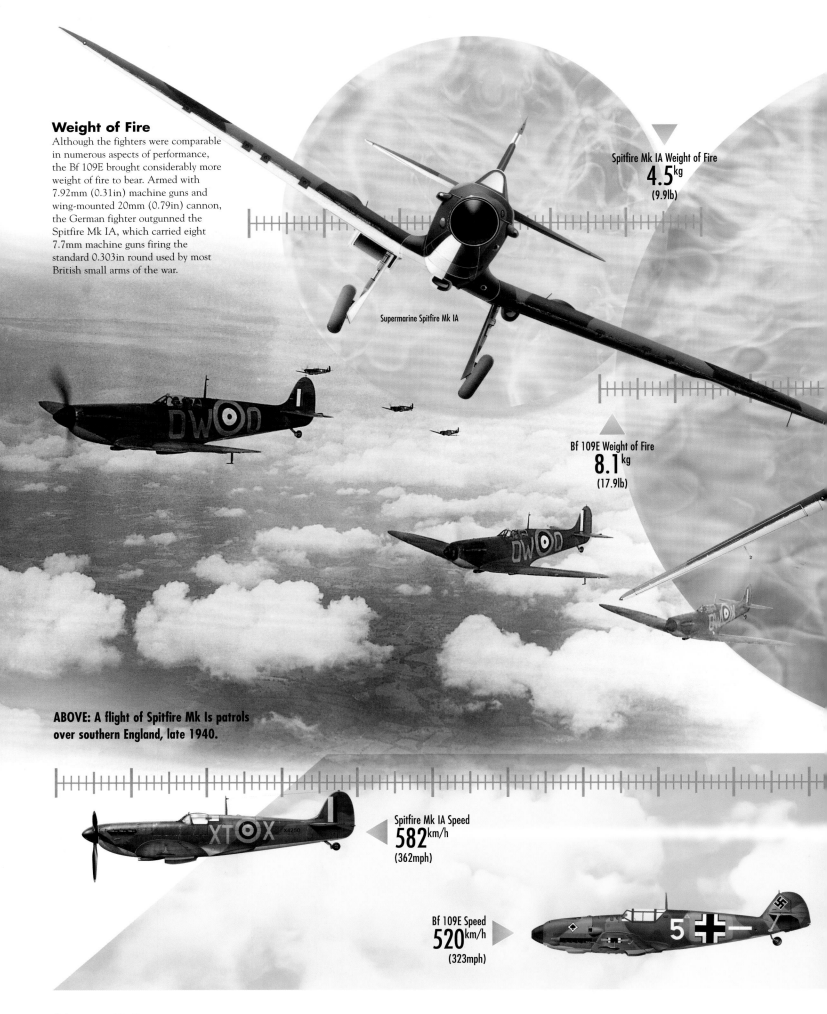

Weight of Fire

Although the fighters were comparable in numerous aspects of performance, the Bf 109E brought considerably more weight of fire to bear. Armed with 7.92mm (0.31in) machine guns and wing-mounted 20mm (0.79in) cannon, the German fighter outgunned the Spitfire Mk IA, which carried eight 7.7mm machine guns firing the standard 0.303in round used by most British small arms of the war.

Spitfire Mk IA Weight of Fire
4.5kg
(9.9lb)

Supermarine Spitfire Mk IA

Bf 109E Weight of Fire
8.1kg
(17.9lb)

ABOVE: A flight of Spitfire Mk Is patrols over southern England, late 1940.

Spitfire Mk IA Speed
582km/h
(362mph)

Bf 109E Speed
520km/h
(323mph)

Battle of Britain Fighters: 1940

Weight of Fire and Maximum Speed

▶ **Supermarine Spitfire Mk IA**
▶ **Messerschmitt Bf 109E**

Messerschmitt Bf 109E

The Supermarine Spitfire Mk IA and the Messerschmitt Bf 109E emerged from the Battle of Britain as icons of the air war. Both the Spitfire and the Bf 109 were developed in the 1930s, and variants served with the RAF and the *Luftwaffe* respectively throughout World War II.

During the Battle of Britain, which lasted from July to October 1940, the Royal Air Force fielded two primary fighter aircraft, the Spitfire and the Hawker Hurricane. The slower Hurricane was available in greater numbers, and British aerial tactics evolved with Hurricanes attacking German bomber formations while Spitfires engaged the enemy's front-line fighter escort, the Bf 109E.

While the Rolls-Royce Merlin engine of the Spitfire was capable of greater speed in level flight than the Messerschmitt's Daimler-Benz DB 601, pilots of both aircraft reported that their plane outclimbed its adversary. However, one distinct advantage for the Bf 109E was its weight of fire. Mounting two 7.92mm (0.31in) machine guns and 20mm (0.79in) cannon in each wing, the Messerschmitt outgunned the Spitfire Mk IA, which carried eight 7.7mm (0.303in) Browning machine guns. In combat conditions, the 20mm (0.79in) cannon could easily cause sufficient damage to send a Spitfire down in flames.

Aside from the Bf 109's advantage in firepower, the opposing fighters were well matched. However, the Messerschmitt expended the majority of its fuel during the flight across the Channel, allowing the aircraft only about 20 minutes in combat areas to preserve enough fuel for the return flight. Conversely, Spitfires and Hurricanes flew shorter distances from their bases, enabling them to remain in the air longer. Victory or defeat often hinged upon the skills of the pilots, which aircraft spotted the other first and the advantages of altitude and position of attack – such as out of the sun. During the Battle of Britain, the opposing aircraft proved comparable in overall performance. German losses in fighters and bombers were more than 1800 aircraft, and the British lost more than 1500 planes.

Maximum Speed
In level flight, the British Spitfire Mk I was capable of greater maximum speed than its German rival. In most respects, however, the performance of the two fighter planes was evenly matched, and victory in an aerial duel was determined by the relative skill of the opposing pilots.

Early Fighters: Pacific Theatre, 1941

Operational Range

- ▶ **Mitsubishi A6M Zero**
- ▶ **Brewster B-239 Buffalo**
- ▶ **Grumman F4F-4 Wildcat**
- ▶ **Aichi D-3**
- ▶ **Curtiss P-36 Hawk**
- ▶ **Nakajima Ki-27**

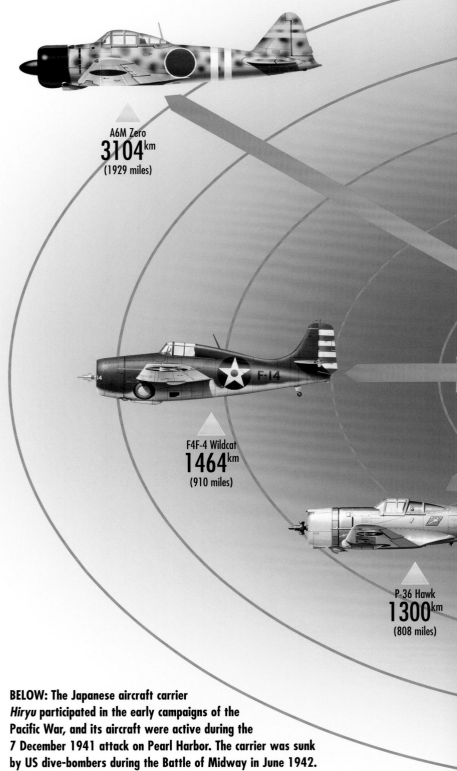

A6M Zero
3104^{km}
(1929 miles)

F4F-4 Wildcat
1464^{km}
(910 miles)

P-36 Hawk
1300^{km}
(808 miles)

Japanese aircraft designers relied on long range and high performance to maintain an edge in aerial combat, and during the early days of the Pacific War such an advantage was telling. In part, operational enhancements were achieved at the expense of such basic safeguards as self-sealing fuel tanks and armour protection for pilots and aircrew. Nimble fighters such as the Mitsubishi A6M Zero and Nakajima Ki-27 outclassed virtually every opposing fighter encountered early in the war. While the Zero, or Zeke as it was known to the Allies, served as the front-line carrier-based Japanese fighter throughout the war, the Ki-27 Nate was the primary fighter of Japan's air force during combat in China in the 1930s. By 1940, it was being replaced by the Nakajima Ki-43 Oscar.

The Aichi D-3 Val dive-bomber proved successful against both naval and land targets. The Val was distinguished by its fixed landing gear, while its heavy bomb load limited range somewhat, though not enough to prevent it taking part in the 7 December 1941 strike on Pearl Harbor from a distance of more than 322km (200 miles).

US fighter aircraft such as the Curtiss P-36 Hawk and Brewster Buffalo were designed in the mid-1930s. By the start of World War II, both were obsolete and saw limited action during the early days of the Pacific War. The emergence of the Grumman F4F Wildcat somewhat evened the odds against the Zero; indeed the Wildcat offered its pilot greater protection and survivability.

BELOW: The Japanese aircraft carrier
Hiryu **participated in the early campaigns of the Pacific War, and its aircraft were active during the 7 December 1941 attack on Pearl Harbor. The carrier was sunk by US dive-bombers during the Battle of Midway in June 1942.**

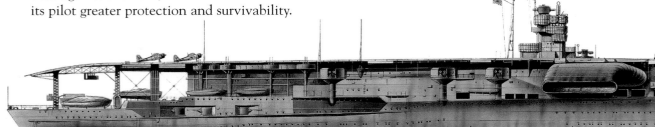

Operational Range

Outstanding range was an essential requirement of Japanese aircraft developed during the 1930s, as both the Imperial Army and Navy envisioned campaigns covering the Pacific Ocean and the interior of China and the Asian continent. However, high performance came at the cost of armour protection and self-sealing fuel tanks. Early US fighter aircraft were routinely outperformed until a new generation of combat planes eclipsed the Japanese models with lethal combinations of range, performance and survivability.

Aichi D-3
1352km
(840 miles)

B-239 Buffalo
1600km
(994 miles)

Ki-27
630km
(391 miles)

BELOW: Smoke billows from the aft section of the US aircraft carrier *Belleau Wood,* struck by a Japanese kamikaze suicide plane. Damage-control parties play fire hoses across the flight deck. As the Pacific War progressed, the Japanese became convinced that conventional air tactics utilizing bombs and torpedoes were insufficient to stem the American advance towards the home islands. Therefore, kamikaze attacks against US warships were initiated and caused extensive damage, particularly off the coast of Okinawa in the spring of 1945.

Torpedo-bombers

Bomb Load

▶ **Junkers Ju 88A-17**

▶ **Grumman TBF-1 Avenger**

▶ **Nakajima B5N**

▶ **Bristol Beaufighter TF Mk X**

▶ **Fairey Swordfish Mk I**

The development of the torpedo-bomber transformed war at sea, making the transit of warships and merchant vessels hazardous, particularly in the absence of air cover. Often, coordinated torpedo attacks involved several planes approaching from multiple directions to disperse anti-aircraft fire and increase the chance of a hit on the target.

Aerial torpedoes delivered by swarms of Japanese Nakajima B5N Kate torpedo-bombers crippled the US Pacific Fleet at Pearl Harbor on 7 December 1941, and three days later contributed to the sinking of the Royal Navy's *Prince of Wales* and *Repulse* off Malaya. Known for its speed and manoeuvrability, the Kate served with the Imperial Japanese Navy throughout World War II. Meanwhile, the US Navy struggled to deploy a torpedo-bomber with acceptable performance. Obsolescent types were replaced by the stout Grumman TBF Avenger, capable of carrying a single torpedo of substantial payload or conventional bombs and proving a robust carrier mainstay as the war progressed.

In the European Theatre the maritime variant of the Junkers Ju 88 carried a pair of torpedoes and frequently attacked Allied shipping in the Channel, combining speed and manoeuvrability to evade enemy fighters. The Bristol Beaufighter and Fairey Swordfish were contemporary British torpedo-bombers, with the Beaufighter beginning service as a heavy, long-range fighter variant of the Bristol Beaufort torpedo-bomber. As the war went on, the redesigned Beaufighter assumed the torpedo role as well.

The Swordfish was a flying anachronism, its biplane configuration and wood-and-canvas construction outdated by 1940. However, the aircraft performed admirably during the Fleet Air Arm attack on the Italian fleet anchored at Taranto in November of that year, following up with a decisive blow against the German battleship *Bismarck* the following May.

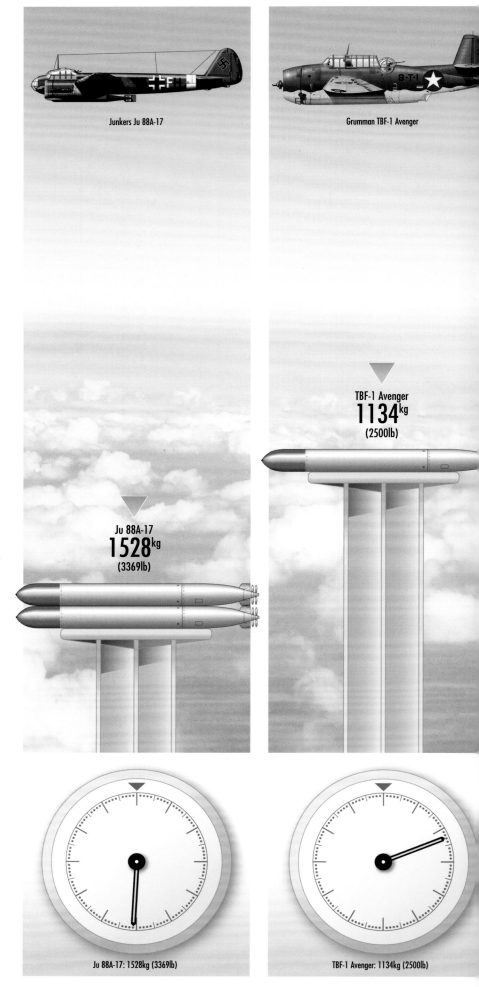

Junkers Ju 88A-17

Grumman TBF-1 Avenger

TBF-1 Avenger
1134kg
(2500lb)

Ju 88A-17
1528kg
(3369lb)

Ju 88A-17: 1528kg (3369lb)

TBF-1 Avenger: 1134kg (2500lb)

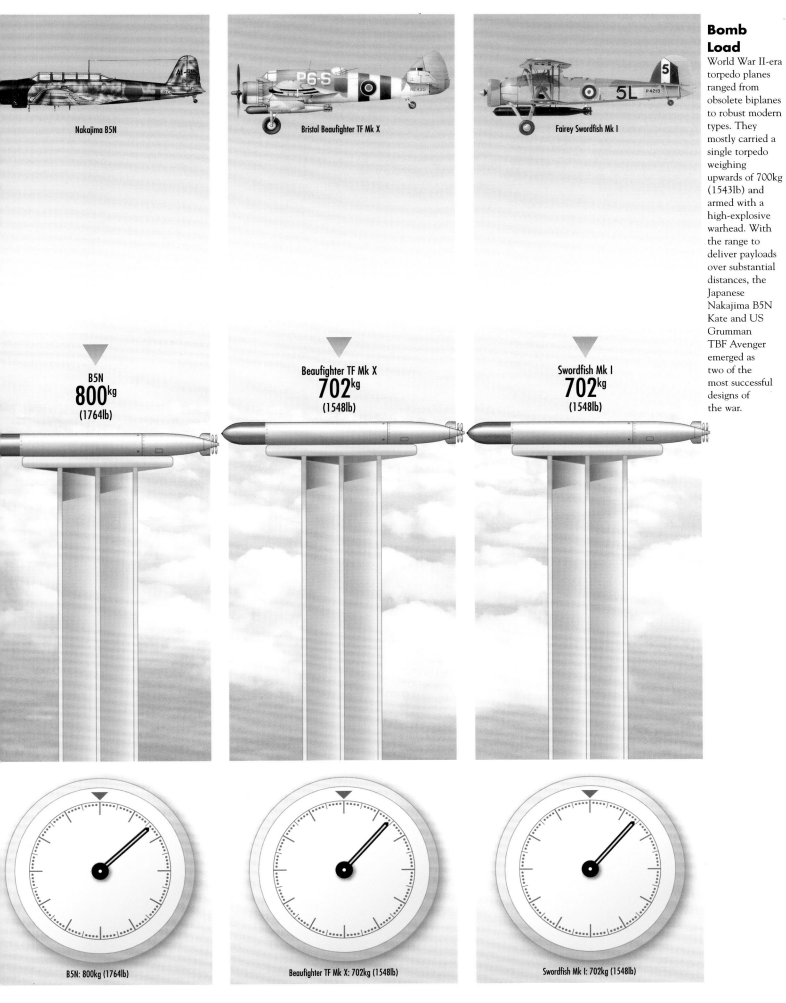

Bomb Load

World War II-era torpedo planes ranged from obsolete biplanes to robust modern types. They mostly carried a single torpedo weighing upwards of 700kg (1543lb) and armed with a high-explosive warhead. With the range to deliver payloads over substantial distances, the Japanese Nakajima B5N Kate and US Grumman TBF Avenger emerged as two of the most successful designs of the war.

Nakajima B5N

Bristol Beaufighter TF Mk X

Fairey Swordfish Mk I

B5N
800kg
(1764lb)

Beaufighter TF Mk X
702kg
(1548lb)

Swordfish Mk I
702kg
(1548lb)

B5N: 800kg (1764lb)

Beaufighter TF Mk X: 702kg (1548lb)

Swordfish Mk I: 702kg (1548lb)

Allied Ground-attack Aircraft 1

Bomb Load

- ▶ **Lockheed P-38J Lightning**
- ▶ **Republic P-47D Thunderbolt**
- ▶ **Hawker Typhoon Mk IB**
- ▶ **Hawker Tempest Mk V**
- ▶ **Supermarine Spitfire Mk XVIE**

The role of tactical air support was critical to the Allied victories in the Pacific and European theatres. In numerous cases, ground-attack aircraft were designed with multiple roles in mind. The exigencies of war dictated that improved aircraft enter service as soon as possible, and versatile designs were cost-efficient and eased pilot training.

Originally conceived as escort and air-supremacy fighters, the Lockheed P-38 Lightning and Republic P-47 Thunderbolt proved highly effective in the ground-attack role. Each was capable of carrying a variety of ordnance, including bombs and rockets, while the Lightning carried 12.7mm (0.5in) machine guns and 20mm (0.79in) cannon. The eight 12.7mm (0.5in) machine guns of the Thunderbolt were devastating to ground targets from troop concentrations to rail traffic.

Although the British Hawker firm envisioned the Typhoon as a capable air-to-air fighter, the type and its successor, the powerful Tempest, earned reputations as superb ground-attack planes. Following its combat debut in late 1943, the Typhoon ranged across northern Europe attacking convoys, bridges and enemy installations. In autumn 1944, the Spitfire Mk XVIE entered service uniquely armed for ground combat with up to four 20mm (0.79in) wing-mounted cannon.

American General George S. Patton Jr praised the ground-support efforts of the IX Tactical Air Force during his Third Army drive across France, and marauding Allied fighters restricted German troop and armour movement during daylight hours. Perhaps the most striking example of the devastation wrought by Allied ground-attack aircraft occurred at the Falaise Pocket in the summer of 1944. Thousands of German troops, tanks and vehicles were trapped, and Allied planes flew countless sorties against them.

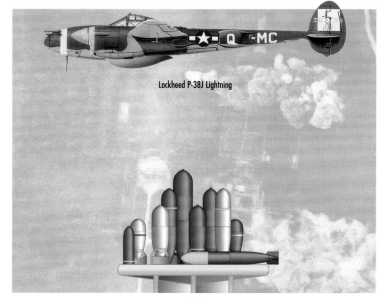

Lockheed P-38J Lightning

P-38J Lightning
1814 kg
(3999lb)

Bomb Load

Affixed to external hard points, significant bomb loads were carried by Allied ground-attack aircraft. These loads ranged from smaller fragmentation and anti-personnel bombs to heavy ordnance capable of penetrating fixed fortifications or destroying armoured vehicles. Often, fighter-bombers carried weapons that penetrated the thin upper armour of German tank turrets and chassis.

ABOVE: The Hawker Typhoon was a powerful, heavily armed aircraft that entered service with the RAF in 1943. Although its production run ended within a year, more than 3200 were built. The destructive power of the bombs and other ordnance carried by a single Typhoon has been compared to the broadside of a Royal Navy destroyer.

Republic P-47D Thunderbolt

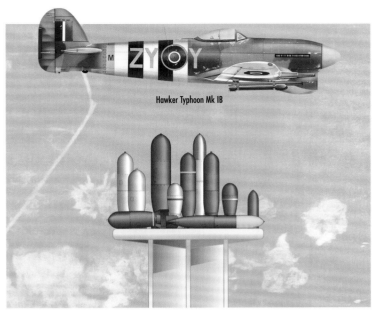

Hawker Typhoon Mk IB

P-47D Thunderbolt
1134kg
(2500lb)

Typhoon Mk IB
908kg
(2002lb)

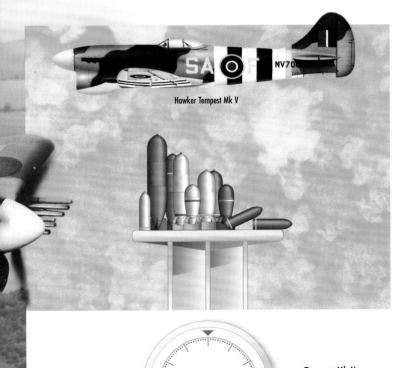

Hawker Tempest Mk V

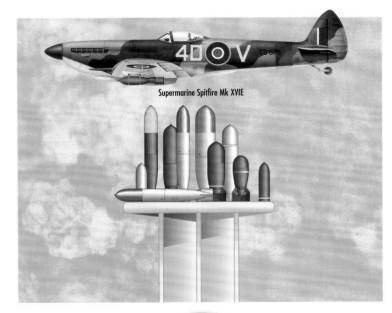

Supermarine Spitfire Mk XVIE

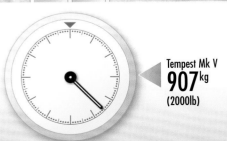

Tempest Mk V
907kg
(2000lb)

Spitfire Mk XVIE
456kg
(1005lb)

P-38J Lightning Speed
666 km/h
(414mph)

P-38J Lightning Ceiling
13,410 m
(43,996ft)

Maximum Speed

Often performing double duty as tactical air support and fighter-vs-fighter air cover, Allied ground-attack aircraft relied on adequate speed in order to engage enemy planes or dash out of the range of enemy anti-aircraft batteries, thus epitomizing the term 'fighter-bomber'.

Spitfire Mk XVIE Ceiling
12,650 m
(41,503ft)

Spitfire Mk XVIE Speed
707 km/h
(439mph)

P-47D Thunderbolt Speed
697 km/h
(433mph)

P-47D Thunderbolt Ceiling
12,495 m
(40,994ft)

Service Ceiling

Ground-attack fighters were often required to not only provide tactical support to infantry and armour but also take on enemy fighter aircraft. Service ceiling was an essential element in ground-attack-aircraft performance, allowing Allied planes to defend against enemy fighters attacking with the advantage of altitude and also to identify targets of opportunity.

Tempest Mk V Speed
686 km/h
(426mph)

Tempest Mk V Ceiling
10,975 m
(36,007ft)

Mosquito FB Mk VI Ceiling
10,515 m
(34,498ft)

Mosquito FB Mk VI Speed
595 km/h
(370mph)

Allied Ground Attack Aircraft 2

Maximum Speed, Service Ceiling and Rate of Climb

▶ **Lockheed P-38J Lightning**
▶ **Supermarine Spitfire Mk XVIE**
▶ **Republic P-47D Thunderbolt**
▶ **Hawker Tempest Mk V**
▶ **de Havilland Mosquito FB Mk VI**

Tactical air support was critical to the momentum of the Allied ground offensive in western Europe. Among the legendary ground-attack aircraft of World War II, several were adapted air-superiority fighters. The Republic P-47D Thunderbolt, of which more than 12,600 were built during the war, was nicknamed the 'Jug' and had hard points for bombs or rockets in addition to its machine guns. The Spitfire Mk XVIE, a bomb- or rocket-armed variant of the fighter, appeared late in the war, while the Hawker Tempest Mk V, based on the Typhoon, entered service in spring 1944. Noted for high performance at low altitudes, it was well suited to take on V-1 flying bombs launched at British cities.

The American Lockheed P-38J Lightning and British de Havilland Mosquito were versatile aircraft that performed recce and tactical-support functions. The Lightning was considered an outstanding fighter as well, and the Mosquito, constructed partially of wood, was one of the fastest aircraft of its type produced during the war.

Tempest Mk V Rate of Climb
1060 m/min
(3478ft/min)

P-47D Thunderbolt Rate of Climb
976 m/min
(3202ft/min)

Rate of Climb

Allied ground-attack pilots often chose steep-diving approaches when targeting enemy installations, troop concentrations and vehicles. Rate of climb was essential once a strafing or bombing run was completed, since the plane was within range of enemy anti-aircraft and small-arms fire and extremely vulnerable to German fighters attacking from above.

ABOVE: The Republic P-47D Thunderbolt was feared and respected by the Germans both as a ground-attack aircraft and in the bomber-escort role. Pilots loved the P-47D for its performance and firepower, as well as its ability to absorb tremendous punishment and remain aloft.

Night Fighters

Operational Range and Distances from London

▶ **Messerschmitt Bf 110G-4**
▶ **Heinkel He 219A**
▶ **Bristol Beaufighter Mk II**
▶ **Northrop P-61A**

With the advent of airborne radar, the night fighter came into its own as cities were attacked by waves of enemy bombers. The Bristol Beaufighter Mk IIF entered service in early 1941, just as British airborne interception radar was being introduced. The Beaufighter served in all theatres, and 70 Royal Air Force night-fighter pilots became aces flying the plane. The long-range Northrop P-61 Black Widow was the first US aircraft built specifically as a night fighter and the first designed to incorporate radar.

The German Messerschmitt Bf 110G-4 utilized the Lichtenstein airborne radar. Although its performance during daylight combat was disappointing, the Bf 110 was deadly as a night fighter. The advanced Heinkel He-219A mounted improved VHF (Very High Frequency) radar; however, fewer than 300 entered combat from 1943.

Rey

▶ 4200km (2610 miles)   ▶ 3500km (2175 miles)   ▶ 2800km (1740 miles)   ▶ 2100km (1305 miles)   ▶ 14

ABOVE: The Northrop P-61 Black Widow appeared late in the war and served with US squadrons in all theatres. Despite its heavy weight, the twin-boom design was powered by a pair of Pratt & Whitney R2800-10 Double Wasp engines, providing impressive range. The operator of the P-61's SCR-720 radar advised the pilot, who also had a small screen of his own, as to the location of potential targets.

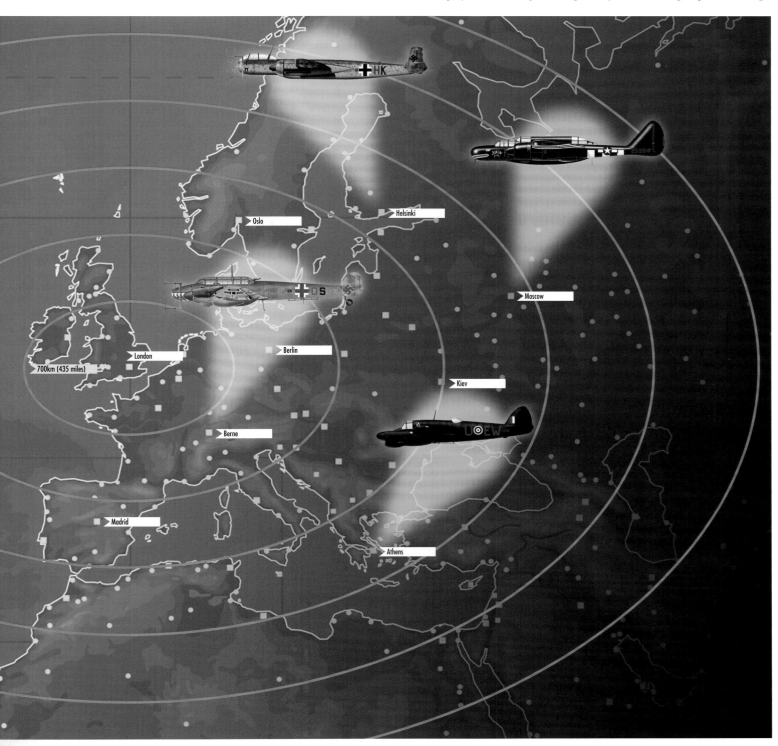

700km (435 miles)

Oslo

Helsinki

Moscow

London

Berlin

Kiev

Berne

Madrid

Athens

Bf 110G-4 Range
775km
(482 miles)

He 219A Range
1850km
(1150 miles)

Beaufighter Mk II Range
2414km
(1500 miles)

P-61A Range
3058km
(1900 miles)

Eastern Front: Tactical Aircraft

Weapons Calibre

- ▶ **Ilyushin Il-2m3**
- ▶ **Henschel Hs 129B**
- ▶ **Petlyakov Pe-2FT**

The pre-eminence of armoured formations on the battlefields of the Eastern Front compelled both the Germans and Soviets to develop tactical aircraft capable of light-bombing, infantry-support and ground-attack roles.

Soviet Premier Josef Stalin proclaimed that the Ilyushin Il-2 Shturmovik was as vital to the defence of the nation as air or bread. The Il-2 was built in greater numbers than any other aircraft of the war and packed a powerful offensive punch against enemy armour, while its pilot was protected by a steel 'bathtub' surrounding the cockpit. The Il-2m3 variant entered service in August 1942. The Petlyakov Pe-2 developed into the best Soviet light bomber of World War II, and its Pe-2FT variant, with a more powerful engine and defensive machine-gun armament, reached the Eastern Front in late 1942.

Luftwaffe planners envisioned the need for a tactical aircraft and developed the Henschel Hs 129 in 1937. The improved Hs 129B entered service in December 1941, serving primarily on the Eastern Front.

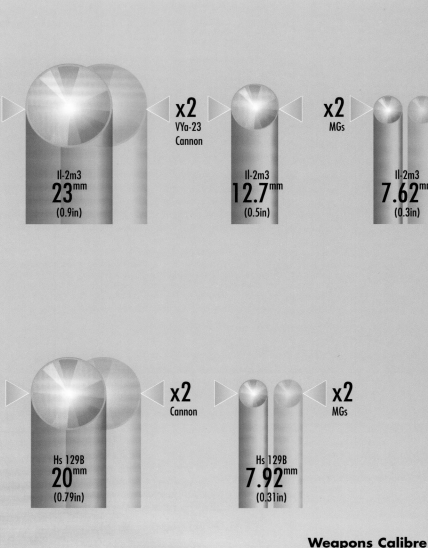

x2
VYa-23
Cannon

x2
MGs

Il-2m3
23mm
(0.9in)

Il-2m3
12.7mm
(0.5in)

Il-2m3
7.62mm
(0.3in)

x2
Cannon

x2
MGs

Hs 129B
20mm
(0.79in)

Hs 129B
7.92mm
(0.31in)

Weapons Calibre

Weapons calibres among tactical aircraft on the Eastern Front were steadily increased as the augmented armour protection of German and Soviet tanks became more challenging to penetrate. The firepower of 20mm (0.79in) and 30mm (1.2in) cannon was complemented by rockets and bombs, while pilots regularly attacked tanks where they were most vulnerable – at the comparatively lightly armoured top and rear.

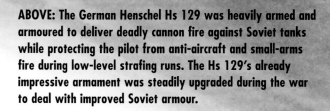

ABOVE: The German Henschel Hs 129 was heavily armed and armoured to deliver deadly cannon fire against Soviet tanks while protecting the pilot from anti-aircraft and small-arms fire during low-level strafing runs. The Hs 129's already impressive armament was steadily upgraded during the war to deal with improved Soviet armour.

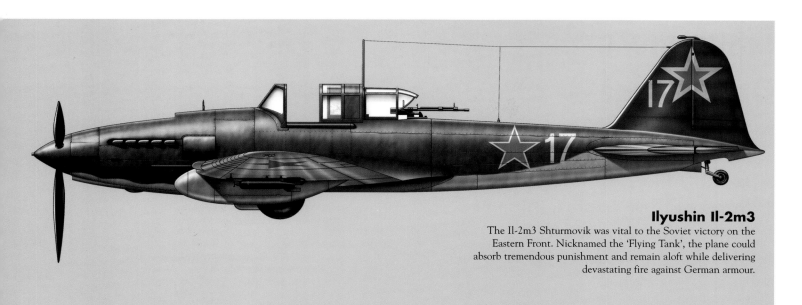

Ilyushin Il-2m3

The Il-2m3 Shturmovik was vital to the Soviet victory on the Eastern Front. Nicknamed the 'Flying Tank', the plane could absorb tremendous punishment and remain aloft while delivering devastating fire against German armour.

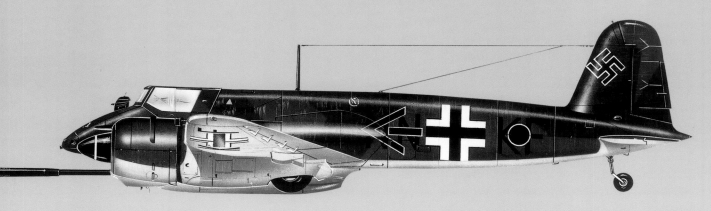

Henschel Hs 129B

The 20mm (0.79in) cannon and machine-gun armament of the Henschel Hs 129B were fired accurately from a steady aerial platform. The cannon was capable of penetrating the top or rear armour of the later Soviet T-34 and Josef Stalin series tanks.

Petlyakov Pe-2FT

The pilot and gunner of the Pe-2FT flew a versatile aircraft initially designed as a high-altitude fighter. As a light bomber, the plane was extremely agile, delivering a bomb load of up to 1200kg (2646lb).

x3
ShKAS MGs

Pe-2FT
7.62mm
(0.3in)

Interceptors Over Europe

Wing Span and Maximum Speed

▶ **North American P-51D**

▶ **Supermarine Spitfire Mk XIV**

▶ **Focke-Wulf Fw 190A-6**

▶ **Messerschmitt Bf 109G-6**

▶ **Yakovlev Yak-9**

ABOVE: P-51D Mustangs carry out a patrol somewhere over western Europe. A total of 8,156 were built.

During much of the air war over occupied Europe, Allied air forces struggled to develop a fighter that could escort bomber formations on long-range flights deep into Germany. German fighters such as the sleek Messerschmitt Bf 109G-6 and the Focke-Wulf Fw 190A-6 took a fearful toll of US heavy bombers during daylight raids. The late-production, high-performance Bf 109G-6, powered by a 1070.2kW (1455hp) Daimler-Benz DB 605 engine, was heavily armed, while the Fw 190A-6, introduced in the summer of 1943, compensated for earlier modifications that added weight with the introduction of a lighter wing; it also had substantially increased armament. While the comparatively shorter wing spans of these German aircraft produced less drag and additional air speed, they limited performance and manoeuvrability at high altitude, as the surface failed to generate the lift of opposing fighters with longer wing spans.

To counter improved German fighter variants, a new laminar-flow wing was installed on the top-performing British fighter, the Spitfire, and the resulting Mk XIV with a new aerofoil profile increased top speed by 89km/h (55mph) over its predecessor, the Mk XXI. Meanwhile, the German fighters of the late-war period met their match when US squadrons were equipped with the North American P-51 Mustang. The Mustang combined range and speed to deliver outstanding performance at high altitudes.

On the Eastern Front, Soviet aircraft engineers were faced with the necessity of rapidly developing an aircraft comparable to the latest German Messerschmitt and Focke-Wulf variants that decimated outmoded Red Air Force fighters. The Yakovlev Yak-9 entered service in late 1942, incorporating both metal and wood construction. It was produced in greater numbers than any other Soviet fighter in history.

Spitfire Mk XIV Speed
720km/h
(447mph)

P-51D Mustang Speed
703km/h
(437mph)

P-51D Mustang Wing Span
11.28ᵐ
(37ft)

Spitfire Mk XIV Wing Span
11.23ᵐ
(36.8ft)

Fw 190A-6 Wing Span
10.49ᵐ
(34.4ft)

Bf 109G-6 Wing Span
9.92ᵐ
(32.5ft)

Yak-9 Wing Span
9.74ᵐ
(32ft)

Wing Span

The wing span and wing surface of an aircraft are critical to generating sufficient lift to maintain performance as altitude increases. As World War II progressed, the introduction of redesigned wings along with higher-performance engines resulted in enhanced fighter capability.

ABOVE: A aerial view of a Yakovlev Yak-9. The Yak-9 entered service in October 1942.

Maximum Speed

Theoretically, a shorter wing span produces less drag and better aerodynamics in fighter aircraft, resulting in greater maximum speed and manoeuvrability at lower altitudes while sacrificing some degree of lift. During World War II, more powerful engines and lighter materials compensated somewhat for limitations in lift capacity.

Fw 190A-6 Speed
683km/h
(424mph)

Bf 109G-6 Speed
653km/h
(406mph)

Yak-9 Speed
591km/h
(367mph)

Normandy Campaign: Tactical Fighters

Weight of Fire and Weapons Calibre

▶ **Messerschmitt Bf 109G**
▶ **Hawker Typhoon 1B**
▶ **Republic P-47D Thunderbolt**

The Messerschmitt Bf 109G was one of the best multi-role fighters of the late war. The backbone of *Luftwaffe* fighter defence against Allied bombing raids, it was also responsible for ground support and air-to-air combat with Allied air-superiority fighters. To accomplish these missions, the 'G' series was equipped with numerous armament kits, including 13mm (0.51in) machine guns and 20mm (0.79in) cannon capable of delivering tremendous weight of fire and taking down an Allied bomber. The Bf 109G was also fitted with hard points for rockets and bombs, and its Daimler-Benz DB 605 engine was equipped with a supercharger.

The British Hawker Typhoon excelled in the tactical ground-support role, although its air-to-air performance was somewhat disappointing. The rocket- and cannon-firing Typhoon became one of the most successful aircraft of its type in the Allied arsenal, capable of destroying enemy tanks and other ground targets with a fusillade of 20mm (0.79in) shells. Painted with alternating black and white D-Day identification stripes, the Typhoon wreaked havoc during low-altitude attacks across the Norman countryside. Based on the success of the Typhoon, its successor, the Hawker Tempest, refined the art of tactical support in the waning months of the war.

The heavy Republic P-47 Thunderbolt proved an outstanding aircraft in the fighter-bomber role during the Normandy campaign and came to be known to the Germans as the 'Jabo'. Its eight wing-mounted 12.7mm (0.5in) machine guns produced withering fire in combat against German fighter aircraft and during strafing runs against ground targets, while its rockets and bombs proved devastating to German tanks, troop concentrations and rail and road transport. The Thunderbolt was capable of absorbing tremendous punishment; however, its low-level tactical-support missions required prolonged exposure to enemy flak, and significant numbers were shot down or damaged.

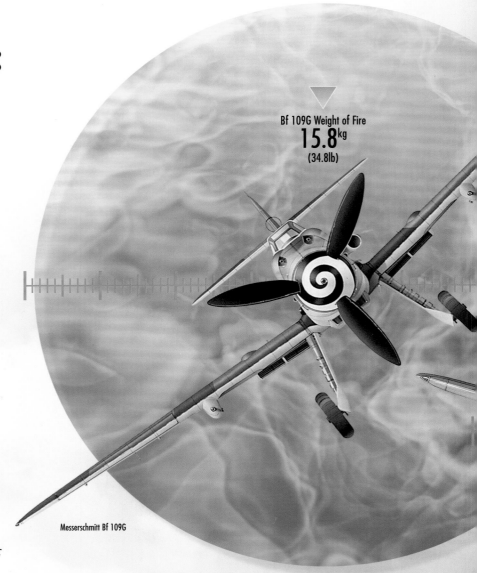

Bf 109G Weight of Fire
15.8kg
(34.8lb)

Messerschmitt Bf 109G

Weapons Calibre

Tactical fighter aircraft deployed during the Normandy campaign were heavily armed in anticipation of either aerial combat or operations against ground targets. To fulfil the requirements of multiple roles, both cannon and machine guns were mounted in substantial numbers.

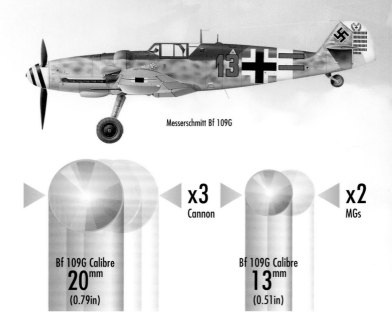

Messerschmitt Bf 109G

x3 Cannon   **x2** MGs

Bf 109G Calibre
20mm
(0.79in)

Bf 109G Calibre
13mm
(0.51in)

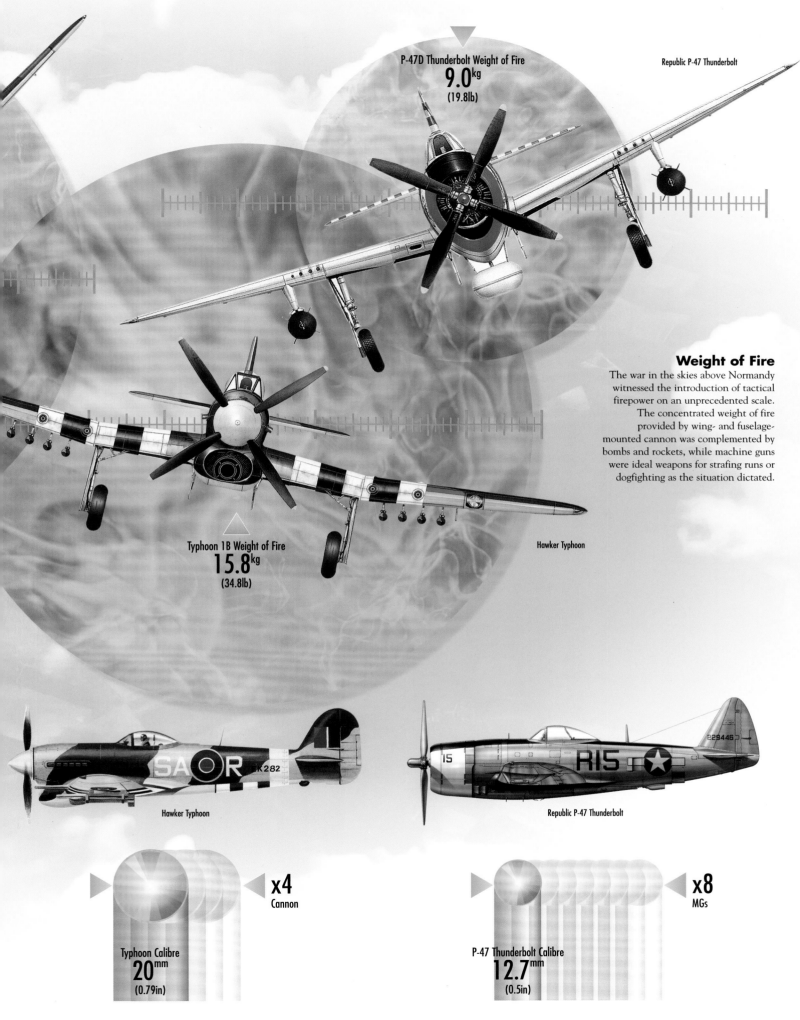

P-47D Thunderbolt Weight of Fire
9.0kg
(19.8lb)

Republic P-47 Thunderbolt

Weight of Fire

The war in the skies above Normandy witnessed the introduction of tactical firepower on an unprecedented scale. The concentrated weight of fire provided by wing- and fuselage-mounted cannon was complemented by bombs and rockets, while machine guns were ideal weapons for strafing runs or dogfighting as the situation dictated.

Typhoon 1B Weight of Fire
15.8kg
(34.8lb)

Hawker Typhoon

Hawker Typhoon

Republic P-47 Thunderbolt

Typhoon Calibre
20mm
(0.79in)

x4
Cannon

P-47 Thunderbolt Calibre
12.7mm
(0.5in)

x8
MGs

Allied Aircraft Durability

Vulnerability to German Aerial Cannon

▶ **Boeing B-17G Flying Fortress**
▶ **Avro Lancaster Mk III**
▶ **Supermarine Spitfire**

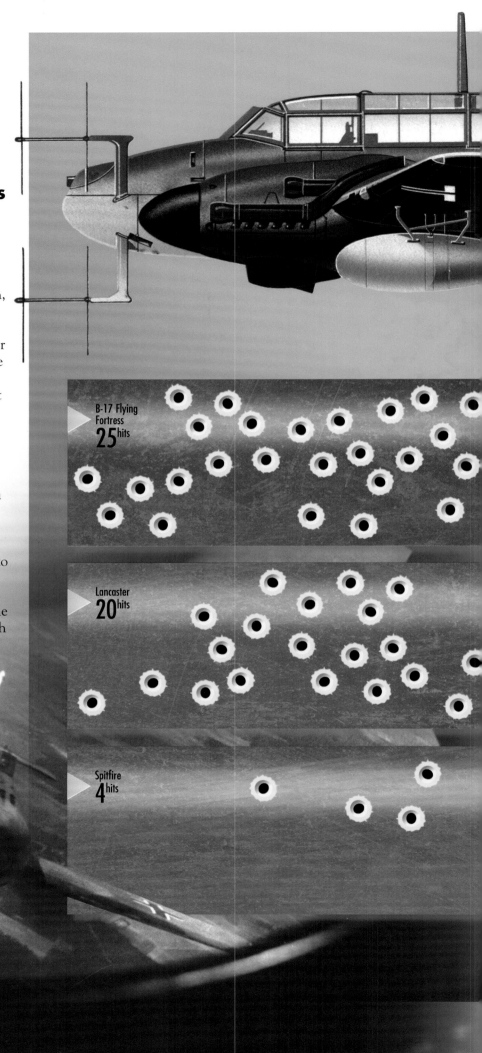

The 20mm (0.79in) MG 151/20 aerial cannon, produced by Waffenfabrik Mauser, and the drum-fed MG FF/M, designed by Ikaria Werke Berlin, were in widespread use in *Luftwaffe* fighter aircraft during the defensive struggle against large formations of Allied bombers striking cities and industrial targets across Germany. *Luftwaffe* night fighters such as the modified Messerschmitt Bf 110 as well as variants of the potent Focke-Wulf Fw 190 by day mounted these cannon with reasonably good performance against the British Avro Lancaster and US Boeing B-17 Flying Fortress heavy bombers. Both cannon delivered a relatively high rate of fire for such large-calibre weapons. *Luftwaffe* records indicate that German pilots were required to maintain contact and deliver an average of 25 hits from these cannon to bring down the rugged B-17, while an average of 20 was usually enough to send a Lancaster plunging earthwards in flames. Comparatively, the lighter airframes of Allied single-seat fighters such as the British Supermarine Spitfire were usually capable of sustaining only four 20mm (0.79in) hits before succumbing.

B-17 Flying Fortress
25 hits

Lancaster
20 hits

Spitfire
4 hits

Messerschmitt Bf 110 night fighter

Boeing B-17G Flying Fortress

Avro Lancaster Mk III

Supermarine Spitfire

Vulnerability

While a single well-placed 20mm (0.79in) cannon round could tear the wing off an RAF Spitfire or sufficiently disable its engine, the Spitfire's speed made it a difficult target for this weapon. Allied heavy bombers often withstood significant fire from German aerial cannon and returned to base.

OPPOSITE: The German Focke-Wulf Fw 190A demonstrated immediate superiority over its Allied fighter adversaries when it entered service in late 1941, and it was employed as an interceptor against Allied bombers for the rest of the war.

Allied Strategic Bombers 1

Range (from the North Pole)

▶ **Boeing B-29 Superfortress**
▶ **Consolidated B-24H Liberator**
▶ **Short Stirling Mk III**
▶ **Boeing B-17G Flying Fortress**
▶ **Avro Lancaster Mk III**

1 A prototype RAF Lancaster Mk III bomber stands on an airfield somewhere in Britain.

As Allied four-engine strategic bombers were required to traverse great distances to deliver their bomb loads during World War II, extended range became a primary goal of aircraft designers as the conflict progressed. The Boeing B-17 Flying Fortress remains the most recognized strategic bomber of the war; however, its 1930s design was limited in overall range and bomb-load capacity, eclipsed by its British counterparts the Avro Lancaster and Short Stirling and by the American Consolidated B-24 Liberator, introduced in large numbers by 1943. Nevertheless, the B-17 was loved by its crews for its survivability in combat. Stories abound of the B-17 absorbing tremendous battle damage and bringing its crew safely back to base in England. Even so, the range of the B-24 was nearly twice that of the B-17, while its bomb capacity was easily 25 per cent greater.

When it entered service with the RAF in February 1942, the Avro Lancaster quickly overshadowed the Short Stirling, the first operational four-engine British bomber of the war, which first flew in combat in 1941 and carried a heavier bomb load. The backbone of RAF night air raids against Germany, the Lancaster was also greatly loved by its crews and proved to be a rugged aircraft that absorbed considerable damage. The Lancaster could deliver heavier bomb tonnage than the B-24 or B-17 and outranged the latter by more than 1000km (621 miles).

Late in World War II, the innovative Boeing B-29 Superfortress entered service in the Pacific Theatre. The B-29 introduced substantially greater standard bomb-load capacity and such advances as the pressurized crew compartment and remote fire-control systems. The B-29 delivered the atomic bombs against Hiroshima and Nagasaki and was the primary weapon of the fire-bombing raids against other major Japanese cities during the closing months of the war.

Operational Range

Allied heavy bombers were obliged to cover great distances to complete their missions in both the European and Pacific theatres. Lighter airframes and greater fuel capacity improved range substantially. However, demand for bigger ordnance payloads remained in play as well, and achieving reasonable balance was an arduous task for Allied aircraft designers.

Washington DC

B-24H Liberator Range
5955km
(3700 miles)

Panama City

B-29 Superfortress Range
9382km
(5830 miles)

B-17G Flying Fortress Range
3219km
(2000 miles)

Stirling Mk III Range
3750km
(2330 miles)

NORTH POLE

Trondheim, Norway

Fairbanks, Alaska

Lancaster Mk III Range
4313km
(2680 miles)

Moscow

Boeing B-17 Flying Fortress

Maximum Speed

Aerodynamic improvements and more efficient powerplants provided Allied four-engine heavy bombers with greater maximum speed and range during World War II, although most basic designs had been developed in the 1930s with defence against enemy fighters in mind and maximum speed a somewhat secondary concern.

B-17G Speed
462 km/h
(287mph)

B-17G Ceiling
10,850 m
(35,597ft)

B-29 Speed
576 km/h
(358mph)

B-29 Ceiling
9710 m
(31,857ft)

B-24H Ceiling
8535 m
(28,002ft)

B-24H Speed
467 km/h
(290mph)

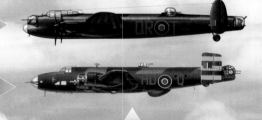

Lancaster Ceiling
7460 m
(24,475ft)

Lancaster Mk III Speed
452 km/h
(281mph)

Halifax Mk III Speed
454 km/h
(282mph)

Halifax Ceiling
7315 m
(23,999ft)

Service Ceiling

Higher service ceilings offered Allied strategic bombers some degree of defence against German fighters, particularly early variants whose performance was markedly diminished at greater altitudes, while the effective range of enemy anti-aircraft weapons was also stretched substantially. The increased service ceilings of later Allied bombers were countered by high-performance German fighters modified specifically to intercept bomber formations.

Stirling Ceiling
5030 m
(16,503ft)

Stirling Speed
410 km/h
(255mph)

Allied Strategic Bombers 2

Bomber Formation, Service Ceiling and Maximum Speed

▶ **Boeing B-17G Flying Fortress**
▶ **Boeing B-29 Superfortress**
▶ **Consolidated B-24H Liberator**
▶ **Avro Lancaster Mk III**
▶ **Handley Page Halifax Mk III**
▶ **Short Stirling Mk III**

The strategic-bombing campaign against the Third Reich was meant to degrade German industrial and armaments-manufacturing capacity and demoralize the civilian population. Debate continues to this day as to the success of its overall mission in light of the substantial cost in men and equipment to the US Army Air Forces and Royal Air Force Bomber Command.

The American Boeing B-17 Flying Fortress and the British Avro Lancaster remain iconic symbols of the air war over Europe. While the B-17, flying in tight box formation, bombed by day, the RAF Lancaster conducted nocturnal raids inside Germany. More than 7300 Lancasters were produced, and the plane was capable of carrying massive Blockbuster and Tallboy bombs in raids against hard targets. Essentially replacing the slower Short Stirling, the Lancaster was complemented by the Handley Page Halifax, which was capable of carrying 5800kg (12,787lb) of ordnance.

Combat Box Formation

The combat box was designed to provide maximum defensive support for bomber formations. The bombers were arranged in such a way that their various machine guns could provide interlocking fire against German fighter aircraft.

LEFT: The Avro Lancaster entered service with the Royal Air Force in February 1942 and became the mainstay of Bomber Command's offensive capability. The Lancaster developed a reputation as a versatile aircraft, bombing at night and during daylight precision attacks.

Supply Aircraft

Troop Capacity and Payload

▶ **Junkers Ju 52/3**
▶ **Douglas C-49K Skytrooper**
▶ **Curtiss C-46A Commando**
▶ **Messerschmitt Me 323 Gigant**

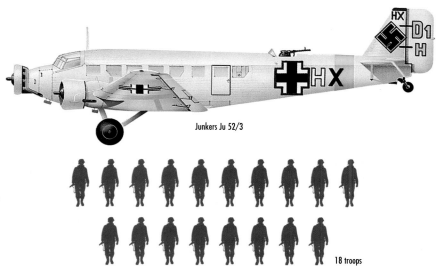

Junkers Ju 52/3

18 troops

Easily distinguishable with its three radial engines and corrugated-aluminum-alloy construction, the German Junkers Ju 52/3 was a workhorse of supply and troop movement for the German armed forces during World War II. In addition to delivering ground troops or airborne forces, the Ju 52/3 could carry a light cargo payload. Nicknamed 'Auntie Ju' by German airmen, the plane was susceptible to anti-aircraft fire, and large numbers were lost in operations in the Netherlands and Crete. Another German transport, the Messerschmitt Me 323 Gigant, was the largest transport aircraft of the war. It was derived from an earlier glider design and around 300 were placed in service up to 1944.

The US-built Curtiss C-46 Commando earned lasting fame – alongside the Douglas C-47 Skytrain, the military version of the commercial DC-3 airliner – as the primary supply aircraft flying the 'Hump', the route across the Himalayas from India to China. At the time of its introduction in 1941, the C-46 was the heaviest twin-engine aircraft in the world. More than 3100 were produced. A number of civilian DC-3s were acquired by the US military during World War II. Some of these were designated as the C-49K Skytrooper, with operational and design characteristics quite similar to the C-47.

Troop Capacity and Payload

Logistical supply and movement of troops by air came into their own during World War II. Often, transport capabilities spelled the difference between victory and defeat, as evidenced by the failure of the *Luftwaffe* to adequately supply the besieged German Sixth Army at Stalingrad.

Curtiss C-46A Commando

50 troops

LEFT: The German Ju 52/3mg5e was powered by three BMW radial engines and fitted with interchangeable floats or skis. This variant of the transport aircraft was particularly valuable during operations in Scandinavia and on the Eastern Front.

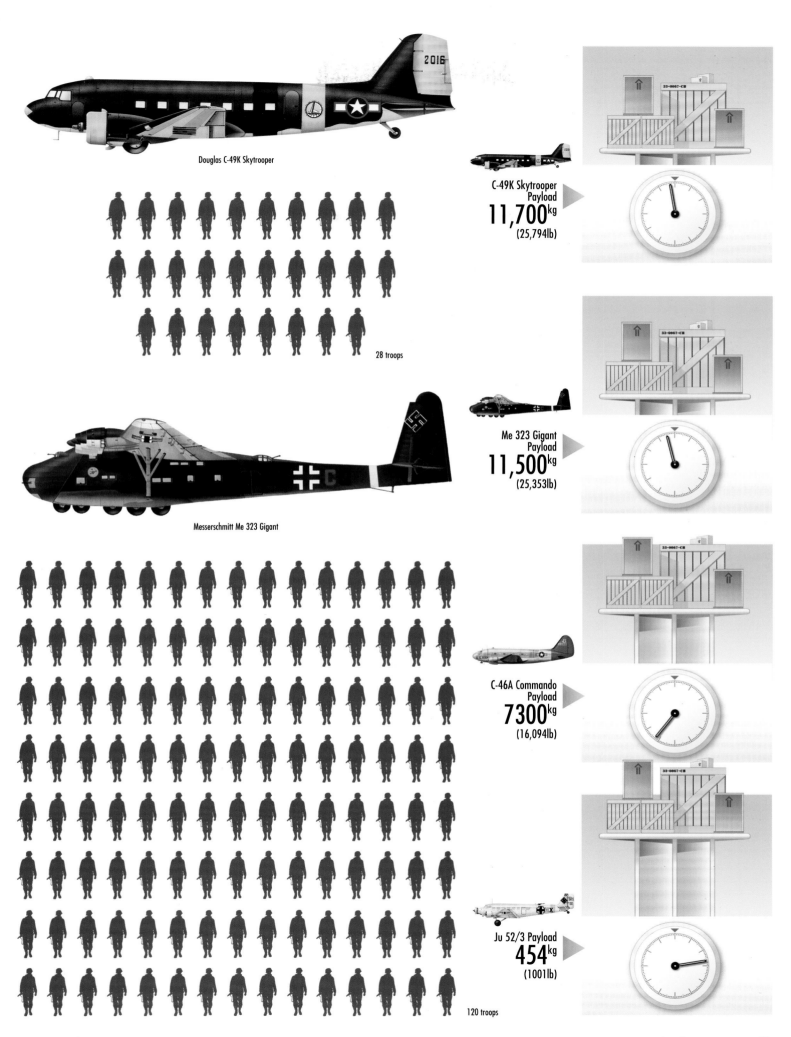

Douglas C-49K Skytrooper

28 troops

Messerschmitt Me 323 Gigant

120 troops

C-49K Skytrooper
Payload
11,700kg
(25,794lb)

Me 323 Gigant
Payload
11,500kg
(25,353lb)

C-46A Commando
Payload
7300kg
(16,094lb)

Ju 52/3 Payload
454kg
(1001lb)

Maximum Speed

The emergence of a relative few operational jet aircraft such as Germany's Messerschmitt Me 262 late in the war changed the dynamics of aerial combat. In terms of speed, jet engines far outclassed the highest performance piston engines, although the speeds achieved by some propeller aircraft such as the Focke-Wulf Fw-190A-4 were impressive.

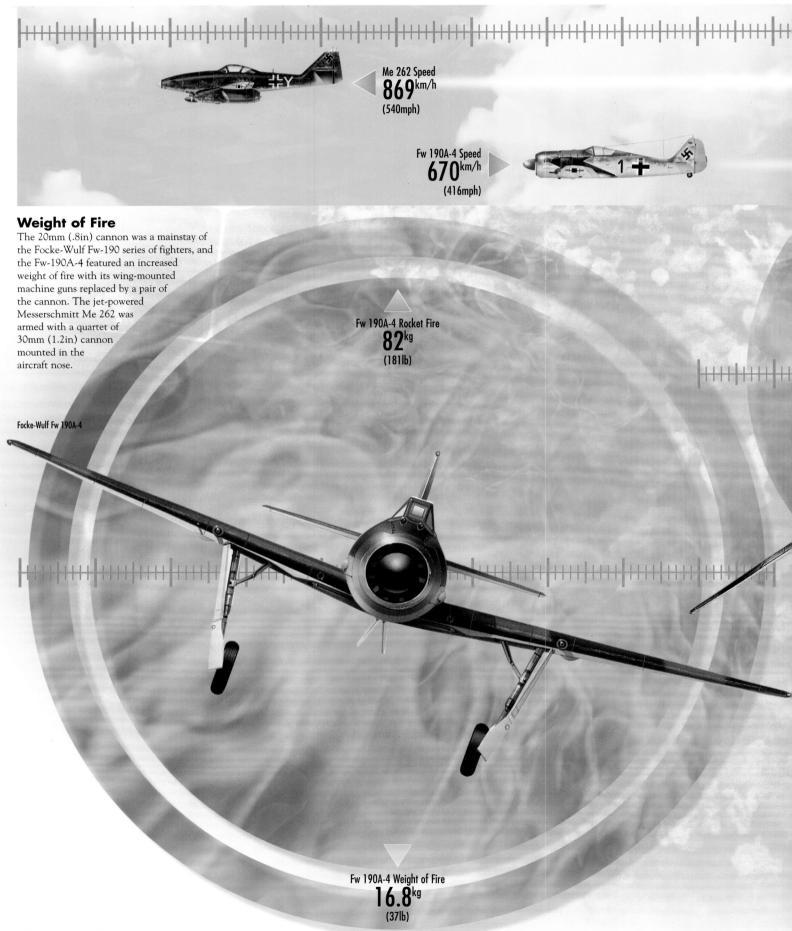

Me 262 Speed
869km/h
(540mph)

Fw 190A-4 Speed
670km/h
(416mph)

Weight of Fire

The 20mm (.8in) cannon was a mainstay of the Focke-Wulf Fw-190 series of fighters, and the Fw-190A-4 featured an increased weight of fire with its wing-mounted machine guns replaced by a pair of the cannon. The jet-powered Messerschmitt Me 262 was armed with a quartet of 30mm (1.2in) cannon mounted in the aircraft nose.

Fw 190A-4 Rocket Fire
82kg
(181lb)

Focke-Wulf Fw 190A-4

Fw 190A-4 Weight of Fire
16.8kg
(37lb)

Late-war Luftwaffe Fighters

Maximum Speed and Weight of Fire

▶ **Focke-Wulf Fw 190A-4**
▶ **Messerschmitt Me 262**

Me 262 Rocket Fire
24kg
(53lb)

Messerschmitt Me 262

Me 262 Weight of Fire
43kg
(95lb)

BELOW: Allied pilots were astonished when the Messerschmitt Me 262 jet fighter made its combat debut in the spring of 1944, slashing through bomber formations and outperforming piston-engine fighter adversaries. Armed with 30mm (1.2in) cannon, the Me 262 was most vulnerable during take-off and landing.

When the *Luftwaffe* introduced the jet-powered Messerschmitt Me 262 Schwalbe in April 1944, its twin Junkers Jumo turbojet engines produced far greater speed than any propeller-driven aircraft in service with the Allies. However, production was limited to slightly more than 1400, far too few to tip the balance of the air war in favour of Germany. To the detriment of German jet-aircraft deployment, Hitler had insisted that the Me 262 be developed primarily as a bomber. By the time he relented, production of the fighter was insufficient.

The Me 262 carried a heavy weight of fire. The Me 262A-1a fighter had four nose-mounted 30mm (1.2in) cannon, and in time 50mm (2in) R4M unguided rockets were also fitted. Even so, the 30mm (1.2in) weapon was rather inaccurate, particularly beyond a range of 590m (645yd). In the fighter-bomber role the Me 262 could carry 500kg (1102lb) of bombs.

The Focke-Wulf Fw 190A-4 fighter made its first combat appearance during the summer of 1942, retaining the substantial weight of fire of the preceding A-3 variant. With a pair of 7.92mm (0.31in) machine guns in the engine cowling and four wing-mounted 20mm (0.79in) cannon, the Fw 190A-4 was one of the most heavily armed fighters of World War II. In addition, its BMW 801D23 engine generated 1250.4kW (1700hp) with the MW-50 fuel boost of a water and methanol mixture.

170059

Maximum Speed

Rocket-powered *Luftwaffe* interceptors were capable of blinding speed; however, massive fuel consumption limited the length of time the aircraft could remain aloft. The jet engine proved to be more sustainable as a combat powerplant for the late-war fighters and bombers produced by several major aircraft firms.

Ba 349 Speed
1000km/h
(621mph)

Me 163 Speed
960km/h
(597mph)

Me 262A-1a Speed
870km/h
(541mph)

He 162A-2 Speed
840km/h
(522mph)

OPPOSITE: The rocket-powered Bachem Ba 349 Natter was controlled by an autopilot and functioned essentially as a manned missile. The unskilled pilot pointed the Ba 349 at its bomber target and fired its complement of rockets. Subsequently, the nose section was discarded, with the pilot and the remainder of the aircraft parachuting to earth. Reportedly, 10 were deployed but never launched.

Me 262B Speed
800km/h
(497mph)

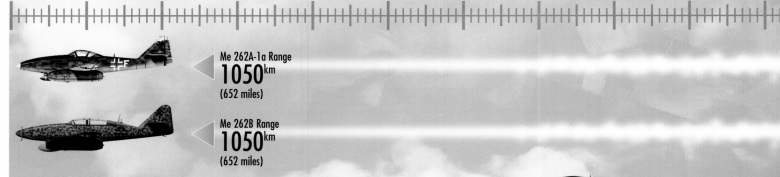

Me 262A-1a Range
1050km
(652 miles)

Me 262B Range
1050km
(652 miles)

He 162A-2 Range
660km
(410 miles)

Operational Range

For the late-war rocket-powered aircraft deployed by the *Luftwaffe*, the advantage of incredible speed was somewhat diminished by limited range and vulnerability while gliding to a landing with fuel expended. Conversely, jet-powered *Luftwaffe* fighter designs benefited from more fully developed technology and demonstrated the potential of such powerplants in future aerial combat.

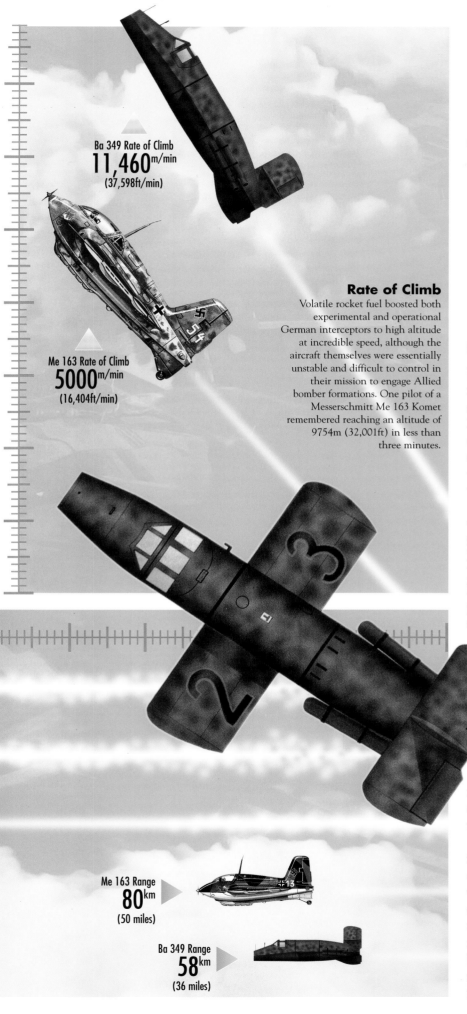

Ba 349 Rate of Climb
11,460 m/min
(37,598ft/min)

Me 163 Rate of Climb
5000 m/min
(16,404ft/min)

Rate of Climb
Volatile rocket fuel boosted both experimental and operational German interceptors to high altitude at incredible speed, although the aircraft themselves were essentially unstable and difficult to control in their mission to engage Allied bomber formations. One pilot of a Messerschmitt Me 163 Komet remembered reaching an altitude of 9754m (32,001ft) in less than three minutes.

Me 163 Range
80 km
(50 miles)

Ba 349 Range
58 km
(36 miles)

Luftwaffe Jet and Rocket Fighters

Maximum Speed, Range and Rate of Climb

▶ **Bachem Ba 349**
▶ **Messerschmitt Me 163**
▶ **Messerschmitt Me 262A-1a**
▶ **Heinkel He 162A-2**
▶ **Messerschmitt Me 262B**

German aircraft designers and engineers were developing jet engines even before the war began, and experimentation with rocket-powered interceptors was ongoing, too. By far the most successful German jet fighter of the war was the Messerschmitt Me 262, the first operational aircraft of its type in the world. A viable combat design as a fighter (Me 262A-1a), it was also produced as a tactical bomber (Me 262A-2a); a night-fighter variant, the Me 262B, was introduced as well.

Other German efforts to produce a jet fighter were plagued by a scarcity of production skills, facilities and qualified pilots. Although the *Luftwaffe* leadership had high hopes for the Heinkel He 162 Salamander, the type was hurriedly developed, going from drawings to production contracts within five weeks. The top speed of the He 162 was comparable to that of the Me 262, but the aircraft lacked range. The prototype first took to the air in December 1944 and exhibited significant instability during test flights. There was little time to remedy some of the design's shortcomings, and the He 162 was deployed to *Luftwaffe* squadrons in 1945. Around 275 were built.

A pair of notable rocket-powered interceptors, the Messerschmitt Me 163 Komet and the Bachem Ba 349 Natter, emerged late in the war. The Me 163 was in design as early as 1940, and its first test flight occurred the following year. By 1944, the Komet had become operational, and more than 300 were built by the war's end. Armed with either 30mm (1.2in) cannon or rockets, the Komet had been conceived to streak through Allied bomber formations, inflict as much damage as possible, then glide back to earth, landing on a skid. The Komet remains the only operational rocket-powered fighter aircraft in history.

Maritime Aircraft

Bomb Load

▶ **Kawanishi H6K**

▶ **Short Sunderland**

▶ **Consolidated PBY-6A Catalina**

▶ **Focke-Wulf Fw 200C-8/U-10**

▶ **Blohm & Voss Bv 138C-1/U-1**

BELOW: The Focke-Wulf Fw 200 Condor was an outstanding military conversion of a prewar civilian airliner that had set numerous range and endurance records. The Condor was operated by a crew of seven and armed with 20mm (0.79in) cannon and 13mm (0.51in) and 7.92mm (0.31in) machine guns.

Consolidated PBY-6A Catalina

Maritime aircraft performed a variety of roles during World War II, including reconnaissance, search and rescue, transport, supply, anti-submarine, and even anti-shipping and ground attack. The US Consolidated PBY Catalina served throughout the war, most notably in the Pacific Theatre, and demonstrated a range of around 4000km (2485 miles) and a speed of 288km/h (179mph).

The Kawanishi H6K Mavis flying boat had a top speed of 385km/h (239mph) with an impressive range of 6775km (4210 miles). In keeping with other Japanese aircraft, the H6K lacked armour protection and self-sealing fuel tanks and was vulnerable to enemy fire.

One of the finest flying boats in the history of maritime aviation, the British Short Sunderland gained lasting fame in the war against the U-boats in the Atlantic. Nicknamed the 'Flying Porcupine' by the Germans for its eight 7.7mm (0.303in) machine guns, it provided air cover for Allied convoys and conducted maritime patrols, with a maximum range of 1609km (1000 miles). The aircraft also served in the Pacific Theatre.

The versatile German Focke-Wulf Fw 200 Condor was noted for its reconnaissance capabilities and prowess as a bomber and torpedo aircraft attacking Allied convoys. The Condor's operational range stretched to nearly 3600km (2237 miles). The Blohm & Voss Bv 138 flying boat performed primarily in a reconnaissance role, shadowing convoys bound for the Soviet Union off the North Cape. Production was halted in 1943. The standard production Bv 138C-1 was armed with two 20mm (0.79in) cannon and multiple 13mm (0.51in) and 7.92mm (0.31in) machine guns. It had a maximum speed of 285km/h (177mph) and a range of 4300km (2672 miles).

Bomb Load

Capable of carrying a variety of ordnance, maritime aircraft of World War II regularly conducted torpedo and bombing runs against enemy shipping and attacked submerged or surfaced submarines, while some engaged in minelaying operations. Due to their great range and reconnaissance role, maritime aircraft were often the first to make contact with an enemy force.

PBY-6A Catalina
1814kg
(3999lb)

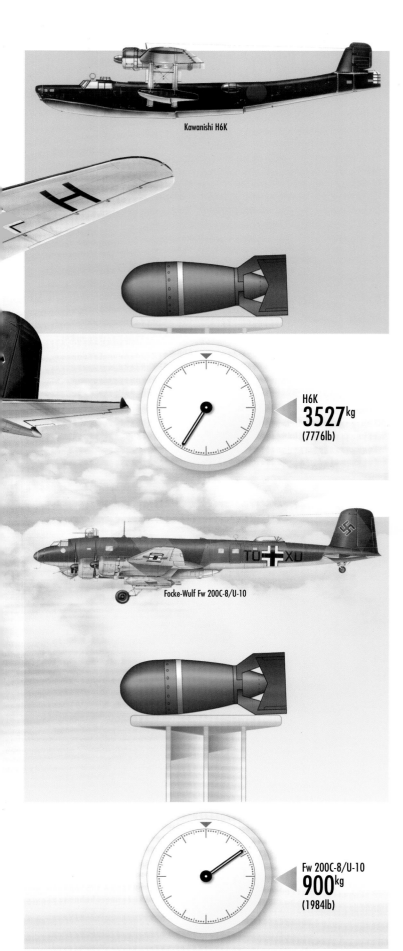

Kawanishi H6K

H6K
3527kg
(7776lb)

Focke-Wulf Fw 200C-8/U-10

Fw 200C-8/U-10
900kg
(1984lb)

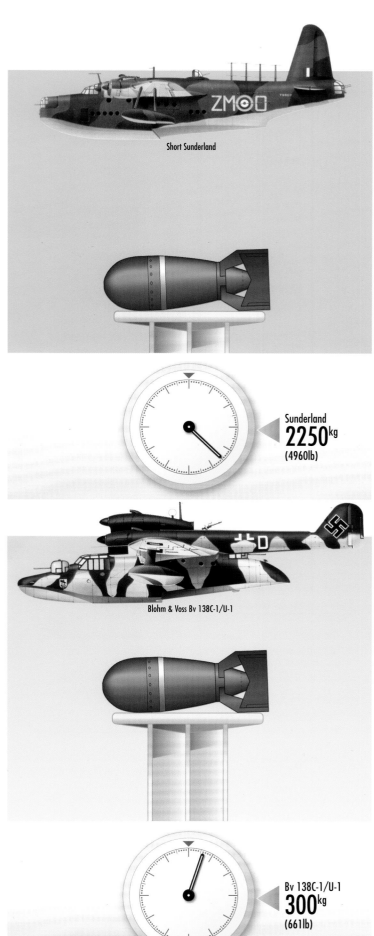

Short Sunderland

Sunderland
2250kg
(4960lb)

Blohm & Voss Bv 138C-1/U-1

Bv 138C-1/U-1
300kg
(661lb)

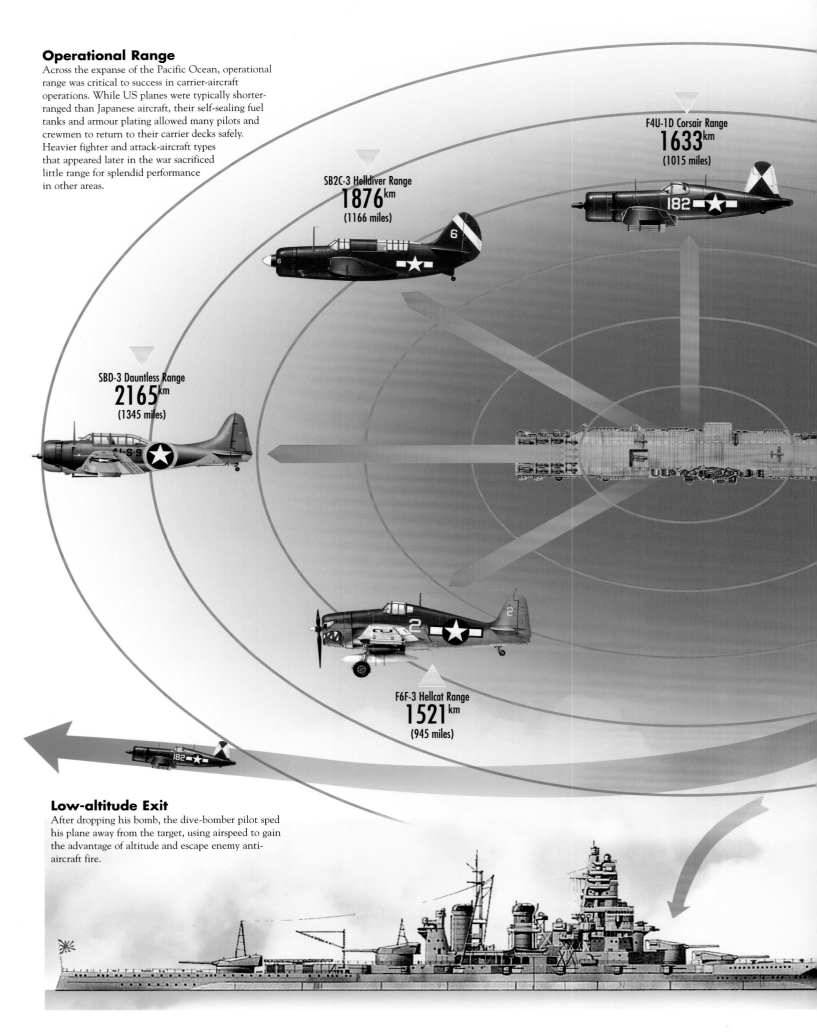

Operational Range

Across the expanse of the Pacific Ocean, operational range was critical to success in carrier-aircraft operations. While US planes were typically shorter-ranged than Japanese aircraft, their self-sealing fuel tanks and armour plating allowed many pilots and crewmen to return to their carrier decks safely. Heavier fighter and attack-aircraft types that appeared later in the war sacrificed little range for splendid performance in other areas.

F4U-1D Corsair Range
1633km
(1015 miles)

SB2C-3 Helldiver Range
1876km
(1166 miles)

SBD-3 Dauntless Range
2165km
(1345 miles)

F6F-3 Hellcat Range
1521km
(945 miles)

Low-altitude Exit

After dropping his bomb, the dive-bomber pilot sped his plane away from the target, using airspeed to gain the advantage of altitude and escape enemy anti-aircraft fire.

US Navy Carrier Strike Power

Operational Range and Dive-bomber Tactics

▶ **Douglas SBD-3 Dauntless**
▶ **Curtiss SB2C-3 Helldiver**
▶ **Vought F4U-1D Corsair**
▶ **General Motors TBM-3 Avenger**
▶ **Grumman F6F-3 Hellcat**

Altitude

The dive-bomber pilot maintained a sufficient altitude of around 4260m (13,976ft) from which to begin an attack. Altitude was critical to avoid detection by enemy warships below and to provide the air speed necessary in a 70-degree dive to deliver the bomb accurately.

TBM-3 Avenger Range
1626km
(1010 miles)

Dive Speed

Holding his aircraft in a steep, steady dive towards the target below, the dive-bomber pilot gained airspeed and maintained course, despite intensifying anti-aircraft fire and the violent manoeuvring of the target vessel. The bomb was released at roughly 300m (984ft) so that the aircraft avoided any blast from the explosion.

As the war continued, heavier, high-performance aircraft provided the US Navy with a formidable offensive capability. Although the Douglas SBD Dauntless had entered service in 1940 and performed admirably, it was one of several naval aircraft supplanted by a new generation of carrier-based planes that emerged rapidly with the exigencies of war. In December 1942, the heavier Curtiss Helldiver began replacing the Dauntless, and while its range was slightly diminished, the Helldiver was capable of greater speed than its predecessor. The Grumman/General Motors TBF/TBM Avenger torpedo-bomber replaced the Douglas TBD Devastator, which had been decimated by nimble Japanese Zero fighters at Midway in 1942.

The robust, well-armed Grumman F6F Hellcat and Vought F4U Corsair fighters reached US carrier decks in significant numbers by 1943, replacing the Grumman F4F Wildcat. The Hellcat and Corsair both proved superior to the Japanese Zero in air-to-air combat, recording positive kill ratios. The Corsair, nicknamed 'Whistling Death' by the Japanese, served into the 1960s as a superb fighter-bomber.

RIGHT: The Douglas SBD Dauntless dive-bomber remains one of the most famous carrier attack aircraft in US naval history due to the exploits of its pilots during the Battle of Midway.

Armoured Fighting Vehicles

Conceived and deployed on the battlefield for the first time only a generation earlier, armoured fighting vehicles became integral components of coordinated land warfare during World War II. With the capacity to achieve and exploit a breakthrough of enemy lines, rapidly gain territory and provide their own source of supporting artillery and direct fire support, armoured fighting vehicles contributed greatly to the war of rapid movement that characterized much of the fighting on the Eastern and Western fronts in Europe.

In the Pacific, the superiority of American armour was telling throughout the island-hopping offensive towards the Japanese home islands. As armoured fighting vehicles grew in firepower and armour protection, a division of labour emerged, with purpose-built vehicles coming into service to take on enemy tanks, support infantry operations, destroy fixed fortifications and provide mobile artillery support. Concurrently, armoured infantry and reconnaissance units fielded an array of troop-carrying halftracks and armoured cars to provide necessary additional support for effective operations.

LEFT: A US infantry squad take shelter behind an American Sherman M4A4 tank somewhere in northern France during the liberation of Europe, 1944. Almost 50,000 Shermans of all types were produced during the war years.

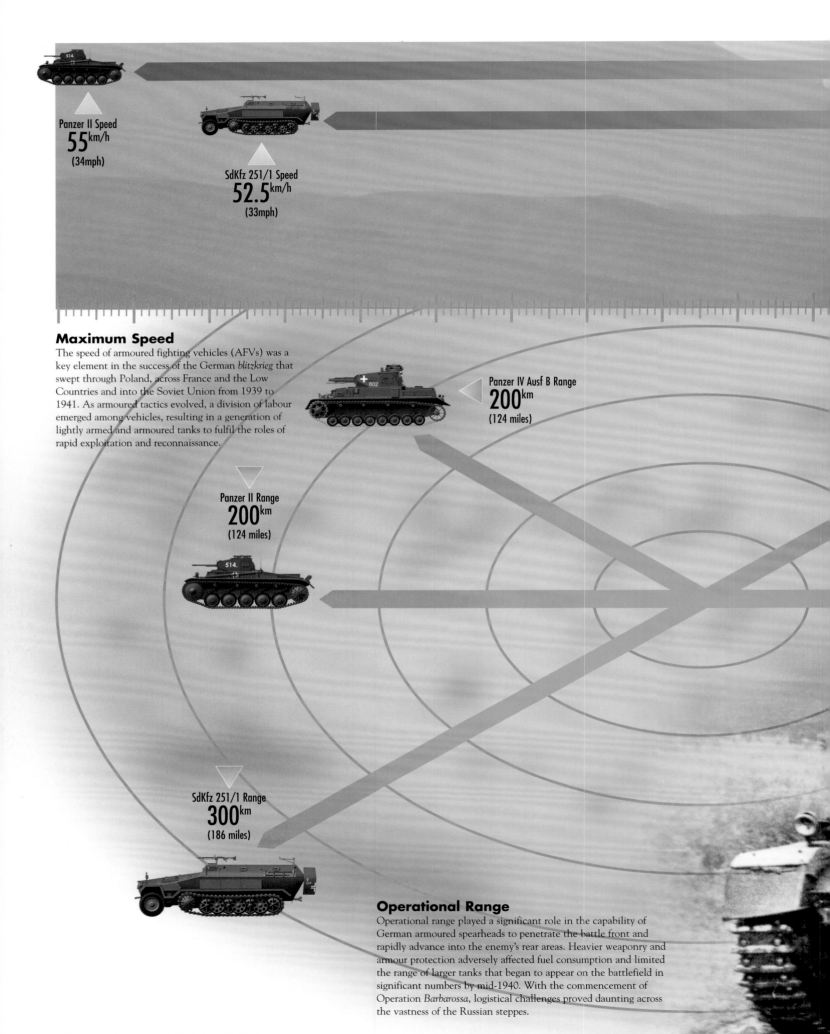

Panzer II Speed
55km/h
(34mph)

SdKfz 251/1 Speed
52.5km/h
(33mph)

Maximum Speed

The speed of armoured fighting vehicles (AFVs) was a key element in the success of the German *blitzkrieg* that swept through Poland, across France and the Low Countries and into the Soviet Union from 1939 to 1941. As armoured tactics evolved, a division of labour emerged among vehicles, resulting in a generation of lightly armed and armoured tanks to fulfil the roles of rapid exploitation and reconnaissance.

Panzer IV Ausf B Range
200km
(124 miles)

Panzer II Range
200km
(124 miles)

SdKfz 251/1 Range
300km
(186 miles)

Operational Range

Operational range played a significant role in the capability of German armoured spearheads to penetrate the battle front and rapidly advance into the enemy's rear areas. Heavier weaponry and armour protection adversely affected fuel consumption and limited the range of larger tanks that began to appear on the battlefield in significant numbers by mid-1940. With the commencement of Operation *Barbarossa*, logistical challenges proved daunting across the vastness of the Russian steppes.

Wehrmacht Blitzkrieg: 1939–41

Maximum Speed and Operational Range

Panzer 38t Speed
42km/h
(26mph)

Panzer IV Ausf B Speed
40km/h (25mph)

Panzer III Ausf E Speed
40km/h (25mph)

Panzer III Ausf E Range
165km
(103 miles)

Panzer 38t Range
250km
(155 miles)

► **Panzer III Ausf E**
► **Panzer 38t**
► **Panzer II**
► **SdKfz 251/1**
► **Panzer IV Ausf B**

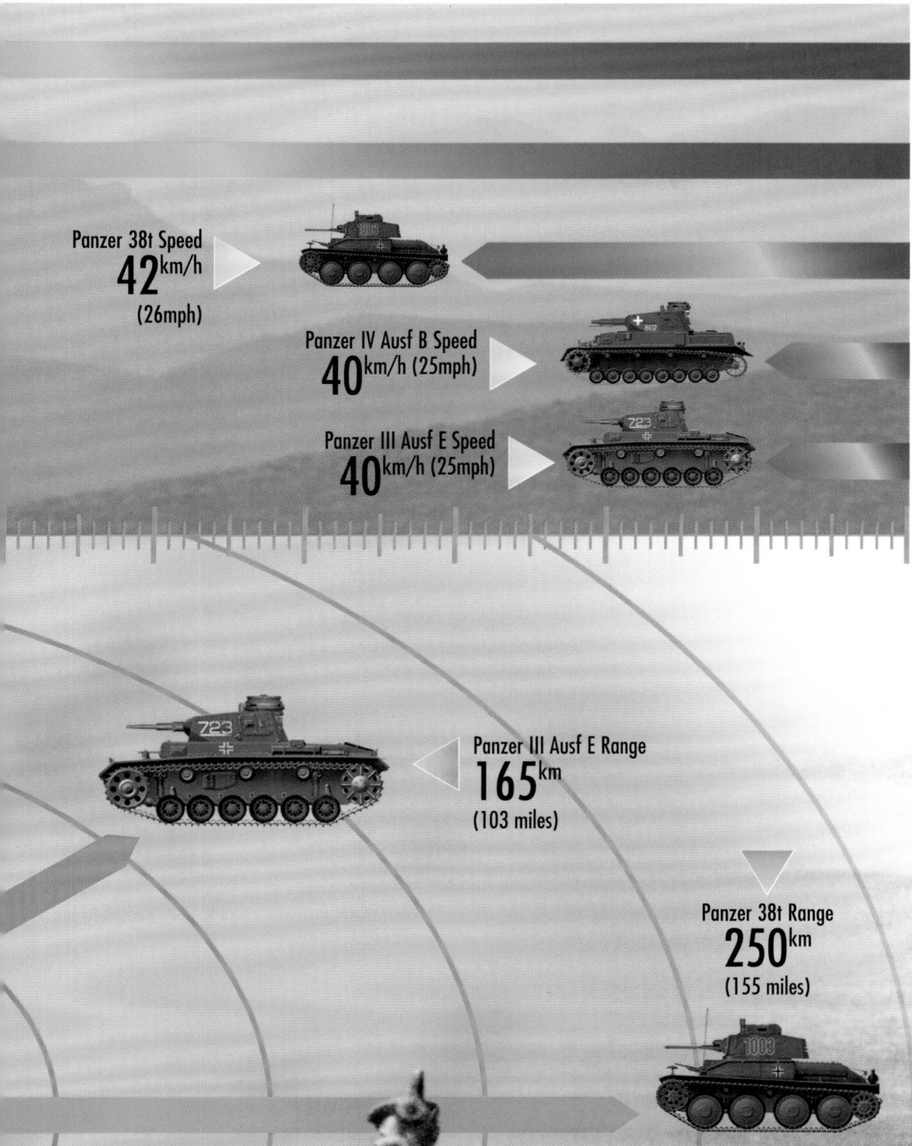

Although the weaknesses in performance inherent in the German Panzerkampfwagen (PzKpfw) I had been laid bare during the Spanish Civil War, the vehicle remained in widespread use at the start of World War II. The speed and range of German armoured vehicles were comparable to and sometimes surpassed those of the best Allied tanks. By this time, however, the emergence of the more heavily armed PzKpfw III, originally conceived to tackle tanks, and the PzKpfw IV, intended to neutralize fixed fortifications, were being deployed on the battlefield. Speed and range were adversely affected, requiring the *Wehrmacht* to provision armoured columns during prolonged combat operations.

ABOVE: A few German armoured units equipped with the PzKpfw IV served in the Polish and French campaigns. Initial armour protection was deemed inadequate against a new generation of Allied anti-tank weapons, and the Ausf H, shown halted along a dirt road, was fitted with thicker armour plating that sacrificed a measure of speed and range.

Early Light Tanks: 1939–41

Maximum Speed and Main Gun Calibre

▶ **T-26 Model 1938**
▶ **Char de Cavalerie 38H**
▶ **7TP Light Tank**
▶ **Cruiser Tank Mk IV A13**
▶ **Panzer 35t**

Achieving balance in speed and firepower constantly challenged the engineering capabilities of the Allied and Axis powers. Always in short supply, the British Cruiser Mk IV tank combined a 2-pounder gun, adequate against German armour into 1941, and a top speed of 48km/h (30mph), which compared favourably with other designs. Many Mk IVs were abandoned at Calais and Dunkirk in 1940. The tank also served early in the Desert War.

The Soviet Union achieved notable success with the T-26, which proved superior to Axis designs in Spain and China with its 45mm (1.8in) gun and speed of 28km/h (17mph), while the French Char de Cavalerie 38H was an improved version of a light tank that entered service in 1935. The 38H featured a longer 37mm (1.5in) gun and thicker armour.

With its 37mm (1.5in) Bofors main gun and top speed of 37km/h (23mph), the Polish 7TP was more than a match for the German PzKpfw I and II, armed only with machine guns and a 20mm (0.79in) cannon respectively. Fewer than 150 were produced, and German and Soviet armour overwhelmed those that reached the battlefield.

Pressed into service with the *Wehrmacht*, the Czech-built Panzer 35t provided the Germans with a stopgap against formidable Allied firepower early in World War II. While heavier German tanks were developed, the 37mm (1.5in) cannon and 35km/h (22mph) speed of the Panzer 35t bolstered the weaker panzer designs during the Polish and French campaigns.

Main Gun Calibre

The proving ground of the battlefield resulted in heavier main weapons as the demanding role of the armoured vehicle expanded early in World War II. Heavier guns, intended for combat with enemy tanks and fortified positions, gradually replaced machine guns and light cannon as primary armament.

Maximum Speed

Often required to deploy through difficult terrain, light tanks seldom achieved maximum speed during cross-country operations, although their rapid-exploitation role remained critical in offensive situations. While speed was sometimes diminished, lighter weight offered better manoeuvrability.

Cruiser Tank Mk I
48km/h
(30mph)

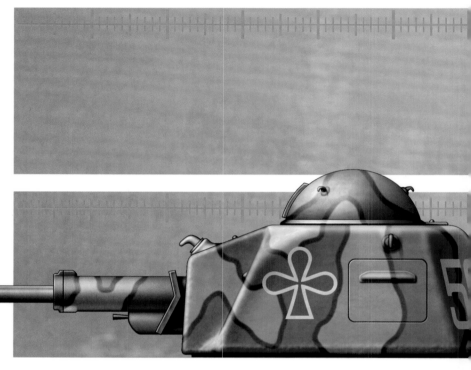

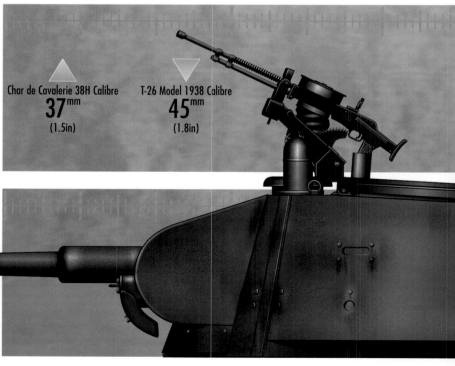

Char de Cavalerie 38H Calibre
37mm
(1.5in)

T-26 Model 1938 Calibre
45mm
(1.8in)

RIGHT: French AMR-33 light tanks parade through Paris before the war. Like many 1930s tanks, the AMR-33 had a small gun and thin armour, making it obsolete by 1939.

7TP Speed
37km/h
(23mph)

Char de Cavalerie 38H Speed
36.5km/h
(22.7mph)

Panzer 35t Speed
35km/h
(22mph)

T-26 Speed
28km/h
(17mph)

Early Medium Tanks: 1939–41

Maximum Speed and Main Gun Calibre

▶ **Char de Cavalerie 35S**
▶ **T-34 Model 1941**
▶ **Matilda II**
▶ **Panzer IV Ausf E**

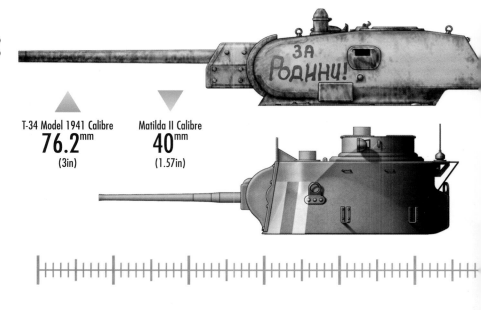

T-34 Model 1941 Calibre
76.2mm
(3in)

Matilda II Calibre
40mm
(1.57in)

T he World War II-era medium tanks, conceived primarily for infantry support, included larger-calibre main armament, thicker armour protection, and larger engines capable of powering the heavier armoured vehicles.

Although it was woefully underpowered and capable only of 13km/h (8mph), the British Matilda II was effective against German and Italian armour with its 2-pounder main gun. Later outclassed in tank-vs-tank combat, the Matilda II remained in production until 1943 and achieved fame in the Desert War of 1940–43.

The French Char de Cavalerie 35S, or S35, was well armed with a 47mm (1.9in) main gun and capable of a respectable 41km/h (25.5mph). Superior to early German tanks, the S35 held its own against the PzKpfw III during the 1940 Battle of France. However, flaws in tactical deployment proved its undoing.

The emergence of the PzKpfw IV was a watershed in German tank development. Originally intended for infantry support, the PzKpfw IV took on an expanded role against Allied tanks. Produced in greater numbers than any other German tank of the war, it had a 75mm (2.9in) gun and top speed of 42km/h (26mph). With increased armour, the Ausf E was produced from December 1939 to April 1941.

The combat debut of the Soviet T-34 in the summer of 1941 shocked the Germans. The T-34 combined the hard-hitting 76.2mm (3in) gun with dazzling speed of up to 53km/h (32.9mph). Produced in greater numbers than any other tank of the period, the T-34 is an icon of the Soviet victory in the Great Patriotic War.

OPPOSITE: Although its silhouette conjured images of World War I-vintage tanks, the French heavy Char B1 bis had a 75mm (2.9in) hull-mounted gun plus a 47mm (1.9in) turret gun. Heavily armoured as well, the Char B1 was superior to German armour deployed during the 1940 Battle of France.

Main Gun Calibre

The increasing calibre of tank weaponry, with greater range and improved muzzle velocity, occurred rapidly in World War II, particularly as anti-tank guns grew more lethal and tank-vs-tank combat became commonplace in the desert of North Africa and on the Eastern Front.

T-34 Speed
53km/h
(32.9mph)

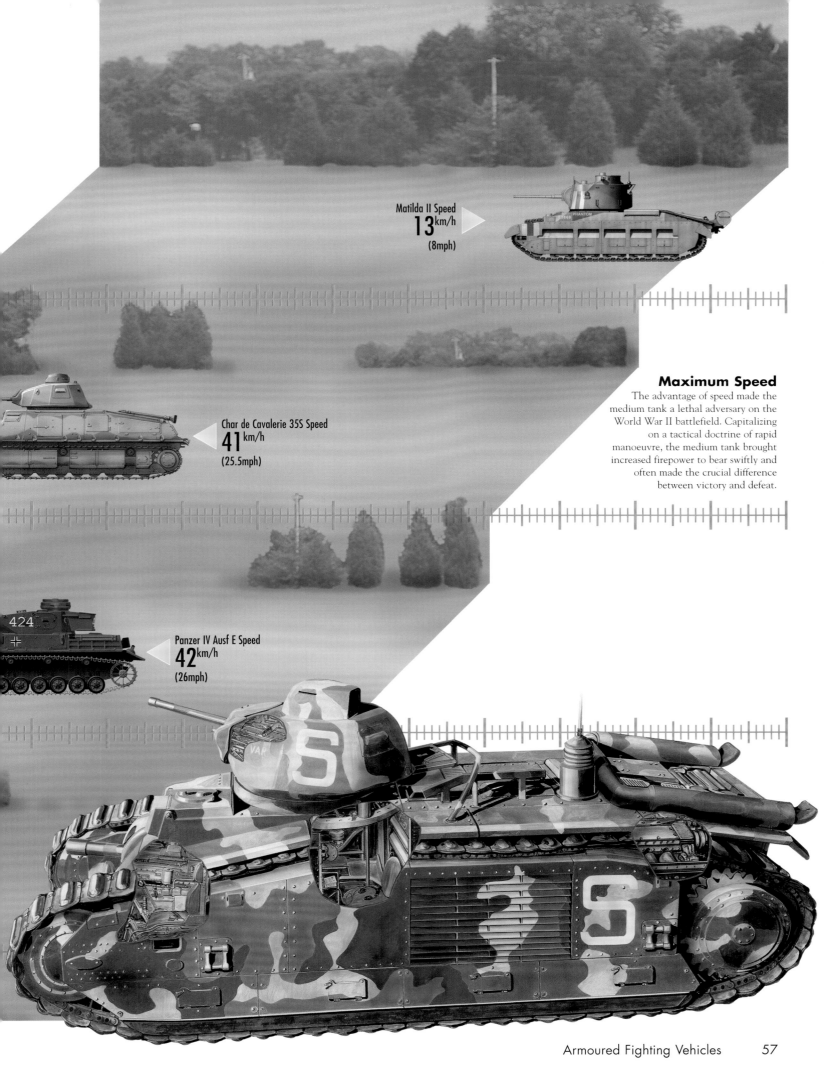

Matilda II Speed
13km/h
(8mph)

Char de Cavalerie 35S Speed
41km/h
(25.5mph)

Maximum Speed

The advantage of speed made the medium tank a lethal adversary on the World War II battlefield. Capitalizing on a tactical doctrine of rapid manoeuvre, the medium tank brought increased firepower to bear swiftly and often made the crucial difference between victory and defeat.

Panzer IV Ausf E Speed
42km/h
(26mph)

Weight

Manoeuvring across the shifting sands of the North African desert became problematic for armoured vehicles during World War II; therefore, light weight was critical to sustaining mobile warfare while easing the tremendous burden of supplying fuel to front-line units.

M3 Stuart Weight
12.7 tonnes
(12.5 tons)

Carro Armato M14/41 Weight
15.8 tonnes
(15.6 tons)

Valentine Mk III Weight
17.7 tonnes
(17.4 tons)

M3 Stuart Weight: 12.7 tonnes (12.5 tons)

Carro Armato M14/41 Weight: 15.8 tonnes (15.6 tons)

Valentine Mk III Weight: 17.7 tonnes (17.4 tons)

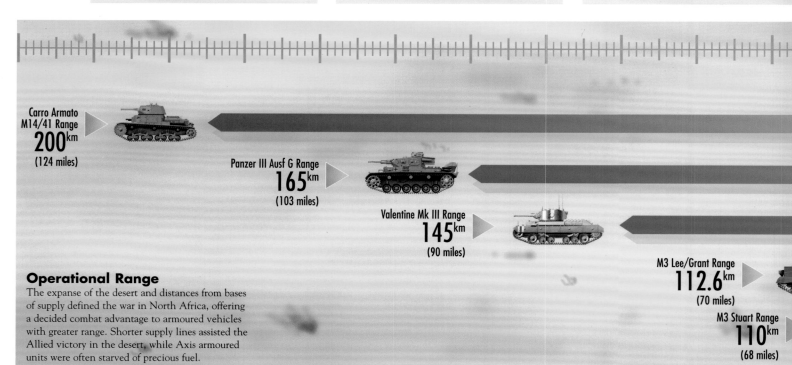

Carro Armato M14/41 Range
200 km
(124 miles)

Panzer III Ausf G Range
165 km
(103 miles)

Valentine Mk III Range
145 km
(90 miles)

M3 Lee/Grant Range
112.6 km
(70 miles)

M3 Stuart Range
110 km
(68 miles)

Operational Range

The expanse of the desert and distances from bases of supply defined the war in North Africa, offering a decided combat advantage to armoured vehicles with greater range. Shorter supply lines assisted the Allied victory in the desert, while Axis armoured units were often starved of precious fuel.

Armour in the Desert: 1940–43

Weight and Operational Range

► **Valentine Mk III**
► **M3 Stuart**
► **Carro Armato M14/41**
► **M3 Lee/Grant**
► **Panzer III Ausf G**

As the war in the desert progressed, heavier armoured vehicles were introduced by both the Allies and the Axis. Each was equipped with a larger main gun and required a more robust powerplant to operate, further straining tenuous supply lines, particularly in the case of the Germans. Lighter tanks such as the US Stuart, the British Valentine and Matilda, and the Italian Fiat Carro Armato M14/41 proved manoeuvrable but susceptible to enemy fire, particularly higher-calibre anti-tank weapons. The German PzKpfw III and IV provided heavier firepower and acceptable ranges, while the US-built M3 Lee/Grant was a match in weaponry with a 37mm (1.5in) turret gun and 75mm (2.9in) hull-mounted cannon but lacked the range of its enemy counterparts.

Panzer III Ausf G Weight
22.4 tonnes
(22 tons)

M3 Lee/Grant Weight
27.9 tonnes
(27.5 tons)

Panzer III Ausf G Weight: 22.4 tonnes (22 tons)

M3 Lee/Grant Weight: 27.9 tonnes (27.5 tons)

LEFT: The final production version of the Panzer III, the Ausf N, entered service in late 1942. Its 75mm (2.9in) gun was intended for use against enemy infantry.

Operation Citadel 1: Kursk, July 1943

Maximum Gradient

- ▶ **T-34 Model 1943**
- ▶ **KV-1S Model 1942**
- ▶ **Panther Ausf D**
- ▶ **Tiger I Ausf E**
- ▶ **Panzer IV Ausf H**

The capability of an armoured vehicle to traverse inhospitable terrain often spelled the difference between life and death for machine and crew during World War II. Such is evidenced by the savage fighting across railway lines and steep gullies at Prokhorovka during Operation Citadel and the critical German offensive against the Soviet Kursk salient. At times, German tanks were required not only to cross streams with steep banks during their advances on the Eastern Front but also to negotiate tank traps dug wide and deep to delay their advance.

The extreme gradient limit of German medium Panther and PzKpfw IV tanks was 60 degrees, and attempting such a climb was perilous, while the ponderous Tiger tank pushed its limit at 50 degrees. Soviet medium T-34 and heavy KV-1 tanks were further limited in their ability to negotiate steep terrain at 40 and 36 degrees respectively. Therefore, Soviet tank commanders chose to avoid uneven surfaces if possible, closing rapidly with the enemy in open country.

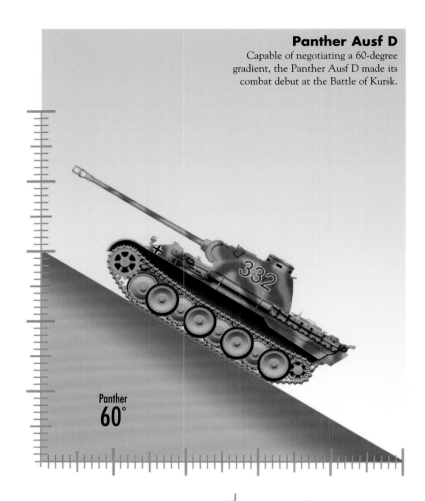

Panther Ausf D
Capable of negotiating a 60-degree gradient, the Panther Ausf D made its combat debut at the Battle of Kursk.

Panther
60°

RIGHT: The heavy Tiger I Ausf E made its combat debut on the Eastern Front in autumn 1942, and with the medium PzKpfw IV and PzKpfw V Panther formed the backbone of the German armoured capability at Kursk. The Tiger I was prone to mechanical breakdowns but was formidable in combat with its 88mm (3.5in) cannon.

Panzer IV Ausf H

The workhorse PzKpfw IV was present in large numbers at Kursk. The Ausf H suffered from an inferior transmission and was hard-pressed to climb a 60-degree gradient.

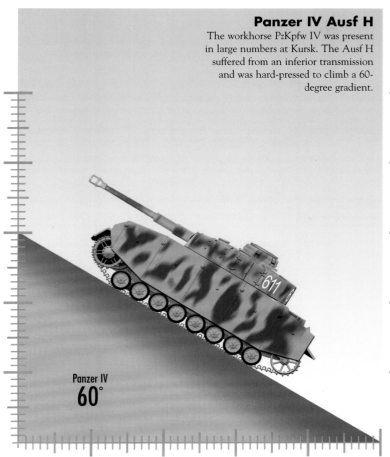

Panzer IV
60°

Tiger Ausf E

The initial combat version of the Tiger tank, the Ausf E weighed nearly 57 tonnes (56 tons), and climbing gradients of 50 degrees strained its powerplant mightily.

Tiger
50°

T-34 Model 1943

The T-34 Model 1943 was capable of negotiating a maximum gradient of 40 degrees but was impressively swift across open country.

T-34
40°

KV-1S Model 1942

The Soviet KV-1S Model 1942 heavy tank was intended as an improvement on earlier versions; however, additional armour was not accompanied by a more powerful engine, limiting its gradient capability to 36 degrees.

KV-1S
36°

Main Gun Calibre

The 88mm (3.5in) cannon of the Tiger I was capable of engaging enemy tanks at distances of more than 1100m (1203yd), while the high-velocity 75mm (2.9in) gun of the PzKpfw V was a potent weapon in its own right.

Maximum Speed

By far the swiftest tank on the battlefield at Kursk, the Soviet T-34 was often employed in rapid advances, closing with the enemy to fight at short range. German armour, meanwhile, relied more heavily on accurate distant gunnery.

T-34 Model 1943 Calibre
76.2mm
(3in)

T-34 Model 1943 Speed
55km/h
(34mph)

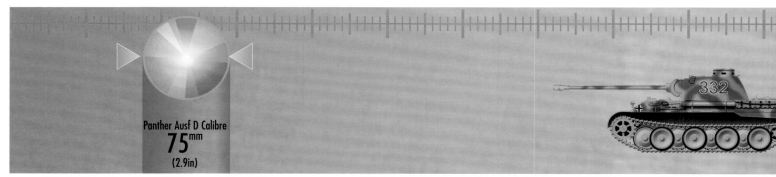

Panther Ausf D Calibre
75mm
(2.9in)

KV-1S Model 1942 Calibre
76.2mm
(3in)

BELOW: A T-34 Model 1943 advances through a Ukrainian village following the Red Army's gains of late 1943.

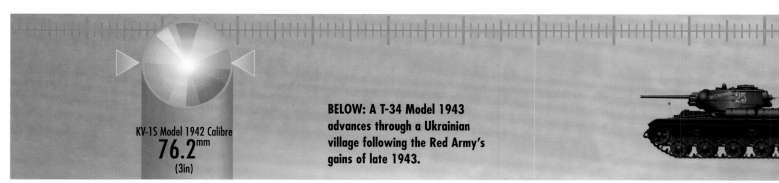

Tiger Ausf E Calibre
88mm
(3.5in)

Panzer IV Ausf H Calibre
75mm
(2.9in)

At 57 tonnes (56 tons), the massive Tiger I heavy tank outweighed its Soviet counterpart, the KV-1S, by nearly 15 tonnes (14.8 tons). Such weight limited the Tiger's cross-country movement and made it susceptible to swarming T-34s probing for vulnerable points of attack.

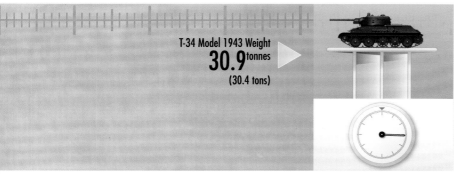

T-34 Model 1943 Weight
30.9 tonnes
(30.4 tons)

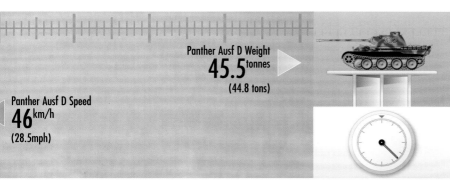

Panther Ausf D Weight
45.5 tonnes
(44.8 tons)

Panther Ausf D Speed
46 km/h
(28.5mph)

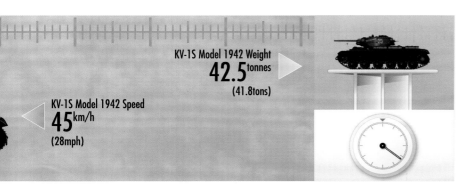

KV-1S Model 1942 Weight
42.5 tonnes
(41.8tons)

KV-1S Model 1942 Speed
45 km/h
(28mph)

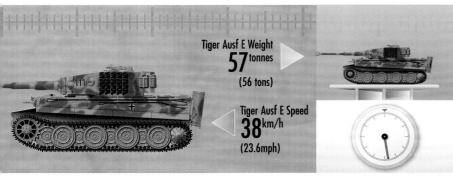

Tiger Ausf E Weight
57 tonnes
(56 tons)

Tiger Ausf E Speed
38 km/h
(23.6mph)

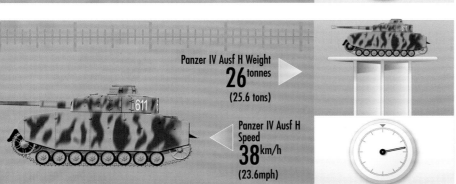

Panzer IV Ausf H Weight
26 tonnes
(25.6 tons)

Panzer IV Ausf H Speed
38 km/h
(23.6mph)

Operation Citadel 2: Kursk, July 1943

Maximum Speed, Main Gun Calibre and Weight

▶ **T-34 Model 1943**
▶ **KV-1S Model 1942**
▶ **Panther Ausf D**
▶ **Tiger Ausf E**
▶ **Panzer IV Ausf H**

In the summer of 1943, the German PzKpfw V Panther made its combat debut less than a year after its prototype had been developed. The first production model, the Ausf D, was plagued by mechanical problems at Kursk, and early reports of its combat prowess were disappointing. The heavy Tiger I was effective at stand-off distances with its powerful 88mm (3.5in) cannon, but crewmen found target acquisition problematic as swift Soviet T-34 medium tanks charged towards the Germans to initiate close-quarter combat.

Initial German momentum was slowed to a crawl as the Panther, originally designed in response to the success of the T-34, experienced mechanical difficulties. In the tank-vs-tank melees that ensued at Kursk, the speed of the T-34 Model 1943 was telling. Despite heavy losses, the agile Soviet tanks, capable of 55km/h (34mph), blunted the German drive against the Red Army salient and forced the attackers to retire. Following the battle it was determined that the 76.2mm (3in) main gun of the T-34 and its heavier counterpart, the KV-1S, were not powerful enough against the new generation of German tanks. As a result, the T-34 was upgunned in 1944 with an 85mm (3.3in) cannon and production of the KV-1S, deemed less effective than the T-34, was curtailed.

Although the performance of the PzKpfw IV was overshadowed by the Panther and Tiger at Kursk, the design shouldered its share of combat duty during the largest tank battle in history. The PzKpfw IV was produced in greater numbers than any other German tank of the war, and while its design was not remarkable, it was durable. The Ausf H had a high-velocity 75mm (2.9in) gun, a top speed of 38km/h (23.6mph), and a weight of 26 tonnes (25.6 tons), significantly less than the almost 31-tonne (30.5-ton) T-34.

Early Assault Guns: 1940–42

Main Gun Range

- ▶ **SU-76**
- ▶ **Bishop**
- ▶ **Semovente DA 75/18**
- ▶ **sIG 33**
- ▶ **StuG Ausf D**

Originally designed as infantry-support weapons, for engaging troop concentrations and fortified positions, self-propelled assault guns were armed with heavy-calibre weapons capable of taking on the enemy at varying ranges. The most recognized of the early assault guns was the German Sturmgeschütz (StuG) III, fielding a 75mm (2.9in) main gun, firing a projectile that could penetrate a target at up to 2000m (2187yd). The Germans produced a variety of assault guns during World War II, several of which were proven excellent designs. One notable exception was the sIG 33, a tracked weapon mounting the standard German 150mm (5.9in) field gun capable of engaging targets at 4700m (5140yd). The sIG 33 did allow German artillery to keep up with tank formations; however, its high profile, lack of onboard ammunition and frequent breakdowns due to an overloaded chassis rendered it ineffective. By 1943, it had virtually disappeared from the battlefield.

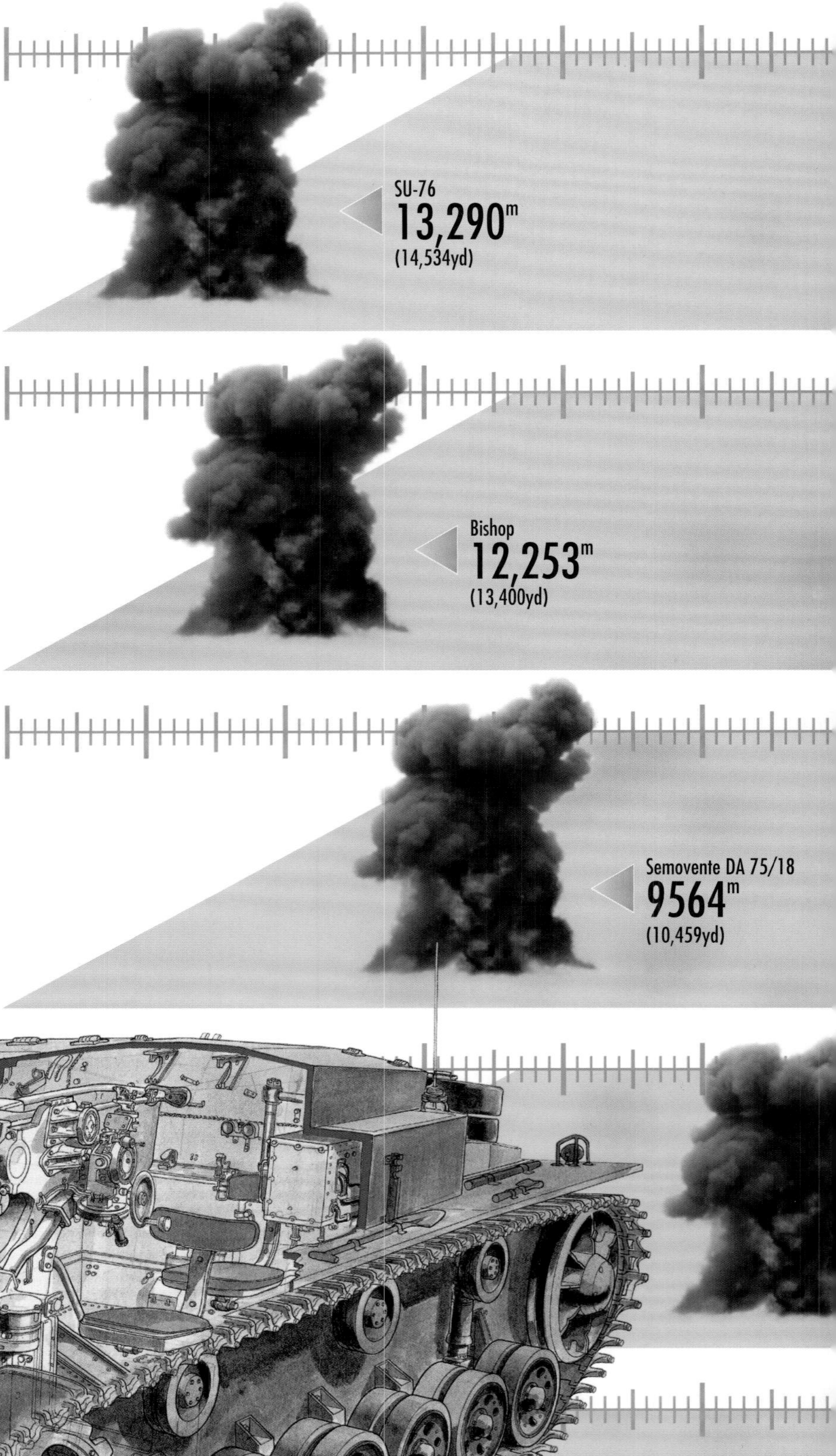

SU-76
13,290ᵐ
(14,534yd)

Bishop
12,253ᵐ
(13,400yd)

Semovente DA 75/18
9564ᵐ
(10,459yd)

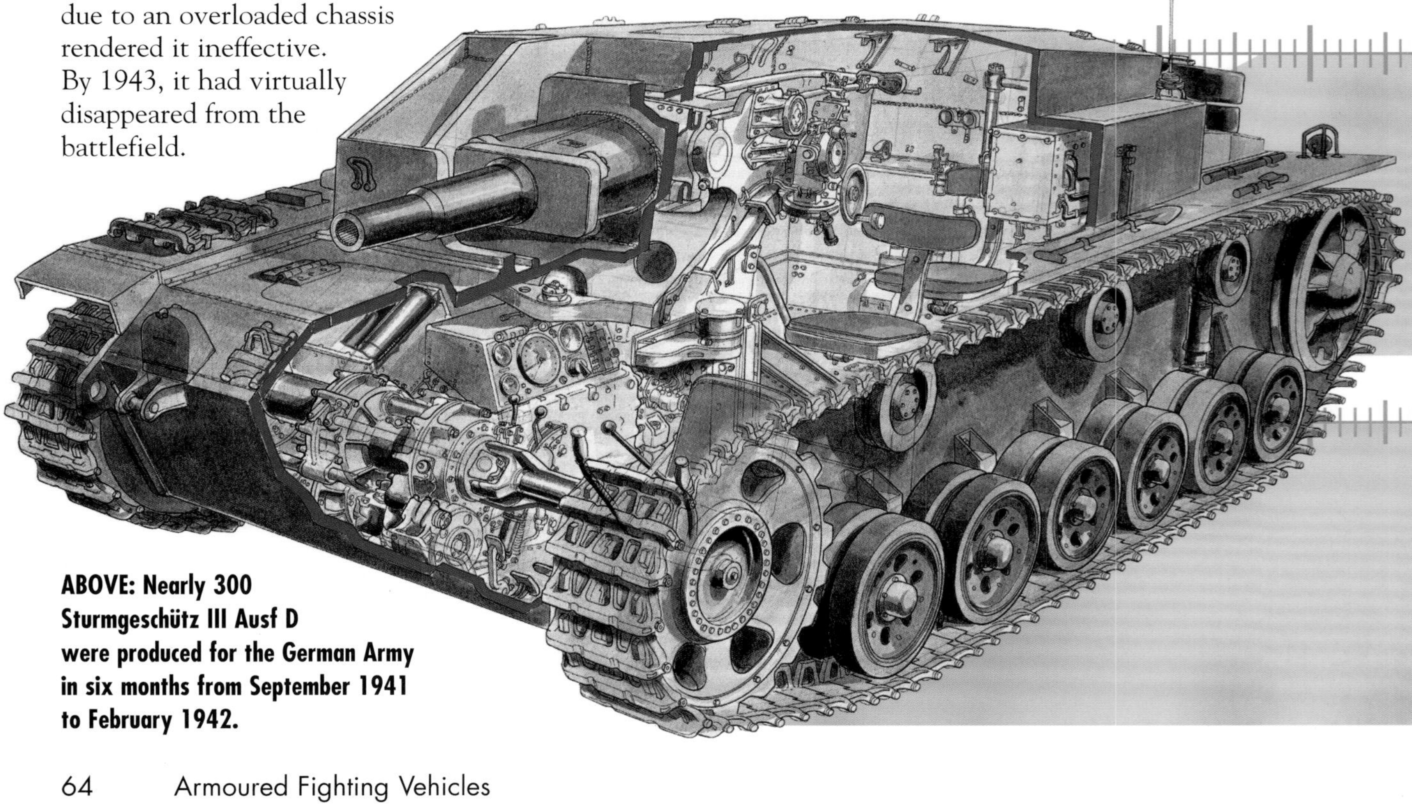

ABOVE: Nearly 300 Sturmgeschütz III Ausf D were produced for the German Army in six months from September 1941 to February 1942.

Effective Main Gun Range

Early-assault-gun range varied widely, depending on the calibre of the main weapon and its corresponding muzzle velocity. The German sIG 33 was developed for heavy infantry support with a 150mm (5.9in) gun, while the British Bishop served as a platform for the 25-pounder cannon, essentially an 88mm (3.5in) gun.

SU-76
The Soviet SU-76 was produced in great numbers, second only to the T-34 tank, and its 76mm (3in) cannon was effective to distances of more than 13,000m (14,217yd).

Bishop
The disappointing Bishop entered service in 1942. It mounted a 25-pounder cannon with a range of 12,253m (13,400yd). The Bishop was intended as a stopgap measure in the Desert War to provide tank-destroyer support until the 6-pounder-armed Valentines and Crusaders were ready.

Semovente DA 75/18
The Italian Semovente DA 75 mounted a 75mm (2.9in) cannon with a range of nearly 9600m (10,499yd).

sIG 33
sIG 33
4700ᵐ
(5140yd)

One of the first infantry support guns to be developed, the sIG 33 was a classic 'lash-up' which combined the 150mm (5.9in) field gun with a Panzer I chassis.

StuG Ausf D
StuG Ausf D
2000ᵐ
(2187yd)

The StuG was the classic early war assault gun, and was used to great effect in the North African desert and Stalingrad.

Armoured Fighting Vehicles   65

Late Assault Guns: 1943–45

Crew and Main Gun Calibre

▶ **StuG III Ausf G**
▶ **Jagdpanzer IV**
▶ **SU-122**
▶ **JSU-152**
▶ **SU-152**

SU-152

JSU-152

SU-122

Jagdpanzer IV

StuG III Ausf G

SU-152 Calibre
152mm
(6in)

JSU-152 Calibre
152mm
(6in)

SU-122 Calibre
122mm
(4.8in)

Jagdpanzer IV Calibre
75mm
(2.9in)

StuG III Ausf G Calibre
75mm
(2.9in)

As World War II dragged on, the role of the self-propelled assault gun expanded from simply one of infantry support to include that of tank destroyer and heavy-artillery platform. German armour designers realized that the turretless assault gun could be produced more rapidly and inexpensively than most tanks.

Therefore, a wave of innovative models and heavy-calibre guns emerged in the German arsenal. Among these were the later variants of the StuG III and the Jagdpanzer IV. The StuG III Ausf G was a high-velocity, long-barrelled 75mm (2.9in) gun mounted on the chassis of the venerable PzKpfw III tank and suitable for taking on fixed targets or Allied tanks. The Jagdpanzer IV was a purpose-built tank destroyer intended to succeed the StuG III and mounting the 75mm (2.9in) Pak 42 L/70 gun. The Jagdpanzer IV was based on the chassis of the PzKpfw IV medium tank, and the decision to produce it adversely affected production of the PzKpfw IV from December 1943. The StuG III and the Jagdpanzer IV were served by crews of four.

Late Soviet heavy assault guns included the SU-122, SU-152 and JSU-152, each with a crew of five and mounting some of the heaviest field guns deployed during the war. More than 1100 examples of the SU-122 were produced from the end of 1942 through to the summer of 1944, and the vehicle mounted the 122mm (4.8in) M-30S howitzer. The SU-152 was conceived as a heavy tank destroyer to counter the German Tiger tank on the Eastern Front and featured a 152mm (6in) gun-howitzer atop the chassis of the KV-1 heavy tank. By the end of 1943, the SU-152 had been replaced by the JSU-152, and this design remained in service with the Red Army into the 1970s. Nearly 1900 JSU-152s were built during World War II as combination infantry-support and anti-tank weapons.

RIGHT: This Soviet tank crewman is wearing standard combat gear, including a leather helmet, coveralls and the typical Red Army high boots.

Main Gun Calibre

The size and calibre of Soviet assault guns grew as the war progressed, partly as a response to the improved armour protection of late war tanks, but also because the red Army emphasised heavy artillery that was capable of offering a bigger 'hit'.

SU-152

SU-152

The five-man crew of the SU-152 included a driver, gunner and loader to the left of the main weapon, and the breech-mechanism operator and commander situated to the right.

5 crew

JSU-152

JSU-152

The multi-role JSU-152 tank destroyer and infantry-support vehicle functioned effectively with a crew of either four or five, sometimes entering combat without the benefit of a second loader.

5 crew

SU-122

SU-122

The poor layout of the SU-122 crew compartment meant that the commander often was required to assist in servicing the main gun, while inadequate ventilation hindered combat operations.

5 crew

Jagdpanzer IV

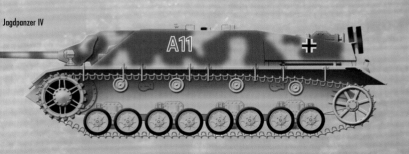

Jagdpanzer IV

The enclosed crew compartment of the Jagdpanzer IV was a departure from earlier open designs and required the commander, driver, gunner and loader to function in cramped quarters.

4 crew

StuG III Ausf G

StuG III Ausf G

StuG units were said to have destroyed some 20,000 enemy tanks during World War II. The vehicle's low silhouette assisted with concealment and provided additional protection for the four-man crew.

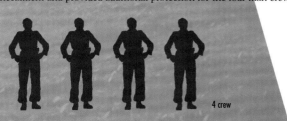

4 crew

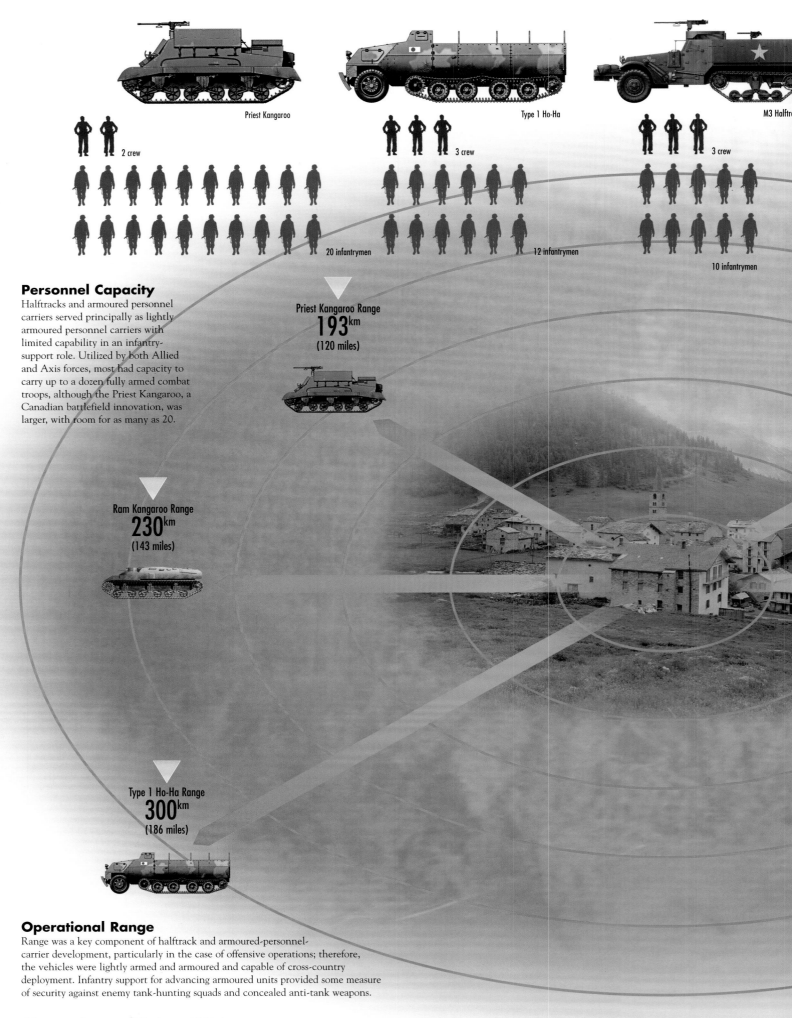

Priest Kangaroo

Type 1 Ho-Ha

M3 Halftrc

2 crew

3 crew

3 crew

20 infantrymen

12 infantrymen

10 infantrymen

Personnel Capacity

Halftracks and armoured personnel carriers served principally as lightly armoured personnel carriers with limited capability in an infantry-support role. Utilized by both Allied and Axis forces, most had capacity to carry up to a dozen fully armed combat troops, although the Priest Kangaroo, a Canadian battlefield innovation, was larger, with room for as many as 20.

Priest Kangaroo Range
193km
(120 miles)

Ram Kangaroo Range
230km
(143 miles)

Type 1 Ho-Ha Range
300km
(186 miles)

Operational Range

Range was a key component of halftrack and armoured-personnel-carrier development, particularly in the case of offensive operations; therefore, the vehicles were lightly armed and armoured and capable of cross-country deployment. Infantry support for advancing armoured units provided some measure of security against enemy tank-hunting squads and concealed anti-tank weapons.

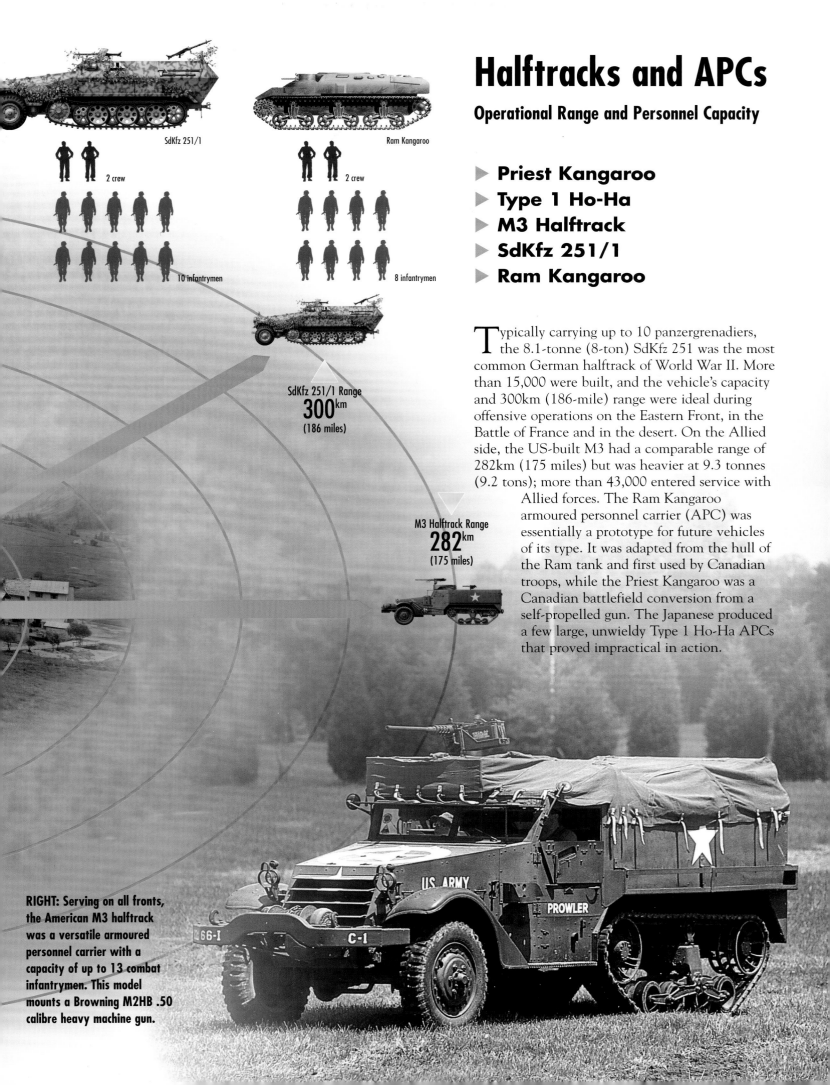

SdKfz 251/1

2 crew

10 infantrymen

Ram Kangaroo

2 crew

8 infantrymen

Halftracks and APCs

Operational Range and Personnel Capacity

▶ **Priest Kangaroo**
▶ **Type 1 Ho-Ha**
▶ **M3 Halftrack**
▶ **SdKfz 251/1**
▶ **Ram Kangaroo**

SdKfz 251/1 Range
300km
(186 miles)

M3 Halftrack Range
282km
(175 miles)

Typically carrying up to 10 panzergrenadiers, the 8.1-tonne (8-ton) SdKfz 251 was the most common German halftrack of World War II. More than 15,000 were built, and the vehicle's capacity and 300km (186-mile) range were ideal during offensive operations on the Eastern Front, in the Battle of France and in the desert. On the Allied side, the US-built M3 had a comparable range of 282km (175 miles) but was heavier at 9.3 tonnes (9.2 tons); more than 43,000 entered service with Allied forces. The Ram Kangaroo armoured personnel carrier (APC) was essentially a prototype for future vehicles of its type. It was adapted from the hull of the Ram tank and first used by Canadian troops, while the Priest Kangaroo was a Canadian battlefield conversion from a self-propelled gun. The Japanese produced a few large, unwieldy Type 1 Ho-Ha APCs that proved impractical in action.

RIGHT: Serving on all fronts, the American M3 halftrack was a versatile armoured personnel carrier with a capacity of up to 13 combat infantrymen. This model mounts a Browning M2HB .50 calibre heavy machine gun.

Armoured Cars

Operational Range and Maximum Speed

▶ **SdKfz 234 Puma**
▶ **M8**
▶ **AEC Mk III**
▶ **BA-10**
▶ **SdKfz 222**

Among the AFVs to come into their own during the interwar years, armoured cars were developed for the purposes of reconnaissance and light infantry support. Speed and manoeuvrability were hallmarks of the armoured car, and those of the Allied and Axis nations were capable of speeds in excess of 55km/h (34mph).

The German SdKfz 234 Puma was protected by armour up to 30mm (1.2in) thick. Its range was an impressive 1000km (621 miles), and it mounted a 50mm (2in) main weapon; however, the Puma was inferior to enemy tanks and primarily engaged machine-gun positions and troop concentrations. The British AEC Mk III was upgunned from previous versions of the wheeled vehicle with a 75mm (2.9in) cannon but had a limited range of 402km (250 miles), while the six-wheeled US M8 Greyhound was armed with a 37mm (1.5in) cannon.

BELOW: The US M8 Greyhound armoured car was still in development when designers realized that its 37mm (1.5in) cannon could not penetrate the thick armour of German tanks. Therefore, its initial planned employment as a tank destroyer was abandoned and a tactical role of reconnaissance and infantry support was stressed.

Operational Range

Operational road ranges among armoured cars varied widely, with the eight-wheeled German SdKfz 234 Puma getting 1000km (621 miles) from its 12-cylinder Tatra diesel engine while the British AEC Mk III, powered by a 6-cylinder gasoline engine, covered less than half that distance.

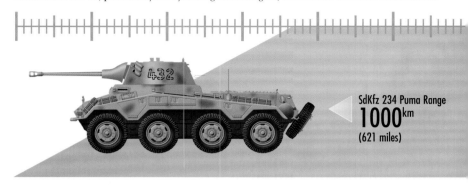

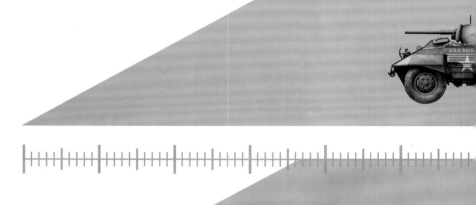

SdKfz 234 Puma Range
1000km
(621 miles)

Maximum Speed

High relative speed capabilities allowed World War II armoured cars to employ the 'fight or flee' option when confronted by hostile forces. Armoured cars served primarily as reconnaissance vehicles and sometimes engaged in infantry support. Generally, these wheeled vehicles were capable of road speeds greater than 55km/h (34mph).

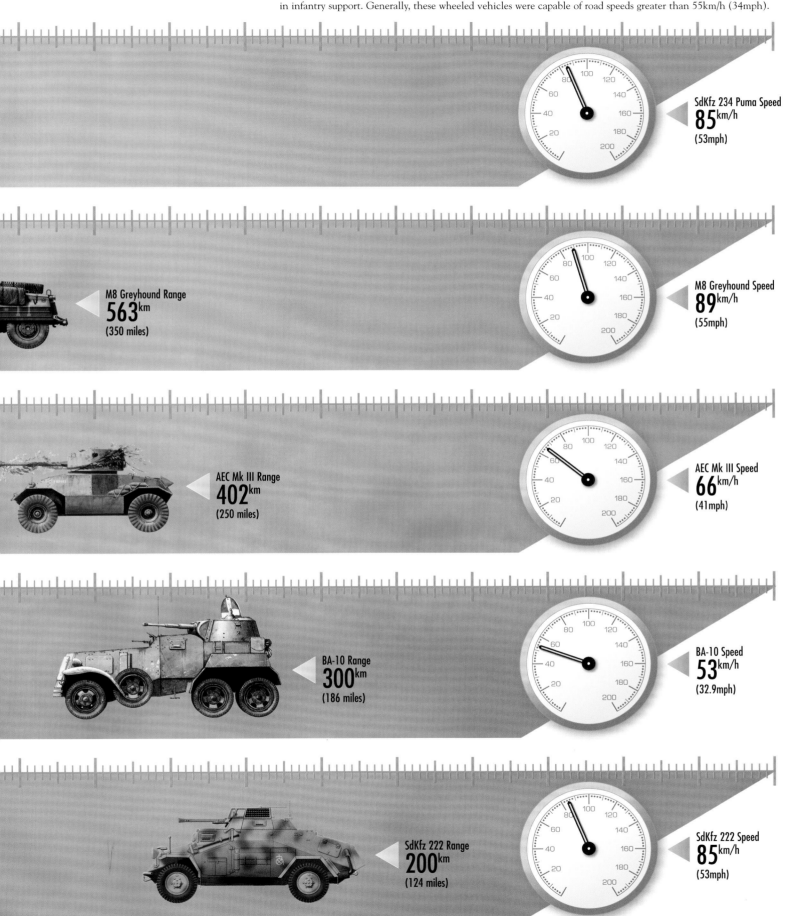

SdKfz 234 Puma Speed
85km/h
(53mph)

M8 Greyhound Range
563km
(350 miles)

M8 Greyhound Speed
89km/h
(55mph)

AEC Mk III Range
402km
(250 miles)

AEC Mk III Speed
66km/h
(41mph)

BA-10 Range
300km
(186 miles)

BA-10 Speed
53km/h
(32.9mph)

SdKfz 222 Range
200km
(124 miles)

SdKfz 222 Speed
85km/h
(53mph)

Maximum Speed on Road

Amphibious vehicles were conceived to carry troops across rough terrain and perform adequately in bad weather. Road speeds for wheeled vehicles were impressive, while tracked craft made up for road deficiencies with cross-country agility. Vehicles that operated in combat zones sacrificed some speed for armour and defensive armament.

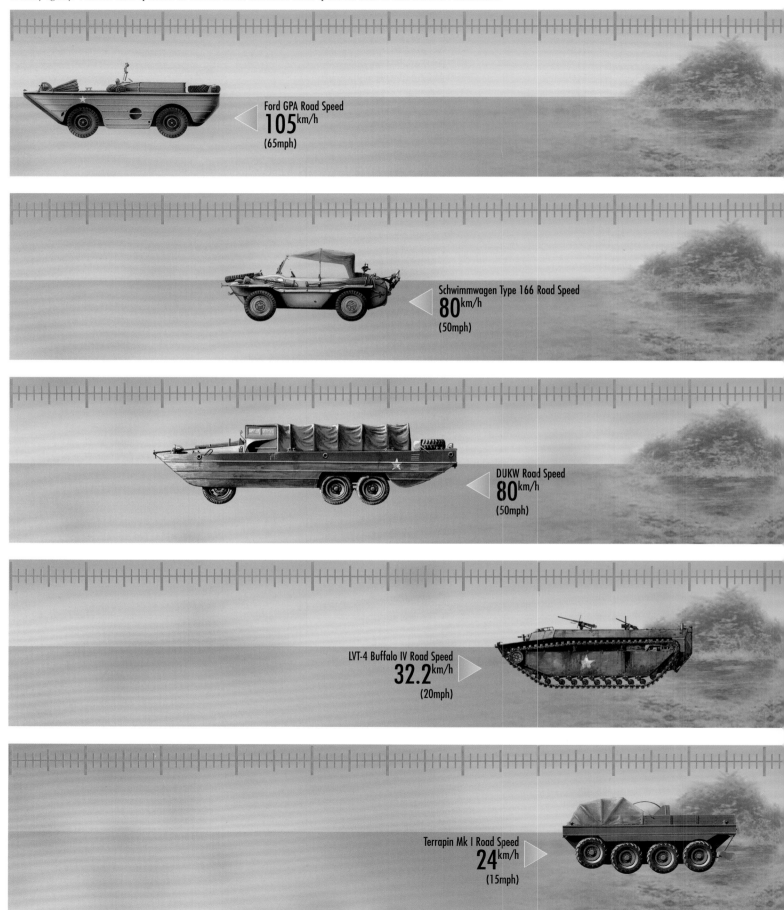

Ford GPA Road Speed
105km/h
(65mph)

Schwimmwagen Type 166 Road Speed
80km/h
(50mph)

DUKW Road Speed
80km/h
(50mph)

LVT-4 Buffalo IV Road Speed
32.2km/h
(20mph)

Terrapin Mk I Road Speed
24km/h
(15mph)

Maximum Speed in Water

Streams and rivers were often encountered in Europe, while churning across the open sea to land troops on hotly contested beaches was a frequent activity in the Pacific. Both required amphibious vehicles to muster some degree of speed through water to minimize exposure to enemy fire.

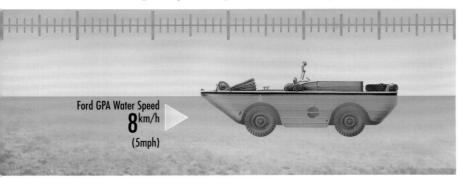

Ford GPA Water Speed
8 km/h
(5mph)

Schwimmwagen Type 166 Water Speed
11 km/h
(6.8mph)

DUKW Water Speed
9.7 km/h
(6mph)

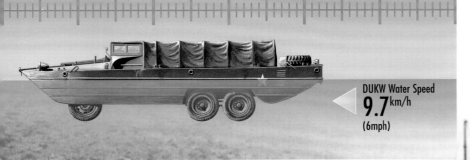

LVT-4 Buffalo IV Water Speed
11 km/h
(6.8mph)

Terrapin Mk I Water Speed
8 km/h
(5mph)

Amphibious Vehicles
Maximum Speed on Road and in Water

▶ **Ford GPA**
▶ **Schwimmwagen Type 166**
▶ **DUKW**
▶ **LVT-4 Buffalo IV**
▶ **Terrapin Mk I**

Varied terrain and weather conditions required that armies deploy some types of amphibious vehicles in all theatres of World War II. The German Schwimmwagen Type 166 served throughout the war as a command vehicle, while the versatile US LVT-4 Buffalo IV developed through practical lessons learned from early Pacific amphibious operations.

More than 21,000 of the ubiquitous American-built DUKW were produced during World War II, transporting troops and supplies, and even serving as ambulances, whereas the Ford GPA failed to perform adequately as an amphibious Jeep. In autumn 1944, the British Terrapin Mk I provided a distinct advantage in mobility for troops clearing the Scheldt estuary near the port of Antwerp.

BELOW: A modification of a General Motors truck design, the DUKW (D = 1942 design, U = utility, K = front-wheel drive, W = two powered rear axles) could haul 2.3 tonnes (2.26 tons) of supplies or carry 12 combat infantrymen.

SU-85 Calibre
85mm
(3.3in)

M18 Hellcat Calibre
76.2mm
(3in)

M10 Calibre
76.2mm
(3in)

M18 Hellcat Speed
88.5km/h
(55mph)

Maximum Speed

Early tank destroyers were configured with open turrets and light armour, offering the advantage of speed during combat with enemy tanks. Later in World War II, purpose-built tank destroyers were designed with enclosed crew compartments for greater survivability, and powerplants were improved to compensate for the vehicles' heavier weight.

M10 Speed
51km/h
(32mph)

SU-85 Speed
47km/h
(29mph)

Archer Calibre
76.2mm
(3in)

Marder III Calibre
75mm
(2.9in)

Tank Destroyers: 1943–45

Maximum Speed and Main Gun Calibre

▶ **M18 Hellcat**
▶ **M10**
▶ **SU-85**
▶ **Marder III**
▶ **Archer**

Main Gun Calibre

World War II-era tank destroyers typically mounted heavy main guns capable of penetrating the armour of enemy vehicles at significant range. As heavier tanks reached the battlefield and armour protection was augmented, Allied and Axis tank destroyers were upgunned proportionately.

As armoured warfare evolved during the war, the multi-purpose self-propelled assault gun assumed the role of tank destroyer as well as infantry-support provider. Sacrificing armour for speed and firepower, the tank destroyer proved a potent weapon, particularly when it had the advantage of concealment. Later tank destroyers afforded greater crew protection, with enclosed turrets or compartments and more powerful engines.

The US open-turreted M10 was the most numerous Allied tank destroyer on the Western Front, while its intended successor, the M18, had the same calibre weapon in an open turret but was the fastest tracked armoured vehicle of the war, capable of up to 88.5km/h (55mph). The Soviet SU-85 mounted an 85mm (3.3in) anti-tank gun and appeared on the battlefield in 1943, while the Germans fielded a variety of tank destroyers, including the Marder III, with a top speed of 42km/h (26mph).

Marder III Speed
42km/h
(26mph)

BELOW: A US Army M10 tank destroyer advances over a pontoon during the final days of the war.

Archer Speed
32.2km/h
(20mph)

Classic Late-war Medium Tanks 1

Maximum Speed and Armour Protection

▶ **T-34/85**
▶ **Cruiser Mk VIII Cromwell VII**
▶ **M4A3 Sherman**
▶ **Panther Ausf G**

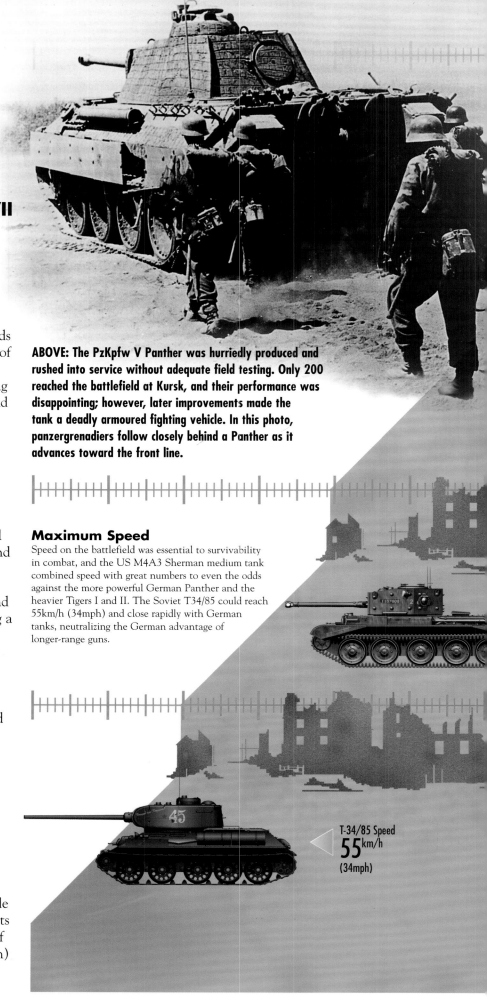

ABOVE: The PzKpfw V Panther was hurriedly produced and rushed into service without adequate field testing. Only 200 reached the battlefield at Kursk, and their performance was disappointing; however, later improvements made the tank a deadly armoured fighting vehicle. In this photo, panzergrenadiers follow closely behind a Panther as it advances toward the front line.

Perhaps the decisive element on the battlefields of World War II in Europe was the presence of the medium tank. Intended for infantry support and evolving into gun platforms capable of taking on one another in tank-vs-tank combat, Axis and Allied medium tanks combined speed, armour protection and firepower to varying degrees of success, and several of these designs became the stuff of legend.

The British Cromwell VII descended from a line of cruiser tanks that had begun design and production in 1940 but did not appear on the battlefield until late in the war. Improved frontal armour of up to 101mm (3.98in), wider tracks and a 75mm (2.9in) cannon kept the tank in service for a decade. Meanwhile, the American M4 Sherman tank was produced in great numbers and sacrificed armour for speed. Eventually mounting a 76mm (3in) gun, the M4A3 carried a maximum of 100mm (3.9in) of protection. At 52km/h (32mph), the top speed of the Cromwell slightly eclipsed the Sherman's 47km/h (29mph).

The most effective combination of speed and firepower to emerge during World War II entered service with the Soviet T-34/85 medium tank. Capable of a top speed of 55km/h (34mph), the T-34/85 was upgunned from the original 76mm (3in) main weapon to an 85mm (3.3in) cannon, while it was protected by up to 75mm (2.9in) of sloped armour.

Developed in response to the appearance on the battlefield of the Soviet T-34, the German PzKpfw V Panther tank made an inauspicious combat debut at the Battle of Kursk but this was followed by performance improvements that made the Panther one of the war's outstanding tanks. Its high-velocity 75mm (2.9in) cannon, top speed of 46km/h (28.5mph) and more than 100mm (3.9in) of frontal armour made the Panther Ausf G a formidable opponent.

Maximum Speed

Speed on the battlefield was essential to survivability in combat, and the US M4A3 Sherman medium tank combined speed with great numbers to even the odds against the more powerful German Panther and the heavier Tigers I and II. The Soviet T34/85 could reach 55km/h (34mph) and close rapidly with German tanks, neutralizing the German advantage of longer-range guns.

T-34/85 Speed
55km/h
(34mph)

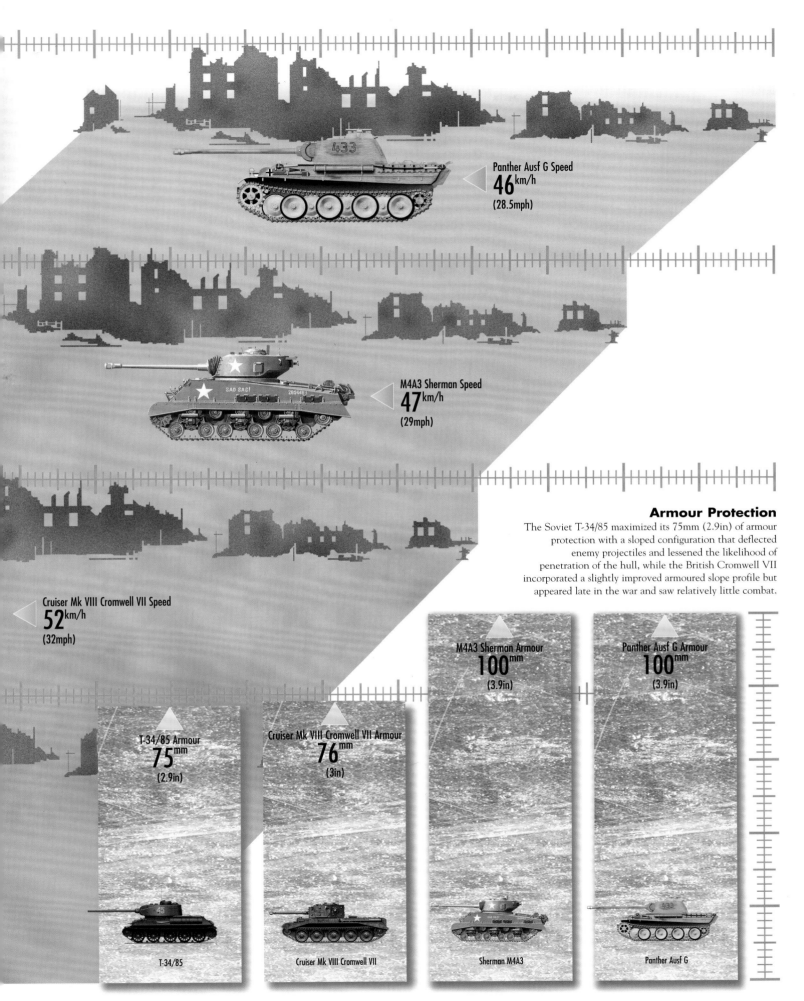

Panther Ausf G Speed
46km/h
(28.5mph)

M4A3 Sherman Speed
47km/h
(29mph)

Cruiser Mk VIII Cromwell VII Speed
52km/h
(32mph)

Armour Protection

The Soviet T-34/85 maximized its 75mm (2.9in) of armour protection with a sloped configuration that deflected enemy projectiles and lessened the likelihood of penetration of the hull, while the British Cromwell VII incorporated a slightly improved armoured slope profile but appeared late in the war and saw relatively little combat.

M4A3 Sherman Armour
100mm
(3.9in)

Panther Ausf G Armour
100mm
(3.9in)

T-34/85 Armour
75mm
(2.9in)

Cruiser Mk VIII Cromwell VII Armour
76mm
(3in)

T-34/85

Cruiser Mk VIII Cromwell VII

Sherman M4A3

Panther Ausf G

Classic Late War Medium Tanks 2

Weight and Operational Range

▶ **Cruiser Mk VIII Cromwell VII**
▶ **T-34/85**
▶ **M4A3 Sherman**
▶ **Sherman Firefly**
▶ **Panther Ausf G**

Heavier weapons and thicker armour protection added to the overall weight of medium tanks as World War II progressed, and often existing powerplants were insufficient to propel the heavier models. However, the trade-off in firepower and survivability was worthwhile for many armoured-vehicle designers.

With its additional armour and 75mm (2.9in) gun, the Cruiser Mk VIII Cromwell VII approached a weight of 28 tonnes (27.6 tons) with a road speed of 52km/h (32mph), while the American M4A3 Sherman was heavier at more than 32 tonnes (31.5 tons) as it incorporated a 76mm (3in) gun with higher muzzle velocity than the earlier Shermans' armament.

British engineers sought a more powerful offensive punch with the Sherman and incorporated a 17-pounder main gun to create the Firefly. While the 17-pounder offered improved penetration, the Firefly's weight soared to more than 35 tonnes (34.4 tons), thereby diminishing the tank's road and cross-country speeds.

Cruiser Mk VIII Cromwell VII Weight
27.94 tonnes
(27.5 tons)

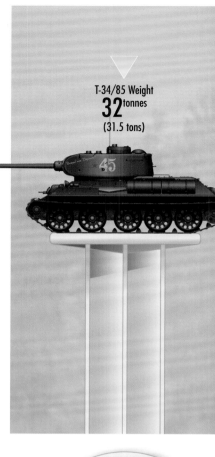

T-34/85 Weight
32 tonnes
(31.5 tons)

Cruiser Mk VIII Cromwell VII Weight: 27.94 tonnes (27.5 tons)

T-34/85 Weight: 32 tonnes (31.5 tons)

T-34/85 Range
360 km
(224 miles)

RIGHT: With its larger 85mm (3.3in) cannon, the Soviet T-34/85 remained a respectable 32 tonnes (31.5 tons) and combined a 55km/h (34mph) top speed in the Red Army surge towards Berlin in 1944–45. Its German counterpart, the Panther, was comparatively ponderous with a top speed of 46km/h (28.5mph).

M4A3 Sherman Weight
32.28 tonnes
(31.8 tons)

Sherman Firefly Weight
35.36 tonnes
(34.8 tons)

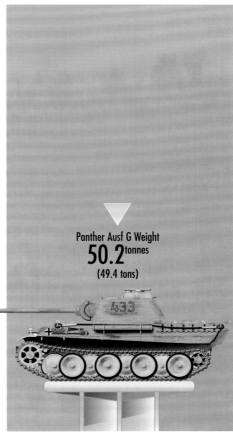

Panther Ausf G Weight
50.2 tonnes
(49.4 tons)

Weight

Heavier armour protection and substantially upgraded weaponry added to the weight of medium tanks during World War II, while speed and mobility were often adversely affected. However, the introduction of larger, more efficient engines eventually improved range and speed. Nevertheless, the issue of weight versus performance has remained at the forefront of tank design into the modern era.

M4A3 Sherman Weight: 32.28 tonnes (31.8 tons)

Sherman Firefly Weight: 35.36 tonnes (34.8 tons)

Panther Ausf G Weight: 50.2 tonnes (49.4 tons)

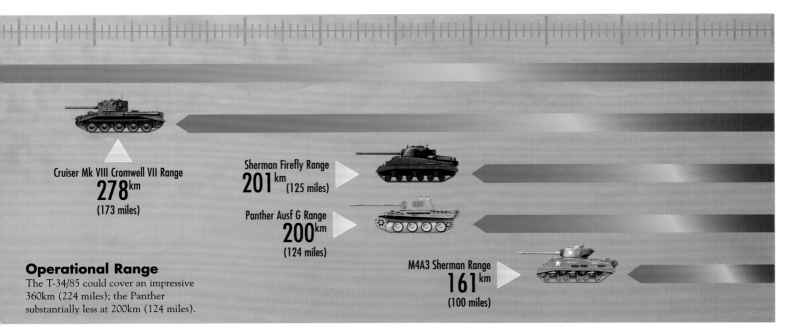

Cruiser Mk VIII Cromwell VII Range
278 km
(173 miles)

Sherman Firefly Range
201 km
(125 miles)

Panther Ausf G Range
200 km
(124 miles)

M4A3 Sherman Range
161 km
(100 miles)

Operational Range

The T-34/85 could cover an impressive 360km (224 miles); the Panther substantially less at 200km (124 miles).

Armour in Normandy: June 1944

Allied Armour Vulnerability

▶ **Churchill Mk VII**
▶ **Cruiser Mk VIII Cromwell**
▶ **Sherman Firefly**
▶ **Panzer VI Tiger I**
▶ **Panzer V Ausf D**
▶ **Panzer IV Ausf H**

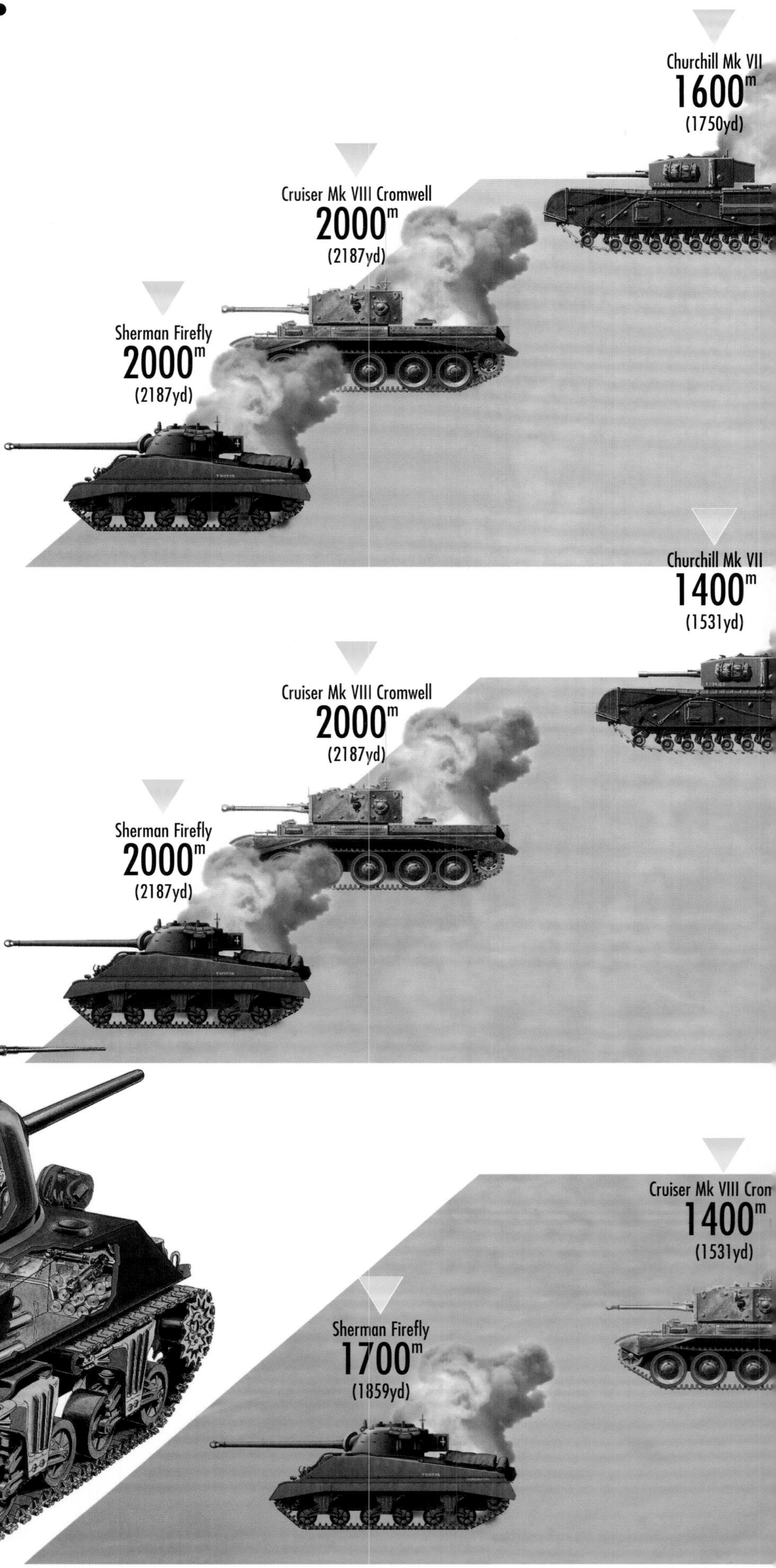

The outstanding armour-piercing capabilities of the German 88mm (3.5in) and 75mm (2.9in) guns mounted on the Tiger I, PzKpfw V Panther, and PzKpfw IV were realized with devastating effect at times during the Normandy campaign. Although the 75mm (2.9in) gun fielded on the Allied Cromwell and Churchill was capable of penetrating the armour of the PzKpfw IV, only the Sherman Firefly's 17-pounder could take on the thick hulls of the Panther and Tiger I.

BELOW: Nearly 50,000 examples of M4 Sherman tank variants were produced during World War II. The Sherman was smaller and faster than its German adversaries but lacked the armour and penetrating power of the enemy tanks. Two significant armament upgrades took place during the war, with the introduction of a high-velocity 76mm (3in) cannon, replacing the early 75mm (2.9in) weapon, and the British introduction of the 17-pounder main gun in the Firefly. The M4A4 Sherman (illustrated, right) featured a lengthened and welded hull.

Churchill Mk VII
1600ᵐ
(1750yd)

Cruiser Mk VIII Cromwell
2000ᵐ
(2187yd)

Sherman Firefly
2000ᵐ
(2187yd)

Churchill Mk VII
1400ᵐ
(1531yd)

Cruiser Mk VIII Cromwell
2000ᵐ
(2187yd)

Sherman Firefly
2000ᵐ
(2187yd)

Cruiser Mk VIII Crom
1400ᵐ
(1531yd)

Sherman Firefly
1700ᵐ
(1859yd)

Armour Penetration

The high-velocity guns of the Tiger and Panther penetrated the armour of the Sherman and Cromwell with virtually equal performance at up to 2000m (2187yd). The PzKpfw IV was effective against the Sherman and Cromwell at 1700m (1859yd) and 1400m (1531yd) respectively, while the effective range dropped to a mere 400m (437yd) against the heavily armoured Churchill. Even the Churchill was vulnerable to the big guns of the Tiger at 1600m (1750yd) and the Panther at 1400m (1531yd).

Effective Main Gun Range

During the Normandy campaign, German medium and heavy tanks regularly engaged Allied armour at significant ranges, utilizing the advantages of large-calibre guns with high muzzle velocity. The Tiger and Panther routinely knocked out Allied tanks at distances of 2000m (2187yd), while the Cromwell and Churchill were required to manoeuvre dangerously close to deliver effective fire. Only the Firefly could engage the German monster tanks at standard ranges.

Panzer VI Tiger I

Panzer V Ausf D

Churchill Mk VII
400ᵐ
(437yd)

Panzer IV Ausf H

British Tank Gun Capability

Vulnerability of German Armour

▶ **Cruiser Mk VIII Cromwell VII**
▶ **M4A3 Sherman**
▶ **Sherman Firefly**

As Allied tanks encountered the heavy armour of the German Panther and Tiger I in Normandy, battlefield tactics evolved to minimize the advantages of range the Germans possessed with their 75mm (2.9in) and 88mm (3.5in) guns. Often, British tank crews manoeuvred in teams to achieve the most advantageous firing positions against German AFVs, which were most vulnerable from their lightly armoured rear.

The 75mm (2.9in) gun of the Cruiser Mk VIII Cromwell VII was effective against the rear of the heavy Tiger at very short ranges only. While the low muzzle velocity of the early 75mm (2.9in) gun mounted on the M4 Sherman was inadequate against thick German armour, the introduction of the high-velocity 76mm (3in) gun and the development of the British Firefly variant, mounting a 17-pounder anti-tank gun, improved the chances of Allied success, particularly when firing at the flank or rear of German tanks.

In March 1944, the British introduced the APDS (armour-piercing discarding sabot) shell, and the high-velocity 17-pounder gun could damage German tanks at much greater range.

BELOW: US infantry move cautiously past an M4A4 Sherman tank during the fighting for France, 1944.

Effective Main Gun Range

High-velocity 76mm (3in) and 17-pounder main weapons dramatically improved the range and penetrating power of British tanks. As the war progressed, the upgunned variants of the original M4 Sherman tank appeared in greater numbers and began to inflict heavier losses on German armour. More than 2000 examples of the Sherman Firefly were built from 1943. The introduction of APDS (armour-piercing discarding sabot) ammunition increased effective range substantially.

Panzer IV Ausf H
1250ᵐ
(1367yd)

Panzer IV Ausf H
1750ᵐ
(1914yd)

Panzer V Ausf D
1250ᵐ
(1367yd)

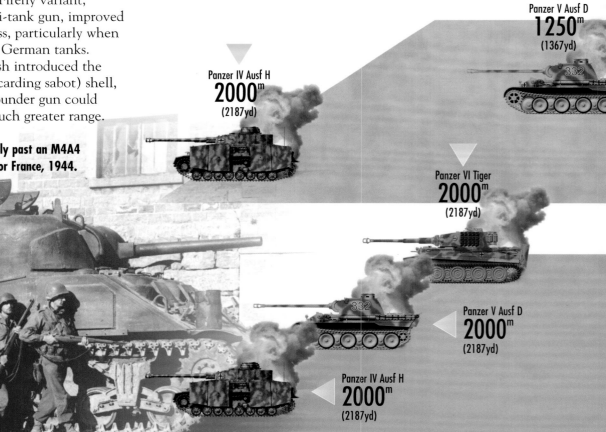

Panzer IV Ausf H
2000ᵐ
(2187yd)

Panzer VI Tiger
2000ᵐ
(2187yd)

Panzer V Ausf D
2000ᵐ
(2187yd)

Panzer IV Ausf H
2000ᵐ
(2187yd)

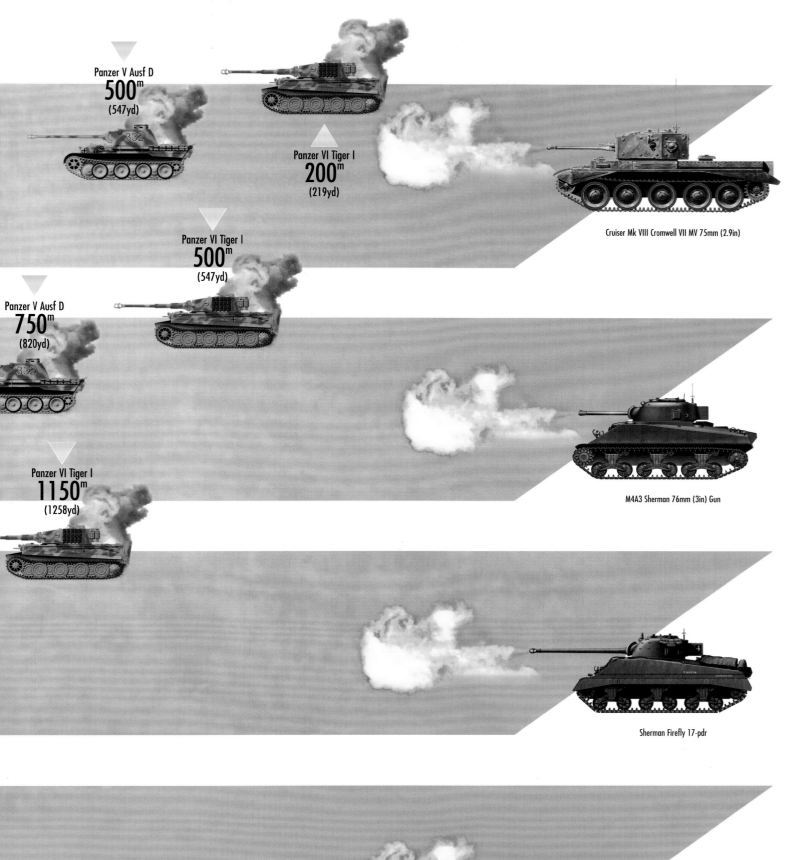

Panzer V Ausf D
500m
(547yd)

Panzer VI Tiger I
200m
(219yd)

Cruiser Mk VIII Cromwell VII MV 75mm (2.9in)

Panzer VI Tiger I
500m
(547yd)

Panzer V Ausf D
750m
(820yd)

M4A3 Sherman 76mm (3in) Gun

Panzer VI Tiger I
1150m
(1258yd)

Sherman Firefly 17-pdr

Sherman Firefly 17-pdr APDS

Armour Protection

The World War II-era Sherman Firefly incorporated up to 89mm (3.51in) of frontal armour protection and a 17-pounder main weapon, increasing the weight of the vehicle appreciably. However, the development of composite armour in modern main battle tanks affords substantially greater protection than steel, along with lighter weight. The M1A2 Abrams, therefore, is protected by the equivalent of 700mm (27.6in) of steel.

Abrams M1A2

Sherman Firefly

Sherman Firefly Armour
89mm
(3.51in)

42 rounds

Abrams M1A2 Calibre
120mm
(4.7in)

Abrams M1A2 Armour
700mm
(27.6in)

Abrams M1A2

Sherman Firefly

Old and New: Sherman Firefly vs M1 Abrams

Gun Calibre, Armour and Number of Rounds

▶ **Sherman Firefly**
▶ **M1A2 Abrams**

Through more than half a century of warfare, the role of the tank in combat has evolved. Where once there was a division of labour among different types, in the main battle tank (MBT) there is now the embodiment of versatility. Modern tanks and AFVs owe much of their combat prowess to the evolution of the tank brought about by battlefield experience in World War II. As the war progressed, innovative combinations of weapons and protection were developed rapidly and pressed into action. The results have influenced tank design and performance expectations ever since.

Among the most notable Allied improvisations of World War II was the development of the 17-pounder-armed Sherman Firefly by British engineers, who sought to provide their fighting men with a weapon that could take on heavier German tanks such as the medium Panther and heavy Tiger I and II with some expectation of success. The Firefly was successful to an extent, although three tonnes (2.9 tons) heavier than the standard M4A3 Sherman.

Through decades of field trials and improving technology, the MBT has demonstrated generational improvements in capabilities. Tested in combat during the Gulf War and operations in the Balkans, Iraq and Afghanistan, the US-built M1 Abrams has set the standard in modern tank performance. Production of the M1A2 began in 1992, and earlier versions of the Abrams were upgraded between 1996 and 2001. The tank mounts a 120mm (4.7in) smoothbore cannon and carries 42 rounds of specialized ammunition. Protected by composite armour that offers maximum defence against projectiles while minimizing vehicle weight, the M1A2 is powered by turbine engines and has a road speed of 56km/h (35mph) despite a weight of more than 60 tonnes (59.1 tons). Its state-of-the-art fire-control system ensures target acquisition and deadly accuracy.

Sherman Firefly Calibre
76.2mm
(17 pdr/3in)

77 rounds

Main Gun Calibre

The 17-pounder gun of the Sherman Firefly was a marked improvement over the original 75mm (2.9in) weapon in range and muzzle velocity, providing greater capability against German AFVs. More than 60 years on, the M1A2 Abrams mounts a 120mm (4.7in) smoothbore cannon with a startling range of up to 8000m (8700yd) firing specialized ammunition.

Pacific Theatre: AFVs and Tanks

Main Gun Calibre and Armour Protection

- ▶ **M4A1 Sherman**
- ▶ **M3 Lee/Grant**
- ▶ **LVT(A)-4**
- ▶ **Type 97 Chi-Ha**
- ▶ **Type 95 Kyu-Go**

During the November 1943 fight for Tarawa atoll in the Gilbert Islands, a direct hit from the 37mm (1.5in) gun of a Japanese tank turned the turret armour of a US Marine Corps M4 Sherman lemon yellow but did no real damage. In turn, the Sherman blasted the enemy tank with its 75mm (2.9in) gun in a short and unequal contest. The Sherman's 75mm (2.9in) weapon far outclassed the 57mm (2.2in) and 37mm (1.5in) guns mounted on the Japanese medium Type 97 Chi-Ha and light Type 95 Kyu-Go tanks, while the M3 Lee/Grant carried a 37mm (1.5in) cannon in addition to a turreted 75mm (2.9in) weapon.

The armour of Sherman variants ranged from 64 to 76mm (2.5–3in), and the M3 was protected by up to 51mm (2in). Conversely, the Japanese tanks were thin-skinned, with 12mm (0.47in) protecting the Type 95 and 26mm (1in) the Type 97. Both US tanks were capable of neutralizing Japanese armour and fixed fortifications with their heavy weapons while operating in the confines of a small island or in thick Asian jungle.

The LVT(A)-4 variant (left) of the famed Amtrac landing craft entered service in 1944 mounting a 75mm (2.9in) howitzer.

Main Gun Calibre

US armour held a distinct advantage in firepower during the Pacific War, with the 75mm (2.9in) guns of the M4A1 Sherman and M3 Lee/Grant outclassing the 57mm (2.2in) and 37mm (1.5in) guns of the most numerous Japanese AFVs.

M4A1 Sherman Calibre
75mm
(2.9in)

M3 Lee/Grant Calibre
75mm
(2.9in)

LVT(A)-4 Calibre
75mm
(2.9in)

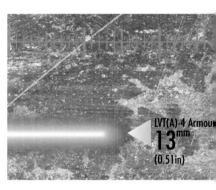
LVT(A)-4 Armour
13mm
(0.51in)

Type 97 Chi-Ha Calibre
57mm
(2.2in)

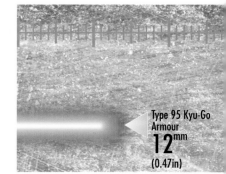

Type 95 Kyu-Go Calibre
37mm
(1.5in)

Type 95 Kyu-Go Armour
12mm
(0.47in)

Armour Protection

The armour of US tanks in the Pacific Theatre afforded protection against most Japanese anti-tank weapons. The Sherman and Lee/Grant were armoured up to 76mm (3in) and 51mm (2in) respectively, while Japanese tanks were thinly protected with only up to half the armour thickness of the Lee/Grant.

M4A1 Sherman

M4A1 Sherman Armour
76mm
(3in)

M3 Lee/Grant

M3 Lee/Grant Armour
51mm
(2in)

LVT(A)-4

Type 97 Chi-Ha

Type 97 Chi-Ha Armour
26mm
(1.1in)

Type 95 Kyu-Go

Late War Heavy Tanks 1: 1944–45

Operational Range and Armour Protection

▶ **Panzer VI Tiger II**
▶ **Tiger I Ausf E**
▶ **M26 Pershing**
▶ **JS-1**
▶ **JS-2**

The 68.5-tonne (67.4-ton) Tiger II was almost impervious to a frontal hit, but its fuel consumption and complex engineering limited its range to 110km (68 miles), somewhat less than the Tiger I at 195km (121 miles). With their thinner armour, Allied heavy tanks weighed less than the Tiger II: the Soviet JS-2 weighed 46 tonnes (45.3 tons) and the US M26 Pershing 42 tonnes (41.3 tons). The former had a range of 240km (149 miles); the M26 could manage only 161km (100 miles), due partially to an inadequate powerplant.

Operational Range

The Soviet JS-1 and JS-2 perhaps provided the finest combination of armour protection and range among the heavy tanks of World War II. With armour as thick as 160mm (6.3in), the JS series managed an operational range of 250km (155 miles) in the case of the JS-1 and 240km (149 miles) with the JS-2. In contrast, the German Tiger I was limited to 195km (121 miles) and the Tiger II to 110km (68 miles).

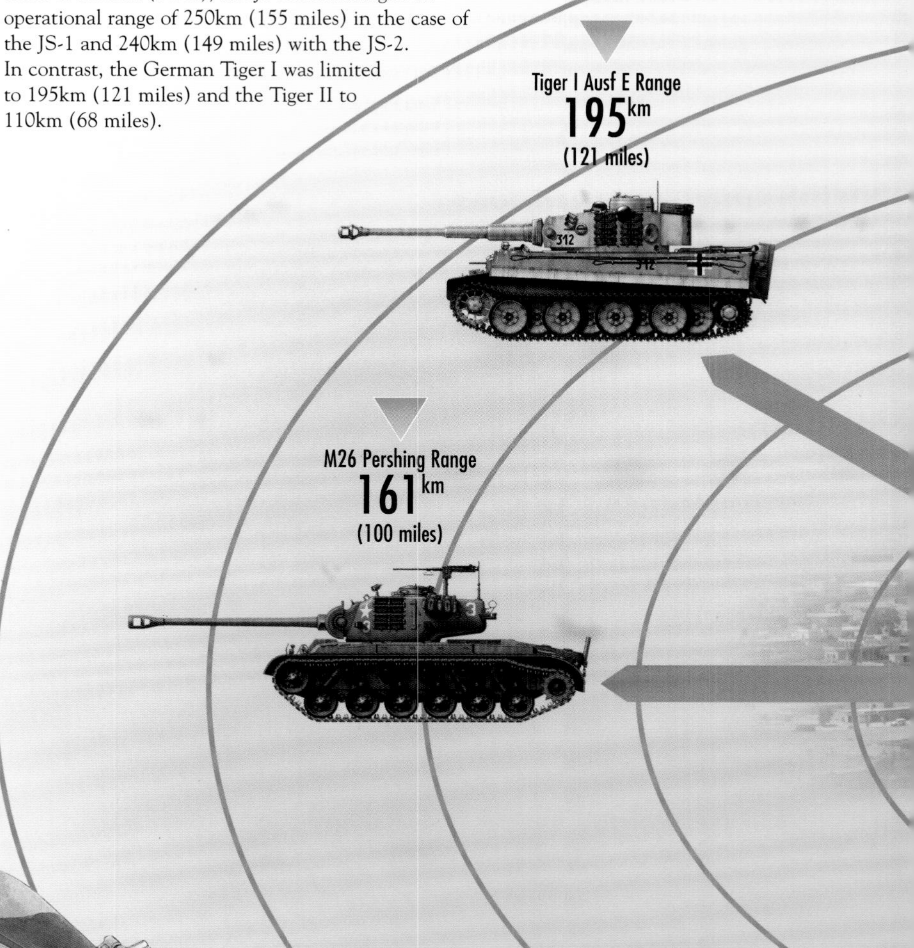

Tiger I Ausf E Range
195 km
(121 miles)

M26 Pershing Range
161 km
(100 miles)

RIGHT: The heavy Tiger II made its combat debut in Normandy in July 1944, incorporating sloped armour and much greater weight than other contemporary tanks, rendering its Maybach engine insufficient to power the vehicle across even the most favourable terrain.

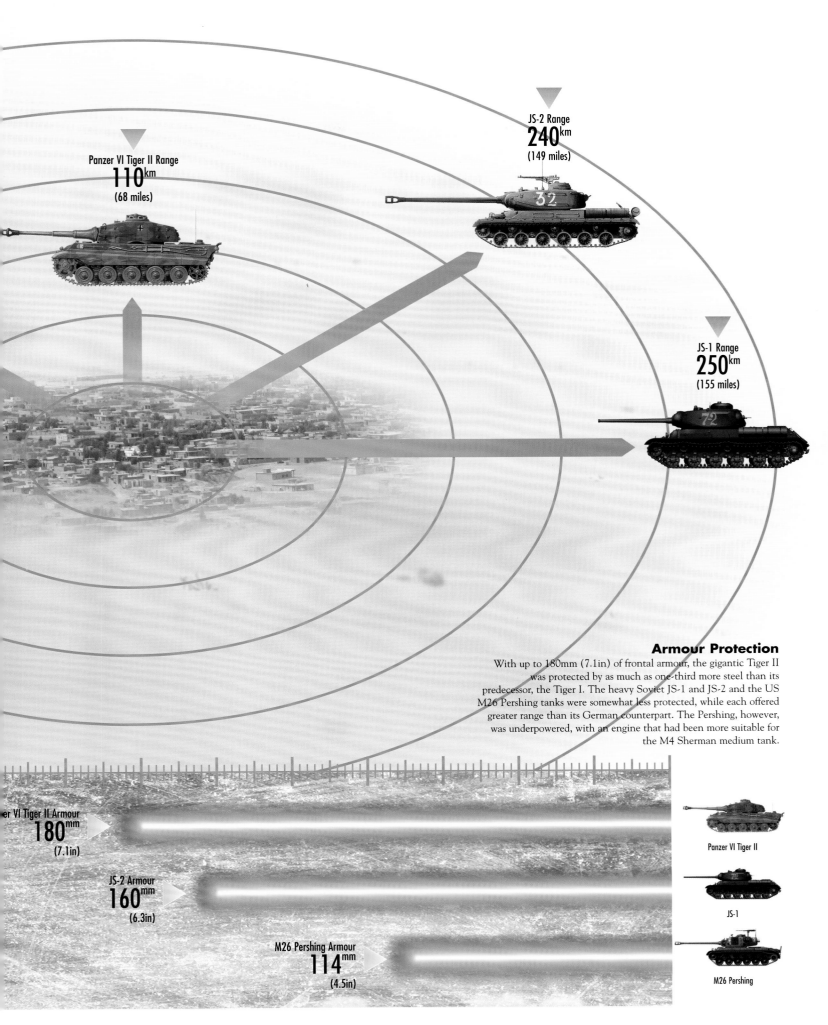

JS-2 Range
240km
(149 miles)

Panzer VI Tiger II Range
110km
(68 miles)

JS-1 Range
250km
(155 miles)

Armour Protection

With up to 180mm (7.1in) of frontal armour, the gigantic Tiger II was protected by as much as one-third more steel than its predecessor, the Tiger I. The heavy Soviet JS-1 and JS-2 and the US M26 Pershing tanks were somewhat less protected, while each offered greater range than its German counterpart. The Pershing, however, was underpowered, with an engine that had been more suitable for the M4 Sherman medium tank.

er VI Tiger II Armour
180mm
(7.1in)

JS-2 Armour
160mm
(6.3in)

M26 Pershing Armour
114mm
(4.5in)

Panzer VI Tiger II

JS-1

M26 Pershing

M26 Pershing

Following great debate in the US over armour protection and firepower, the M26 Pershing emerged with a 90mm (3.5in) gun in a massive cast turret with 100mm (3.9in) of armour on its front glacis.

M26 Pershing Calibre
90mm
(3.5in)

Tiger I Ausf E

With 120mm (4.7in) of frontal armour plating, the turret of the Tiger I mounted the deadly 88mm (3.5in) cannon and accommodated three men – commander, gunner and loader – during combat operations.

Tiger I Ausf E Calibre
88mm
(3.5in)

JS-1

The turret of the JS-1 was positioned according to classic Soviet design, forward on the hull. Early production JS-1s mounted an 85mm (3.3in) gun; however, this was later upgraded to a massive 122mm (4.8in) weapon.

JS-1 Calibre
85mm
(3.3in)

Main Gun Calibre

During World War II, the calibre of Axis and Allied heavy-tank guns steadily increased, particularly in response to advances in anti-tank weaponry, the likelihood of tank-vs-tank combat on both the Eastern and Western fronts and the requirement for high-velocity guns that fired projectiles capable of penetrating heavier enemy armour.

Late War Heavy Tanks 2: 1944–45

Turret, Main Gun Calibre and Engine Power

▶ **M26 Pershing**
▶ **Tiger I Ausf E**
▶ **JS-1**

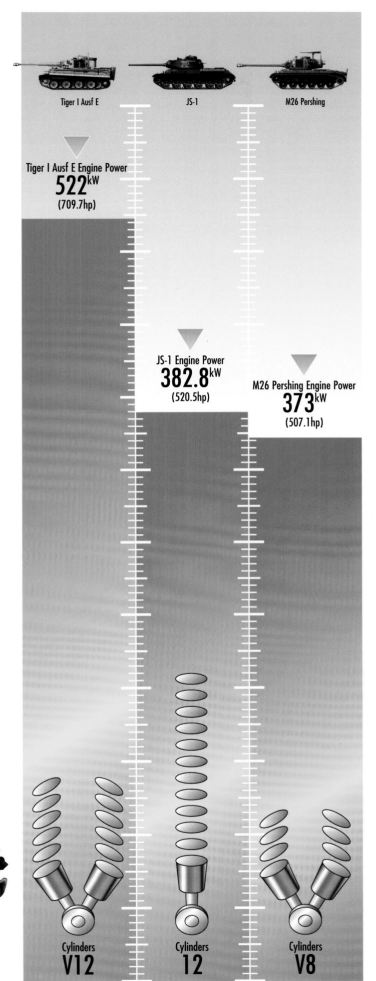

Tiger I Ausf E
JS-1
M26 Pershing

Tiger I Ausf E Engine Power
522kW
(709.7hp)

JS-1 Engine Power
382.8kW
(520.5hp)

M26 Pershing Engine Power
373kW
(507.1hp)

Cylinders
V12

Cylinders
12

Cylinders
V8

As the German Tiger I and Tiger II were fielded, Soviet factories were turning out a new generation of heavy tanks for the Red Army, specifically designed to achieve parity and potentially outperform these battlefield behemoths. The Tiger I mounted an 88mm (3.5in) gun in an 11-tonne (10.8-ton) turret, while the elongated Henschel turret of the Tiger II was equipped with a higher-velocity 88mm (3.5in) gun, some of the finest optics in the world, and 180mm (7.1in) glacis, 80mm (3.15in) side, and 40mm (1.57in) rooftop armour.

The Soviet response was the JS (Josef Stalin) series of heavy tanks. The JS-1 initially mounted an 85mm (3.3in) gun, while late-production JS-1s were equipped with a 122mm (4.8in) gun. The JS-2 followed in the spring of 1944 and offered significant improvements on the earlier KV series, including thicker sloped-armour protection, a heavier 122mm (4.8in) gun, improved top speed, and lighter weight. All this was accomplished through more efficient overall design.

Inadequate engine performance plagued the German designs, and to a somewhat lesser extent the Soviets' as well. Both the Tiger I and the Tiger II were inadequately powered by 12-cylinder Maybach engines, while the JS-1 and JS-2 were powered by a 12-cylinder V-2 diesel that was limited in performance during extremely high temperatures.

In the United States, the need for a production heavy-tank design was recognized early in World War II; however, the development of the M26 Pershing with its 90mm (3.5in) cannon experienced significant delays, and the tank did not enter service in limited numbers until 1945.

Engine Power

The mammoth heavy tanks of World War II consumed extremely large quantities of fuel and required huge engine capacity to power them effectively, particularly in combat. However, available engines often lacked the performance necessary to do this, resulting in mechanical failures and arduous maintenance in the field. Postwar heavy tanks were regularly equipped with larger powerplants.

Artillery & Missiles

Numerous historians have pointed to the effectiveness of Allied artillery as the critical element in winning the ground war in Europe and the Pacific. Throughout the notable campaigns of World War II, massed artillery bombardment was utilized in preparation for offensive operations, literally destroying enemy forward positions, taking rear areas under fire with extended-range weapons and exhibiting the potential to thoroughly demoralize and erode the combat efficiency of those enemy soldiers subjected to prolonged bombardment.

The deployment of heavy artillery, field artillery, self-propelled guns and more specialized anti-aircraft and light weapons, some constructed for use in rugged terrain and easily disassembled and transported by pack animals, often dictated the outcome of battle – providing the edge that decided victory or defeat. Artillery tactically destroyed a massed Japanese assault on Bloody Ridge at Guadalcanal, thundered as a prelude to the Red Army offensive that encircled and annihilated the German Sixth Army at Stalingrad, and paved the way for the British Eighth Army at El Alamein, the offensive which culminated in the defeat of Axis forces in North Africa.

LEFT: US Marines man a 40mm (1.57in) Bofors anti-aircraft gun somewhere in the Pacific region. It was one of the most popular medium anti-aircraft systems during World War II, used by most of the Western Allies as well as by the Axis powers.

Light Anti-tank Guns

Effective Range and Calibre

- ▶ **2.8cm Panzerbüchse 41**
- ▶ **37mm Gun M3**
- ▶ **37mm Pak 36**
- ▶ **QF 2-pdr Mk VII**
- ▶ **47mm Model 01**

Developed primarily during the interwar years, light anti-tank weapons were effective against the thin armour protection of early armoured vehicles; however, with the increase in size and armour thickness of tanks throughout the 1930s, many of these weapons were obsolete by the outbreak of World War II.

The appearance of heavier tanks on the battlefield outpaced the deployment of a new generation of anti-tank guns, often to the consternation of crewmen who watched their well-aimed shots bounce harmlessly off the hulls of enemy vehicles.

BELOW: In early 1943, a pair of American soldiers warily scan the North African landscape beside their light 37mm Gun M3.

The effective range of light anti-tank weapons became problematic for gun crews, who were required to allow enemy tanks to approach dangerously close to their concealed positions to achieve a potentially lethal or disabling hit. Such shortcomings also made the crews vulnerable to enemy infantry.

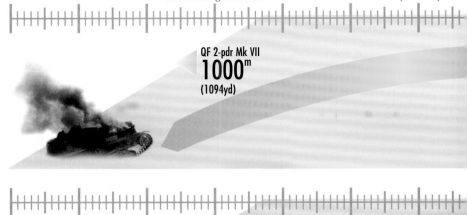

QF 2-pdr Mk VII
1000ᵐ
(1094yd)

47mm Model 01
1000ᵐ
(1094yd)

Calibre

The light calibre of anti-tank weapons, particularly early in World War II, eventually relegated them to secondary roles in most theatres of operations. Heavier armour protection rendered these guns ineffective against enemy tanks, although they were sometimes deployed as infantry support weapons.

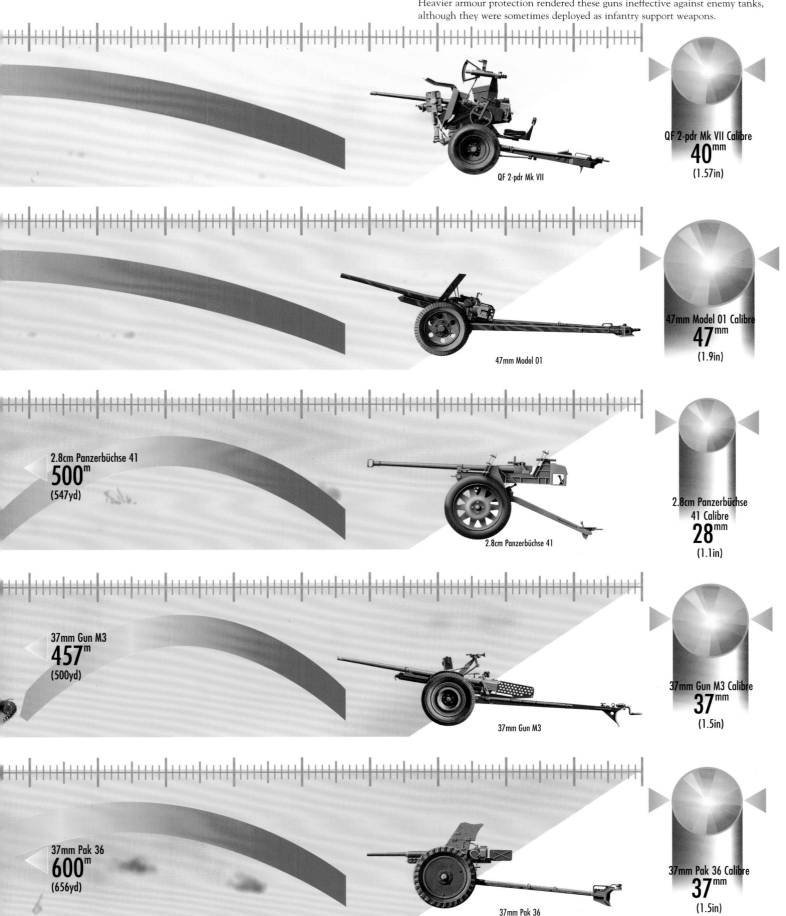

QF 2-pdr Mk VII

QF 2-pdr Mk VII Calibre
40mm
(1.57in)

47mm Model 01

47mm Model 01 Calibre
47mm
(1.9in)

2.8cm Panzerbüchse 41
500m
(547yd)

2.8cm Panzerbüchse 41

2.8cm Panzerbüchse 41 Calibre
28mm
(1.1in)

37mm Gun M3
457m
(500yd)

37mm Gun M3

37mm Gun M3 Calibre
37mm
(1.5in)

37mm Pak 36
600m
(656yd)

37mm Pak 36

37mm Pak 36 Calibre
37mm
(1.5in)

Ordnance QF
460
(503)

88mm Pak 43/41
4000^m
(4374yd)

Ordnance QF 17-pdr
3000^m
(3281yd)

76.2mm Model 1942
2000^m
(2187yd)

75mm Pak 40
7678ᵐ
(8397yd)

Anti-tank Guns

Effective Range

▶ **75mm Pak 40**
▶ **88mm Pak 43/41**
▶ **Ordnance QF 6-pdr**
▶ **Ordnance QF 17-pdr**
▶ **76.2mm Model 1942**

Effective Range
The heavier anti-tank weapons that appeared on the battlefields of World War II in response to a new generation of tanks and armoured fighting vehicles were capable of penetrating increasing armour thicknesses, particularly with the advent of specialized ammunition and longer barrels that raised muzzle velocity.

Financially crippled by the expense of World War I, Britain restricted military spending during the 1920s and early 1930s. One result was that the anti-tank guns deployed with British forces early in World War II were deficient. Rapidly, the QF 2-pounder was outclassed. However, the QF 6-pounder arrived in late 1941 and provided excellent service during a short effective life. In summer 1942, the first 17-pounders became available.

Pressed by British armour at Arras, General Erwin Rommel (1891–1944) ordered 88mm (3.5in) flak guns depressed to level firing lines and stopped the British tanks. Later, he employed the same tactic in North Africa, and the 88mm Pak 43/41 was introduced as a purpose-built anti-tank version of the weapon.

LEFT: The crew of a British anti-tank gun take cover in the face of German counter-battery fire, somewhere in the North African desert. The Ordnance QF 6-pounder was responsible for destroying scores of German and Italian tanks during the British offensive at El Alamein in October 1942.

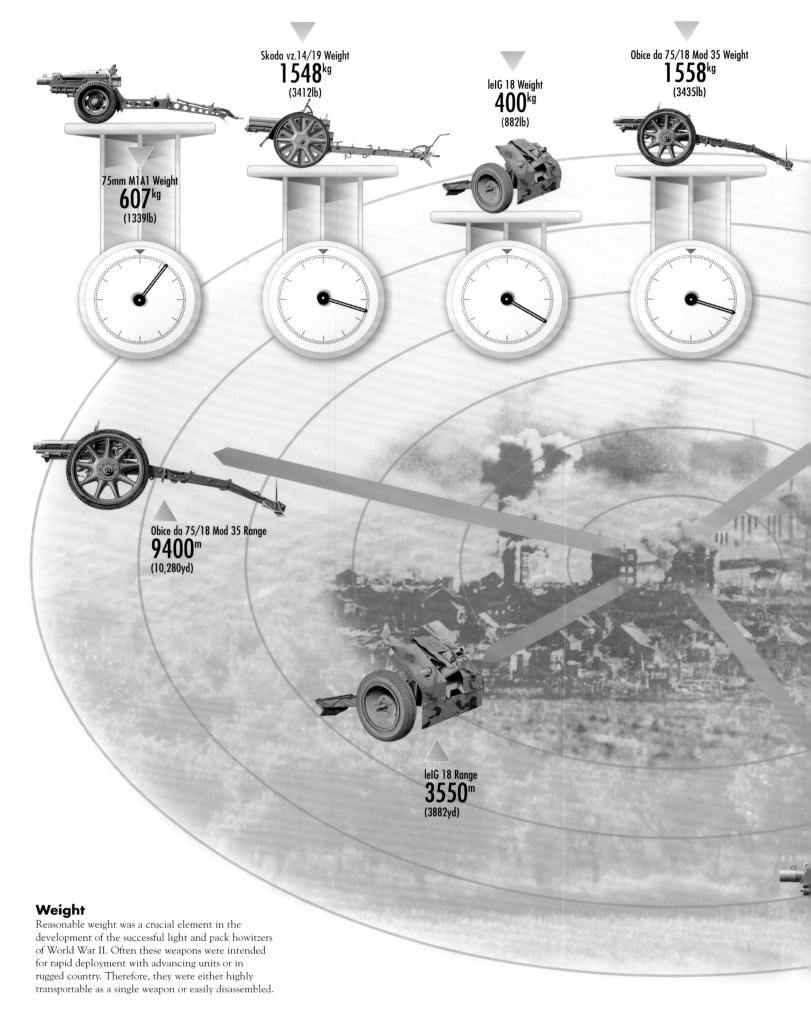

Skoda vz.14/19 Weight
1548kg
(3412lb)

leIG 18 Weight
400kg
(882lb)

Obice da 75/18 Mod 35 Weight
1558kg
(3435lb)

75mm M1A1 Weight
607kg
(1339lb)

Obice da 75/18 Mod 35 Range
9400m
(10,280yd)

leIG 18 Range
3550m
(3882yd)

Weight

Reasonable weight was a crucial element in the
development of the successful light and pack howitzers
of World War II. Often these weapons were intended
for rapid deployment with advancing units or in
rugged country. Therefore, they were either highly
transportable as a single weapon or easily disassembled.

The maximum range of light and pack howitzers was limited due to their calibre, the need for mobility and their deployment often in difficult terrain. The high trajectory of the howitzer was sometimes preferred over distant range due to the advantage of plunging fire against fixed targets or in mountainous areas.

Light/Pack Howitzers

Weight and Effective Range

▶ **75mm Pack Howitzer M1A1**
▶ **10cm Skoda vz.14/19**
▶ **7.5cm leIG 18**
▶ **Obice da 75/18 Mod 35**

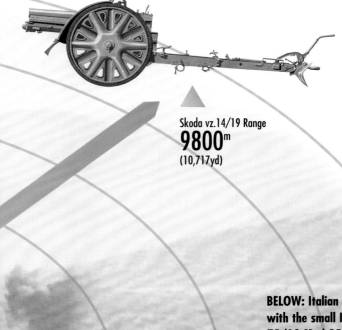

Skoda vz.14/19 Range
9800ᵐ
(10,717yd)

Light artillery often provided a crucial advantage during tactical operations, and the challenge of bringing critical firepower to bear caused weapons designers to recognize the need for optimal weight and mobility, particularly in confined spaces or mountainous terrain. Many of these weapons traced their lineage to the Skoda arms-production facilities of Czechoslovakia or Austrian munitions factories that produced them in volume during World War I.

Pack howitzers such as the highly successful US 75mm (2.9in) M1A1 were designed to be broken down into component parts, carried by pack animals and reassembled quickly for action. These proved highly effective during the long Italian campaign from 1943 through to the end of the war. The Skoda 10cm (3.9in) vz.14/19 light howitzer equipped numerous armies of Central Europe, and a number were pressed into service by the German Army.

BELOW: Italian soldiers train with the small Italian Obice da 75/18 Mod 35. This field howitzer was the by-product of an original mountain-howitzer design from the Ansaldo firm.

75mm M1A1 Range
8787ᵐ
(9610yd)

Infantry Support Mortars

Effective Range

▶ **82mm Model 1937**
▶ **120mm M1938**
▶ **8cm Granatwerfer 34**
▶ **60mm Mortar M2**
▶ **Ordnance ML Mortar 3-inch**

Perhaps the most immediately available infantry support weapon combining range and firepower that could break the back of an enemy assault was the mortar. From light-calibre weapons of approximately 50mm (2in) to heavier towed versions that required substantial crews to operate, the mortar was generally easy to deploy and was brought rapidly into action.

The German 8cm Granatwerfer 34 was common on all fronts with the *Wehrmacht* and earned the grudging respect of Allied troops for its accuracy and rate of fire. Improvements to ammunition bolstered the deficient range of the standard British infantry mortar, the Ordnance ML Mortar 3-inch. The American 60mm Mortar M2 was a licence-built version of the French Brandt model and operated at the company level. Battalion arsenals included the well-known 81mm Mortar M1.

On the Eastern Front, the Soviet 120mm M1938 mortar was one of the best combinations of firepower and mobility in service during the war. The first 120mm (4.7in) mortar fielded by the armed forces of any country, it entered production in 1939 and remains in service today. After German troops encountered the weapon, a copy was placed in production for the *Wehrmacht* and designated the Granatwerfer 42. At 285kg (628lb), the M1938 was one of the heaviest weapons ever carried into combat by infantrymen, either broken down into three components or towed on a two-wheeled carriage.

TOP RIGHT: During action in Normandy in 1944, soldiers of the Black Watch service an Ordnance ML Mortar 3-inch. These men have positioned the weapon in an open pit that provides some protection from small-arms fire, and camouflage netting lies nearby.

Maximum Range

Mortars offered substantial range at the tactical level and often reached targets beyond 2400m (2625yd). Higher-calibre weapons were as effective as light artillery, capable of reaching enemy assembly areas and even disrupting the advances of enemy assaults that included armoured vehicles.

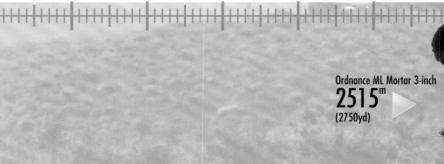

8cm Granatwerf
2400ᵐ
(2625yd)

Ordnance ML Mortar 3-inch
2515ᵐ
(2750yd)

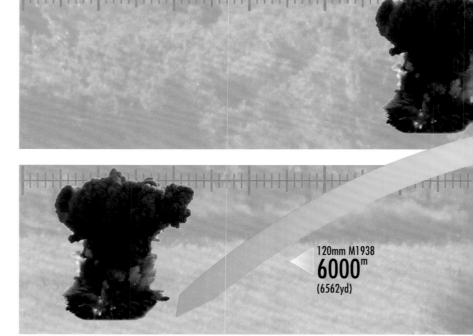

120mm M1938
6000ᵐ
(6562yd)

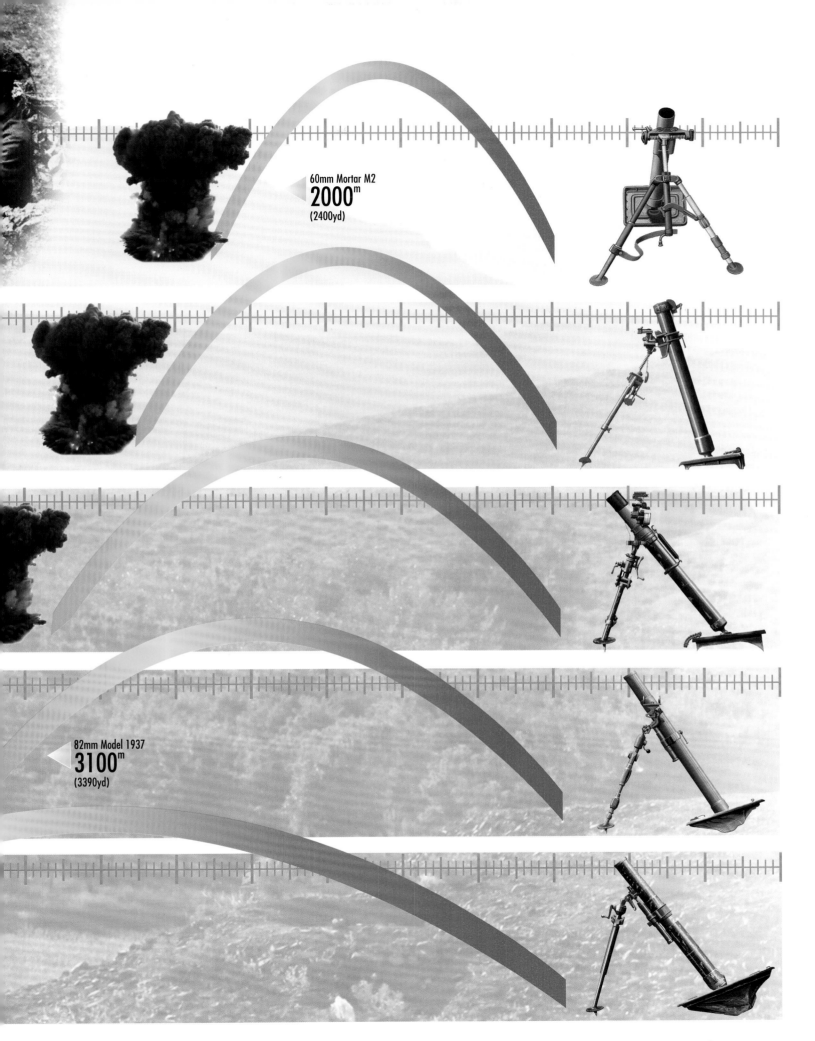

60mm Mortar M2
2000^m
(2400yd)

82mm Model 1937
3100^m
(3390yd)

76mm Model 1942 Weight
1120kg
(2469lb)

Ordnance QF 25-pdr Mk II Weight
1800kg
(3968lb)

75mm Field Gun Type 38 Weight
1910kg
(4211lb)

76.2mm Model 1942 Calibre
76.2mm
(3in)

Ordnance QF 25-pdr Mk II Calibre
87.6mm
(3.45in)

75mm Field Gun Type 38 Calibre
75mm
(2.9in)

Calibre

Heavier-calibre weapons provided greater range, often at the cost of significant weight and more difficult deployment. Finding a balance between firepower and mobility was a great challenge, and weapons designers often determined optimal performance with field artillery of 75mm (2.9in) to 105mm (4.1in).

Weight

The relative weight of field-artillery pieces directly impacted their effectiveness in support of operations. Those that were lighter were deployed more rapidly and brought their fire to bear more efficiently, while the more ponderous weapons required greater commitment of logistics and transport equipment.

105mm Howitzer M2A1 Weight
1934kg
(4264lb)

10.5cm leFH 18(M) Weight
1985kg
(4376lb)

105mm Howitzer M2A1 Calibre
105mm
(4.1in)

10.5cm leFH 18(M) Calibre
105mm
(4.1in)

RIGHT: The Soviet 76.2mm Field Gun Model 1942 was introduced as a lighter, more mobile alternative to its predecessor, the Model 1939. The Model 1942 was produced in greater numbers than any other field-artillery piece of World War II.

Field Artillery 1

Calibre and Weight in Action

▶ **Ordnance QF 25-pdr Mk II**
▶ **10.5cm leFH 18(M)**
▶ **105mm Howitzer M2A1**
▶ **76.2mm Model 1942**
▶ **75mm Field Gun Type 38**

In both an offensive and defensive capacity, artillery has often proved decisive on the battlefield. The advent of field artillery allowed armies to transport mobile fire support with them during extended campaigns. With the outbreak of World War II, artillery was recognized as a key element in land operations.

Early models of the German 10.5cm leFH 18 were manufactured of solid construction with pressed-steel wheels and were discovered to be too heavy for mobile field operations. Later modifications to the original Rheinmetall design lightened this *Wehrmacht* mainstay considerably. The Japanese, on the other hand, relied on Krupp designs that dated from the turn of the twentieth century, such as the 75mm Field Gun Type 38. Britain's QF 25-pounder combined the attributes of a field gun and a howitzer and gained prominence on the battlefields of North Africa. The Mk I version was introduced in limited numbers in the West in 1940, and many were lost at Dunkirk; however, designed in combination with its carriage, the Mk II was a versatile weapon in bombardment and anti-tank roles. From Italy to Normandy and the islands of the Pacific, the 105mm Howitzer M2A1 was the most significant American artillery piece of the war, while the Red Army relied on the 76.2mm Model 1942, which was used as a field gun, anti-tank weapon and configured for use in a tank turret.

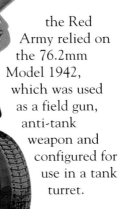

Field Artillery 2

Maximum Range

- ▶ **Ordnance QF 25-pdr Mk II**
- ▶ **10.5cm leFH 18(M)**
- ▶ **105mm Howitzer M2A1**
- ▶ **76.2mm Model 1942**
- ▶ **75mm Field Gun Type 38**

The maximum range and muzzle velocity of World War II-era field artillery contributed directly to its effectiveness in combat, either in preparation for an offensive operation or as a defensive measure that often inflicted heavy casualties on troops, delayed movements and disrupted supply lines. At critical times during the war, artillery is credited with saving a force from annihilation and paving the way to eventual victory. During the Battle of France in 1940, the fast-moving *Wehrmacht* deployed the 10.5cm leFH 18 and utilized superb fire direction to often outduel opposing batteries of the French Army. The Soviets demonstrated effective use of field artillery with the 76.2mm Model 1942 gun, which combined the muzzle velocity necessary to penetrate German armour with the range that allowed the engagement of a variety of targets at advantageous distances. The Model 1942 was the most widely produced weapon of its kind during the war, and examples remain in use today.

During the first sustained American ground offensive of the Pacific War, the Marines of the 1st Raider Battalion fought off waves of attacking Japanese troops as they defended vital Henderson Field on Guadalcanal. Marine artillerymen fired their 105mm M2A1 howitzers furiously, expending nearly 2000 shells and inflicting 1200 Japanese casualties in a single night. The Marine line held firm.

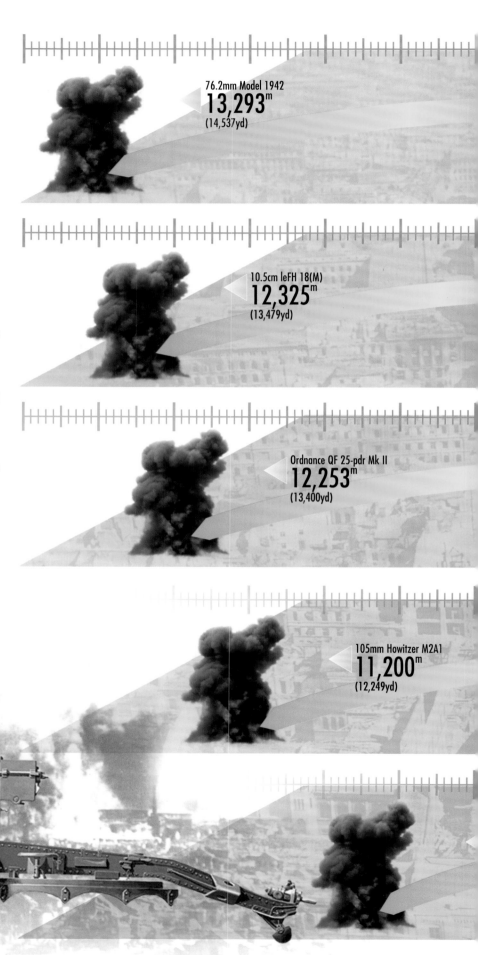

76.2mm Model 1942
13,293ᵐ
(14,537yd)

10.5cm leFH 18(M)
12,325ᵐ
(13,479yd)

Ordnance QF 25-pdr Mk II
12,253ᵐ
(13,400yd)

105mm Howitzer M2A1
11,200ᵐ
(12,249yd)

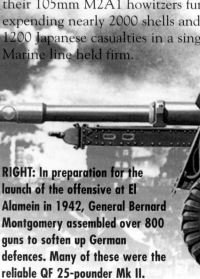

RIGHT: In preparation for the launch of the offensive at El Alamein in 1942, General Bernard Montgomery assembled over 800 guns to soften up German defences. Many of these were the reliable QF 25-pounder Mk II.

Maximum Range

Heavier-calibre weapons often stretched the effective range of field-artillery fire to beyond 12,000m (13,123yd), enabling commanders to suppress the response to their own offensive operations or to break up advancing enemy formations from distant defensive positions.

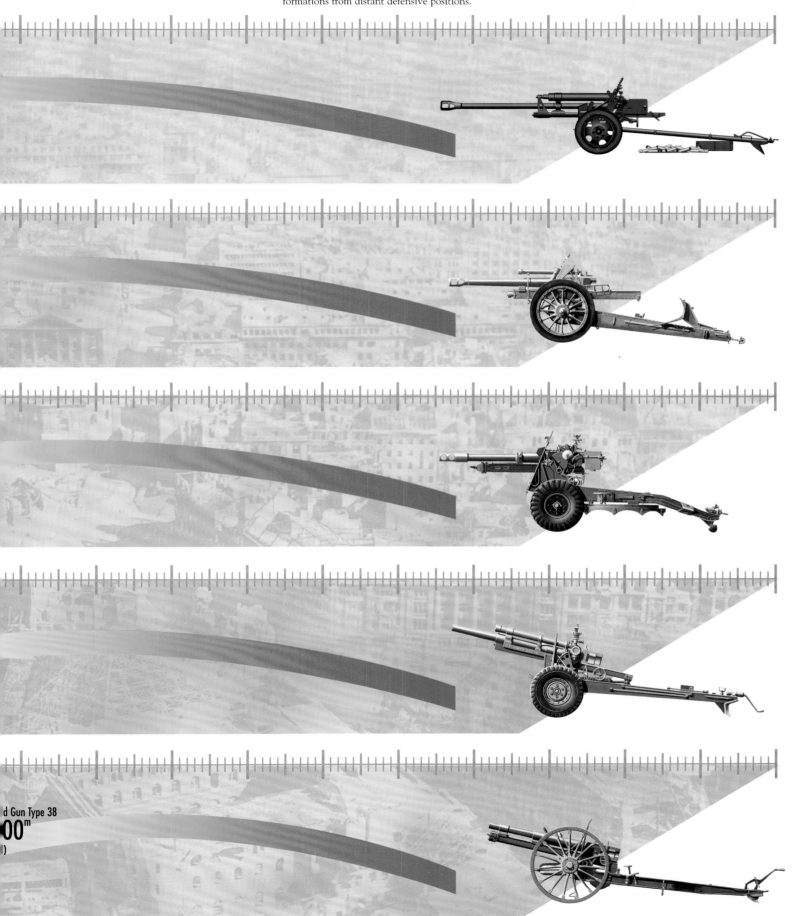

d Gun Type 38
00m
)

Self-propelled Guns 1

Road Range and Weight

▶ **SU-76**
▶ **Wespe**
▶ **Sexton**
▶ **M7 Priest**
▶ **Hummel**

The need for direct fire support for advancing infantry became readily apparent during the early days of World War II as advancing German forces encountered fortified positions and enemy troop concentrations. German efforts to augment mobile firepower capabilities included the Wespe, a self-propelled-gun design which placed a 105mm (4.1in) howitzer atop the chassis of the PzKpfw II tank. The larger Hummel accompanied panzer and panzergrenadier divisions from 1942 and was in production until the end of the war.

In late 1942, the Red Army fielded the SU-76, with a 76.2mm (3in) gun atop the modified chassis of the T-70 tank. Something of a stopgap measure, the SU-76 was intended as a tank killer but was already at a firepower disadvantage by the time it was delivered. The US M7 Priest, named for its pulpit-style supestructure, mounted a 105mm (4.1in) howitzer on the chassis of the M3 tank. The Priest made its combat debut with British troops at El Alamein in October 1942. Britain's self-propelled Sexton was a modified M7 Priest, produced in Canada and mounting the QF 25-pounder gun-howitzer.

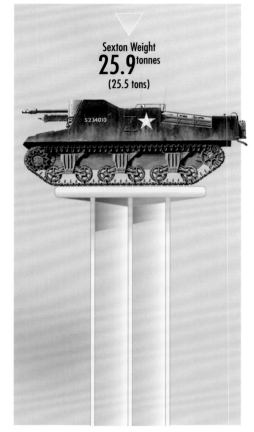

Sexton Weight
25.9 tonnes
(25.5 tons)

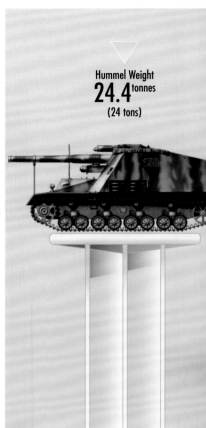

Hummel Weight
24.4 tonnes
(24 tons)

Sexton Weight: 25.9 tonnes (25.5 tons)

Hummel Weight: 24.4 tonnes (24 tons)

SU-76 Range
320 km
(199 miles)

LEFT: Red Army troops go into action under the supporting fire of a self-propelled SU-76.

M7 Priest Weight
22.5tonnes
(22.1 tons)

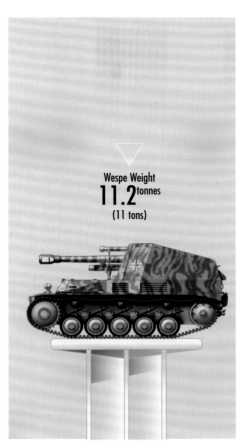

Wespe Weight
11.2tonnes
(11 tons)

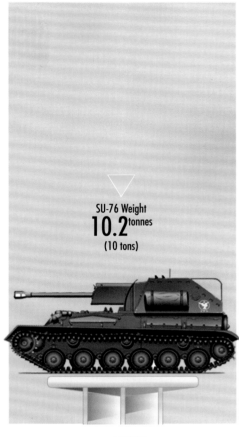

SU-76 Weight
10.2tonnes
(10 tons)

Heavy weight brought about by large-calibre weaponry and increased armour protection negatively impacted the mobility of self-propelled guns, particularly during cross-country movement. Larger engines became necessary to compensate for greater weight, increasing fuel consumption.

M7 Priest Weight: 22.5 tonnes (22.1 tons)

Wespe Weight: 11.2 tonnes (11 tons)

SU-76 Weight: 10.2 tonnes (10 tons)

nel Range
15km
(34 miles)

Sexton Range
201km
(125 miles)

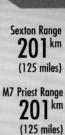

M7 Priest Range
201km
(125 miles)

Road Range

Stretching fuel capacity to the limit across vast expanses of territory, self-propelled guns with extended road range dramatically impacted on the firepower brought to bear at the front. Direct fire support was crucial to a sustained advance.

Wespe Range
140km
(87 miles)

Gun Range

High-velocity weapons with adequate range were critical components of self-propelled guns. Some vehicles mounted gun-howitzers in an attempt to combine the best attributes of both weapons, maximizing muzzle velocity and providing effective plunging fire against hardened targets such as bunkers or pillboxes.

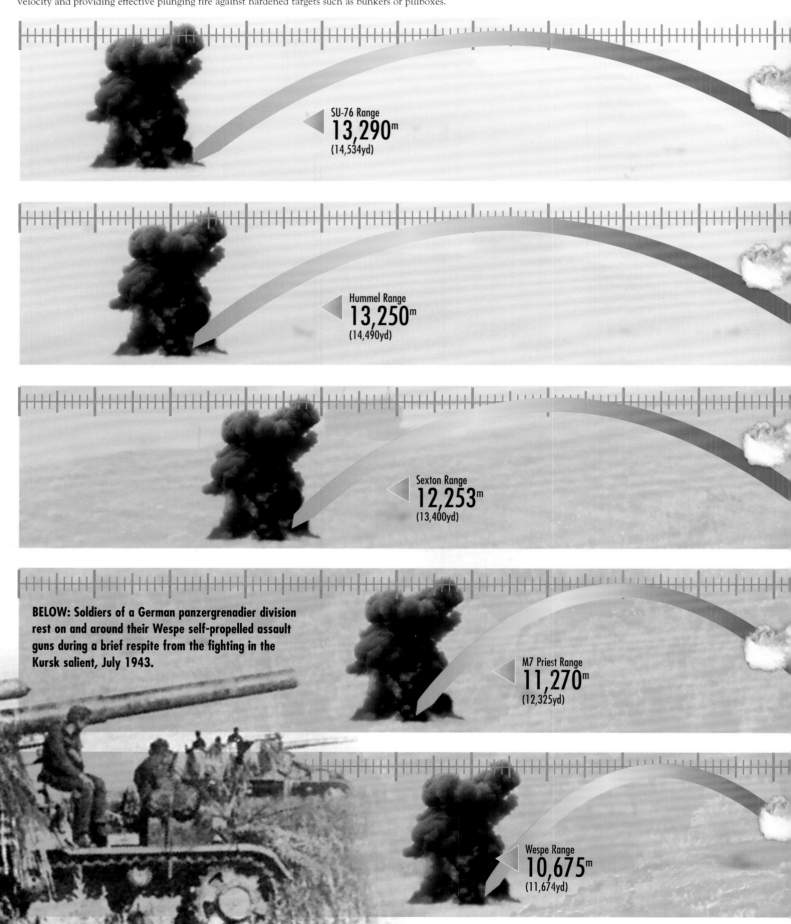

SU-76 Range
13,290ᵐ
(14,534yd)

Hummel Range
13,250ᵐ
(14,490yd)

Sexton Range
12,253ᵐ
(13,400yd)

BELOW: Soldiers of a German panzergrenadier division rest on and around their Wespe self-propelled assault guns during a brief respite from the fighting in the Kursk salient, July 1943.

M7 Priest Range
11,270ᵐ
(12,325yd)

Wespe Range
10,675ᵐ
(11,674yd)

Self-propelled Guns 2

Gun Range and Rate of Fire

SU-76 Rate of Fire
25rpm

▶ **SU-76**
▶ **Wespe**
▶ **Sexton**
▶ **M7 Priest**
▶ **Hummel**

Hummel Rate of Fire
4rpm

The self-propelled gun came into its own on the Eastern Front. All sides recognized the need for mobile artillery and infantry fire support. Although some self-propelled guns were produced with closed turrets, numerous types utilized an open turret mounted generally on existing tank chassis that were readily available. A self-propelled gun could be manufactured faster and more cheaply than a tank. German and Soviet self-propelled guns proved highly effective; however, German production capacity was inferior to that of the Soviets and neither their 11.2-tonne (11-ton) Wespe nor the larger 24.4-tonne (24-ton) Hummel with its 150mm (5.9in) howitzer were available in numbers that approached the Soviet SU-76, of which more than 14,000 were produced from 1942 to 1945. The American M7 Priest, mounting a 105mm (4.1in) howitzer, entered production in the spring of 1942 and impressed the British, who requested more than 5000 of them. Manufactured in Canada, the Sexton, mounting the QF 25-pounder gun, was intended as a replacement for the M7 Priest and served into the mid-1950s.

Sexton Rate of Fire
6-8rpm

BELOW: In the summer of 1943, the highly successful debut of the German Wespe self-propelled gun on the Eastern Front resulted in the cancellation of older self-propelled gun models such as the Marder and reserved all available PzKpfw II chassis for conversion to the open-turret Wespe.

M7 Priest Rate of Fire
4rpm

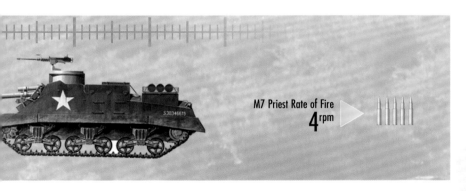

Wespe Rate of Fire
4-6rpm

Close-support SP Guns 1

Muzzle Velocity and Calibre

▶ **Cromwell VI CS**
▶ **M8 Stuart**
▶ **Grille Ausf M**
▶ **SU-122**
▶ **Type 4 Ho-Ro**

Close-support guns were equipped with howitzers to provide plunging fire against fortified positions. Based on the Czech-designed PzKpfw 38(t) chassis, the German Grille Ausf M adapted earlier models with the repositioning of the engine to the centre and the open crew compartment to the rear. The Soviet SU-122 mounted a howitzer atop the T-34 tank chassis. The weapon was versatile enough to serve as close-support and mobile stand-off artillery. Used primarily to provide close fire support to cavalry squadrons, the American M8 Stuart mounted a 75mm (2.9in) howitzer in an open turret on the M5 Stuart light-tank chassis. The British produced nearly 350 Cromwell VI CS support vehicles, replacing the main gun with a 95mm (3.7in) howitzer. The Japanese Type 4 Ho-Ro utilized the chassis of the Type 97 Chi-Ha tank; its small crew compartment gave little protection.

LEFT: The Japanese Type 4 Ho-Ro mounted an old Krupp-designed 150mm (5.9in) howitzer.

Calibre

The howitzers carried by close-support self-propelled weapons were generally of large calibre, sufficient to take on fixed fortifications with plunging fire. Some close-support self-propelled guns also provided a dual-purpose option, having sufficient trajectory and range to serve as mobile artillery.

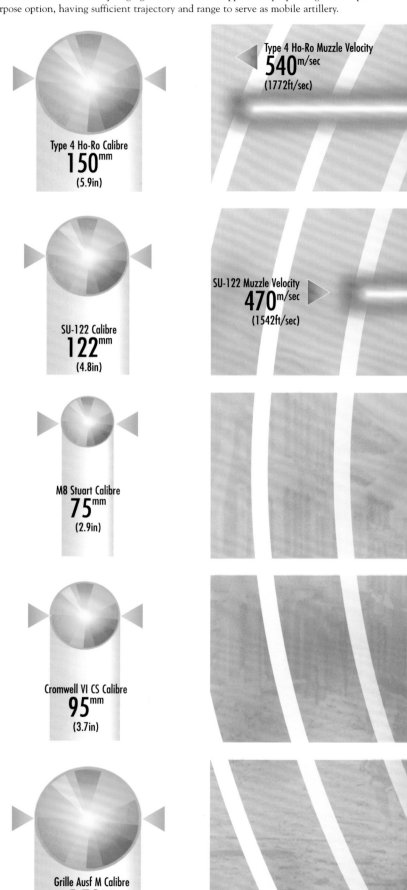

Type 4 Ho-Ro Calibre
150mm
(5.9in)

Type 4 Ho-Ro Muzzle Velocity
540m/sec
(1772ft/sec)

SU-122 Calibre
122mm
(4.8in)

SU-122 Muzzle Velocity
470m/sec
(1542ft/sec)

M8 Stuart Calibre
75mm
(2.9in)

Cromwell VI CS Calibre
95mm
(3.7in)

Grille Ausf M Calibre
150mm
(5.9in)

Muzzle Velocity

The relatively short barrels of the howitzers mounted by close-support self-propelled guns utilized trajectory and typically smaller loads of propellant to achieve the arc and rate of descent required to penetrate fixed targets.

Type 4 Ho-Ro

SU-122

M8 Stuart Muzzle Velocity
381 m/sec
(1250ft/sec)

M8 Stuart

Cromwell VI CS Muzzle Velocity
330 m/sec
(1083ft/sec)

Cromwell VI CS

Grille Ausf M Muzzle Velocity
240 m/sec
(787ft/sec)

Grille Ausf M

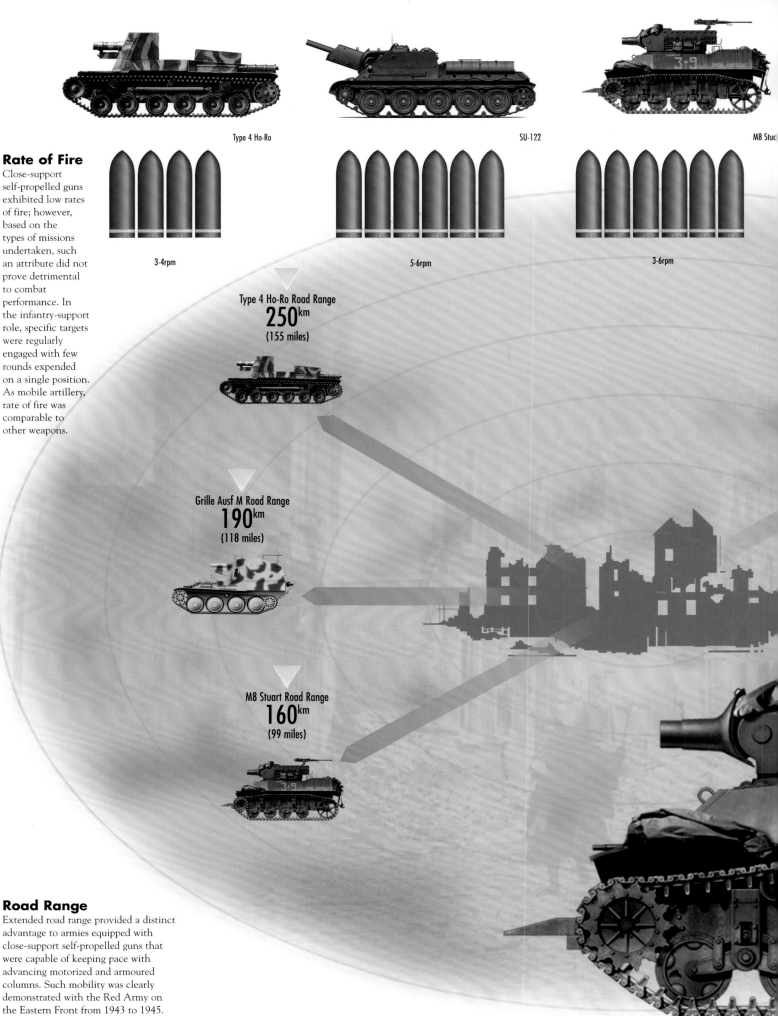

Type 4 Ho-Ro

SU-122

M8 Stuc

Rate of Fire

Close-support
self-propelled guns
exhibited low rates
of fire; however,
based on the
types of missions
undertaken, such
an attribute did not
prove detrimental
to combat
performance. In
the infantry-support
role, specific targets
were regularly
engaged with few
rounds expended
on a single position.
As mobile artillery,
rate of fire was
comparable to
other weapons.

3-4rpm

5-6rpm

3-6rpm

Type 4 Ho-Ro Road Range
250km
(155 miles)

Grille Ausf M Road Range
190km
(118 miles)

M8 Stuart Road Range
160km
(99 miles)

Road Range

Extended road range provided a distinct
advantage to armies equipped with
close-support self-propelled guns that
were capable of keeping pace with
advancing motorized and armoured
columns. Such mobility was clearly
demonstrated with the Red Army on
the Eastern Front from 1943 to 1945.

Cromwell VI CS

Grille Ausf M

7rpm

2-3rpm

Close-support SP Guns 2

Road Range and Rate of Fire

- ▶ **Cromwell VI CS**
- ▶ **M8 Stuart**
- ▶ **Grille Ausf M**
- ▶ **SU-122**
- ▶ **Type 4 Ho-Ro**

Cromwell VI CS Road Range
278km
(173 miles)

SU-122 Road Range
300km
(186 miles)

With the deployment of close-support self-propelled guns, the Soviet Red Army began to develop a generation of armoured vehicles with the intent to provide heavy tactical direct fire against enemy targets. Operating in concert with infantry and tanks, guns such as the SU-122 were purpose-built for close support, although they were capable of executing conventional artillery fire missions. Fewer than 300 examples of the German Grille Ausf M SP gun were built, although a further 120 were produced as ammunition carriers. The British Cromwell VI CS was produced in slightly greater numbers (nearly 350), and the American M8 Stuart was an attempt to combine a heavy howitzer with the mobility of the light-tank chassis. Japan's Type 4 Ho-Ro was obsolescent from its debut, and only a few were fielded.

LEFT: The US M8 Stuart mounted a 75mm (2.9in) howitzer atop the chassis of an M5 Stuart light tank. Nearly 1800 were built from September 1942 to January 1944.

AXATIVE
3-9
USA 4052227

Calibre

The heavy-calibre weapons of late-war self-propelled guns were fielded to support infantry operations in urban areas and with the capability of destroying fortified targets. The 380mm (15in) naval rocket launcher of the Sturmtiger and the 152.4mm (6in) gun-howitzer of the ISU-152 were adequate for such tasks.

Sturmtiger Calibre
380mm
(15in)

ISU-152 Calibre
152.4mm
(6in)

Range

Although its main weapon fired rocket-assisted projectiles, these were of relatively short range since the Sturmtiger was originally conceived for the close-quarter action of urban warfare. The 152.4mm (6in) gun-howitzer of the Soviet ISU-152 provided enough range to allow the self-propelled armoured vehicle to serve as close infantry support, mobile artillery and an assault gun.

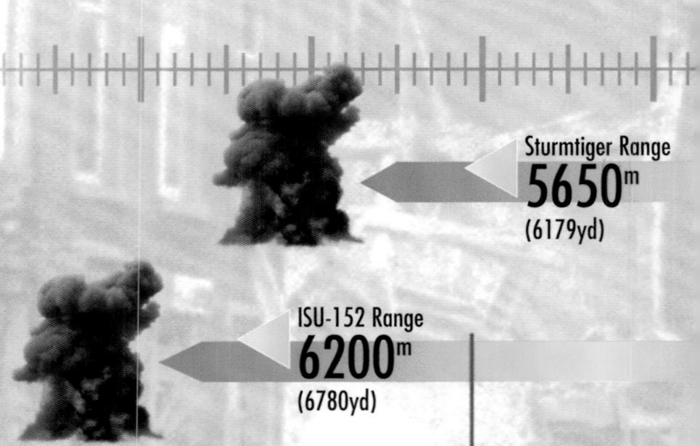

Sturmtiger Range
5650m
(6179yd)

ISU-152 Range
6200m
(6780yd)

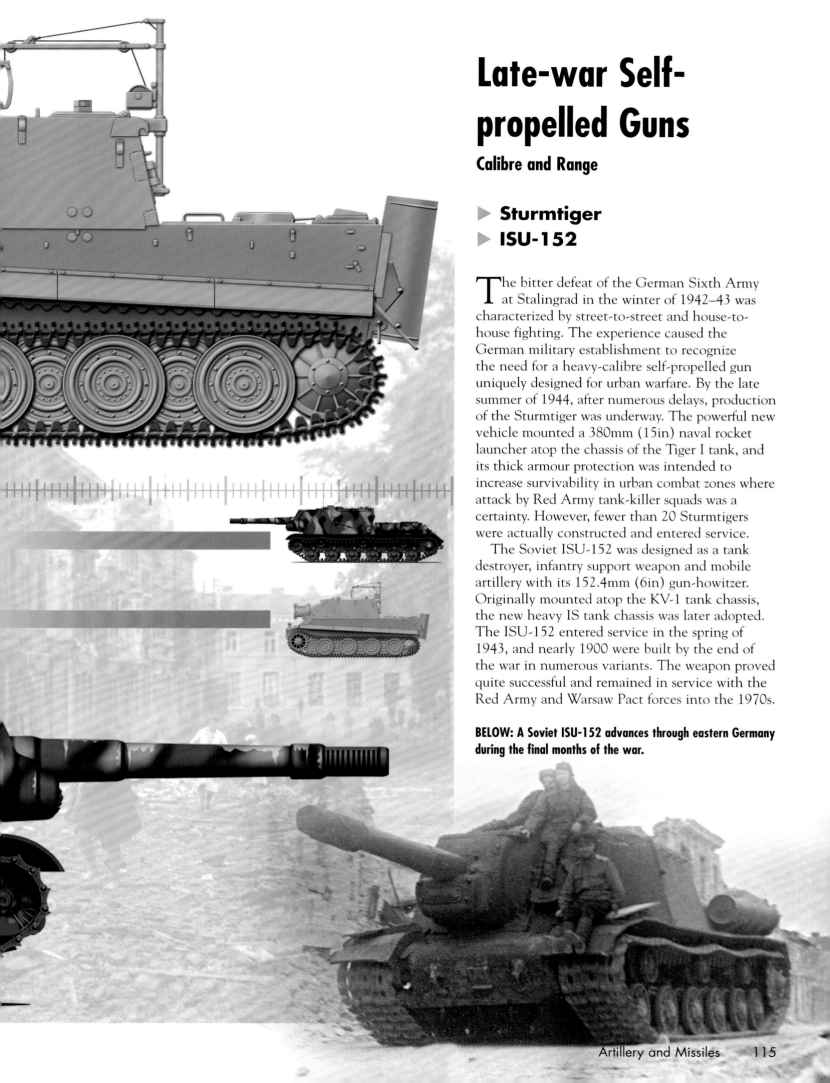

Late-war Self-propelled Guns

Calibre and Range

▶ **Sturmtiger**
▶ **ISU-152**

The bitter defeat of the German Sixth Army at Stalingrad in the winter of 1942–43 was characterized by street-to-street and house-to-house fighting. The experience caused the German military establishment to recognize the need for a heavy-calibre self-propelled gun uniquely designed for urban warfare. By the late summer of 1944, after numerous delays, production of the Sturmtiger was underway. The powerful new vehicle mounted a 380mm (15in) naval rocket launcher atop the chassis of the Tiger I tank, and its thick armour protection was intended to increase survivability in urban combat zones where attack by Red Army tank-killer squads was a certainty. However, fewer than 20 Sturmtigers were actually constructed and entered service.

The Soviet ISU-152 was designed as a tank destroyer, infantry support weapon and mobile artillery with its 152.4mm (6in) gun-howitzer. Originally mounted atop the KV-1 tank chassis, the new heavy IS tank chassis was later adopted. The ISU-152 entered service in the spring of 1943, and nearly 1900 were built by the end of the war in numerous variants. The weapon proved quite successful and remained in service with the Red Army and Warsaw Pact forces into the 1970s.

BELOW: A Soviet ISU-152 advances through eastern Germany during the final months of the war.

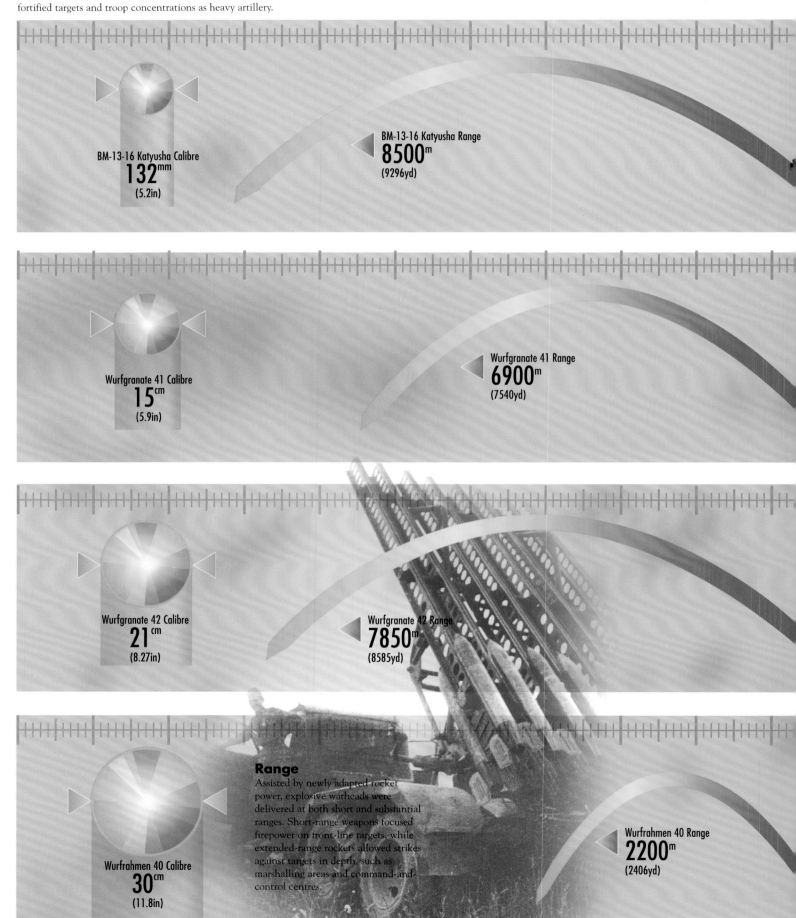

Calibre

High-calibre rockets brought additional tactical firepower to the battlefield. From highly mobile truck-borne launchers to halftrack-mounted tubes, the high-calibre missiles were as effective on fortified targets and troop concentrations as heavy artillery.

BM-13-16 Katyusha Calibre
132mm
(5.2in)

BM-13-16 Katyusha Range
8500m
(9296yd)

Wurfgranate 41 Calibre
15cm
(5.9in)

Wurfgranate 41 Range
6900m
(7540yd)

Wurfgranate 42 Calibre
21cm
(8.27in)

Wurfgranate 42 Range
7850m
(8585yd)

Range

Assisted by newly adapted rocket power, explosive warheads were delivered at both short and substantial ranges. Short-range weapons focused firepower on front-line targets, while extended-range rockets allowed strikes against targets in depth, such as marshalling areas and command-and-control centres.

Wurfrahmen 40 Calibre
30cm
(11.8in)

Wurfrahmen 40 Range
2200m
(2406yd)

Rocket Weight

The weight of rocket-propelled weapons directly affected their operational range, with the lighter projectiles striking deeper behind enemy lines. Heavier rockets proved useful as plunging fire against hard targets, such as pillboxes, bunkers and enemy armour.

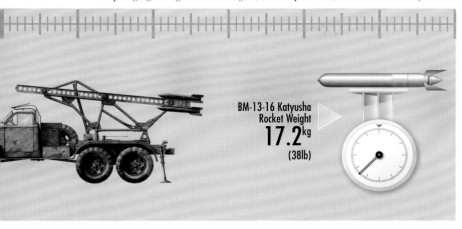

BM-13-16 Katyusha Rocket Weight

17.2kg
(38lb)

Wurfgranate 41 Rocket Weight

2.5kg
(5.5lb)

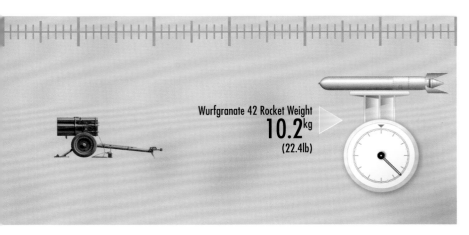

Wurfgranate 42 Rocket Weight

10.2kg
(22.4lb)

Wurfrahmen 40 Rocket Weight

10.2kg
(22.4lb)

Rocket Launchers

Range, Calibre and Rocket Weight

▶ **BM-13-16 'Katyusha'**
▶ **Panzerwerfer 42 (Wurfgranate 41)**
▶ **Nebelwerfer 42 (Wurfgranate 42)**
▶ **SdKfz 251/Wurfrahmen 40**

The deployment of rockets during World War II is most associated with the fighting on the Eastern Front, during which large salvoes of the projectiles often saturated target areas and compensated for the lack of accuracy inherent in these unguided weapons. Rockets were appealing due to their low cost, rapid manufacture and relatively simple operation.

The most famous of the World War II rockets was the Soviet Red Army's 132mm (5.2in) M-13, developed in the 1930s and available only in small numbers when the Germans invaded the Soviet Union in June 1941. However, production was stepped up and the M-13 was in action by the end of the year, shocking German troops who experienced its lethality. Launchers were fitted atop 6x6 trucks with rails for 16 rockets, and the system became known as the BM-13-16 'Katyusha', or 'Little Kate'. The system was improved through the years and served with the Red Army into the 1980s.

The Germans mounted rocket launchers aboard halftracks and also brought them to battle in towed batteries. The Wurfrahmen 40 mounted six launcher frames on the sides of an SdKfz 251 halftrack and these were aimed by pointing the vehicle at the target. Among the rockets used were 28cm (11in) and 32cm (12.6in) weapons that were also used in the Nebelwerfer, perhaps the best-known German rocket-launching system, in this case the 28/32cm 42 variant. This was a six-barrel launcher mounted on a two-wheeled trailer. The weapon was hazardous for its crew in combat due to its backblast.

The 21cm (8.27in) Wurfgranate 42 and 15cm (5.9in) Wurfgranate 41 rockets were also fired from Nebelwerfer launchers; indeed the former was used only with the 21cm Nebelwerfer 42. The 15cm (5.9in) rocket was paired with the 15cm Nebelwerfer 41 but could also be mounted on a halftrack, the 15cm Panzerwerfer 42.

Heavy Artillery 1

Range and Muzzle Velocity

▶ **203mm M1931 B-4**
▶ **152mm ML-20**
▶ **8-inch Howitzer M1**
▶ **15cm sFH 18**
▶ **152mm M1943 (D-1)**

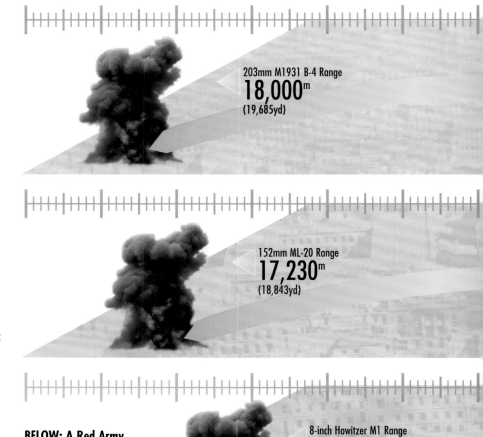

203mm M1931 B-4 Range
18,000ᵐ
(19,685yd)

152mm ML-20 Range
17,230ᵐ
(18,843yd)

8-inch Howitzer M1 Range
16,925ᵐ
(18,509yd)

Heavy artillery maintained its significant role in land warfare during World War II. Just as it had been in previous wars, it was utilized to reduce fortified positions, silence enemy artillery with counterbattery fire and provide long-range preparatory or defensive fire support.

The 203mm Howitzer M1931 B-4 was the heaviest Soviet artillery of the war, while the 152mm ML-20 gun-howitzer was typical of Soviet efforts to balance the lightest possible weight with the heaviest projectile and best range possible. A heavier barrel and large muzzle brake were introduced with the 152mm M1943, which was manufactured in great quantity and later designated the D-1. The American 8-inch Howitzer M1 was heavily influenced by earlier British weapons and proved highly accurate on the battlefield. The German 15cm schwere Feldhaubitze 18 was actually a compromise between designs of the competing Krupp and Rheinmetall firms. The standard German heavy-artillery weapon of the war, the 15cm sFH 18 was also used in static coastal defensive positions.

BELOW: A Red Army 152mm (5.98in) M1937 gun fires in the streets of Berlin during the April 1945 Soviet assault on the German capital.

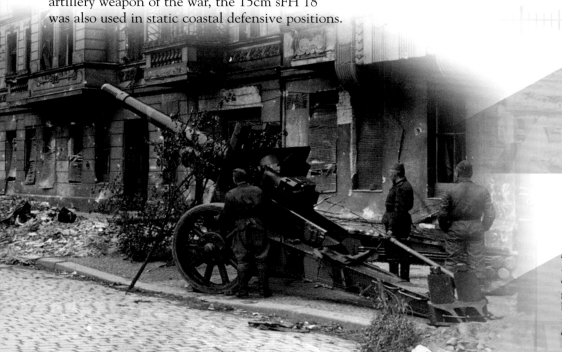

Maximum Range

As a war of mobility became more protracted on certain fronts, the range of heavy artillery gained significance. Without the support of heavy artillery, other land operations involving infantry and armour were quite difficult to execute.

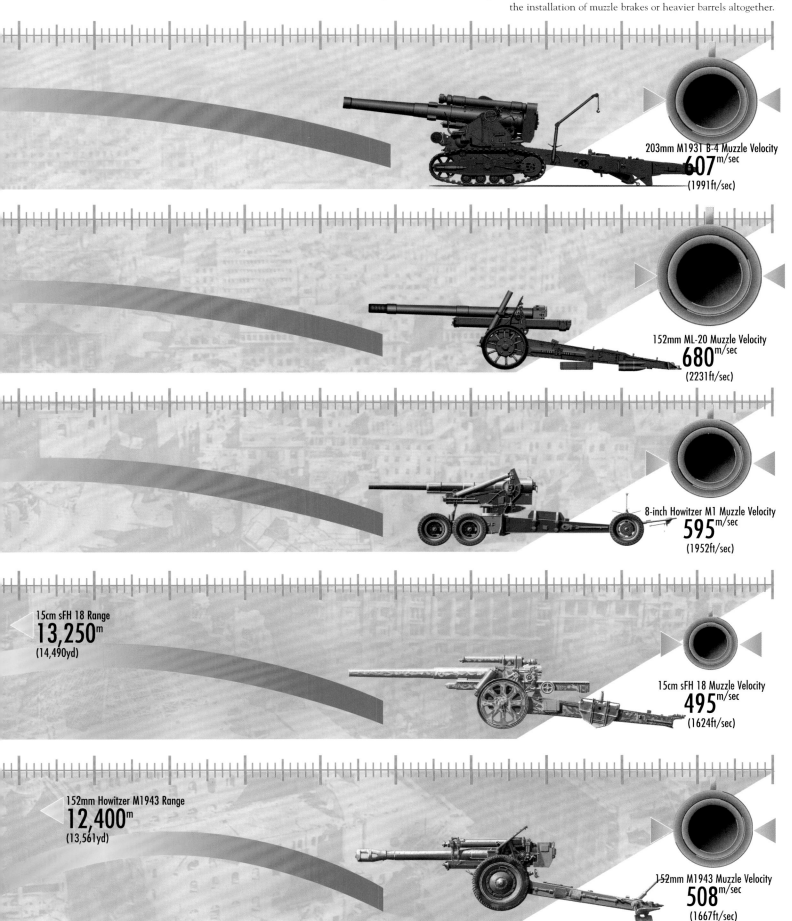

Muzzle Velocity

With heavy artillery, the sheer weight of a projectile often compensated for low muzzle velocity. In some cases, extreme muzzle velocity resulted in excessive wear of heavy-artillery barrels, necessitating the installation of muzzle brakes or heavier barrels altogether.

203mm M1931 B-4 Muzzle Velocity
607 m/sec
(1991ft/sec)

152mm ML-20 Muzzle Velocity
680 m/sec
(2231ft/sec)

8-inch Howitzer M1 Muzzle Velocity
595 m/sec
(1952ft/sec)

15cm sFH 18 Range
13,250 m
(14,490yd)

15cm sFH 18 Muzzle Velocity
495 m/sec
(1624ft/sec)

152mm Howitzer M1943 Range
12,400 m
(13,561yd)

152mm M1943 Muzzle Velocity
508 m/sec
(1667ft/sec)

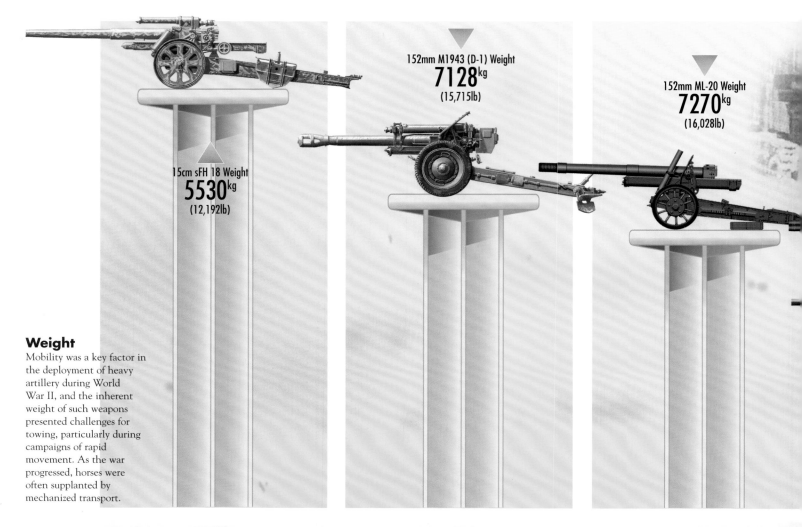

152mm M1943 (D-1) Weight
7128^{kg}
(15,715lb)

152mm ML-20 Weight
7270^{kg}
(16,028lb)

15cm sFH 18 Weight
5530^{kg}
(12,192lb)

Weight

Mobility was a key factor in the deployment of heavy artillery during World War II, and the inherent weight of such weapons presented challenges for towing, particularly during campaigns of rapid movement. As the war progressed, horses were often supplanted by mechanized transport.

15cm sFH 18

152mm M1943 (D-1)

152mm ML-20

Calibre

The most widely deployed heavy artillery of the war spanned calibres from 150mm (5.9in) to 210mm (8.27in). These guns and howitzers combined weight of fire and range to facilitate other offensive land operations or maintain defensive positions with suppressing fire against enemy artillery.

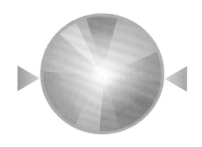

15cm sFH 18 Calibre
149^{mm}
(5.87in)

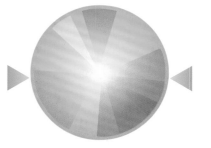

152mm M1943 (D-1) Calibre
152.4^{mm}
(6in)

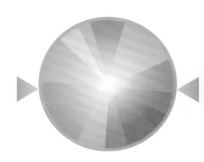

152mm ML-20 Calibre
152^{mm}
(6in)

Heavy Artillery 2

Weight and Calibre

▶ **203mm M1931 B-4**
▶ **152mm ML-20**
▶ **8-inch Howitzer M1**
▶ **15cm sFH 18**
▶ **152mm M1943 (D-1)**

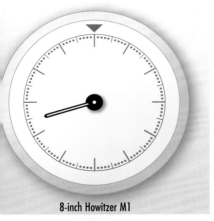

203mm M1931 B-4 Weight
17,700^{kg}
(39,022lb)

8-inch Howitzer M1 Weight
14,380^{kg}
(31,702lb)

8-inch Howitzer M1

203mm M1931 B-4

8-inch Howitzer M1 Calibre
203^{mm}
(8in)

203mm M1931 B-4 Calibre
203^{mm}
(8in)

The Soviet 203mm M1931 B-4 was a workhorse of the Red Army heavy artillery during World War II. As the mobile warfare of the early campaigns on the Eastern Front settled down to more static fighting, the heavy artillery came into its own.

Soviet factories produced incredible numbers of heavy-artillery pieces, and the massed firepower of the M1931 and both the 152mm ML-20 and 152mm M1943 (D-1) devastated German positions and often rendered enemy offensive operations impossible since tanks and infantry cannot advance under concentrated heavy-artillery fire.

When Operation Uranus, the offensive that encircled the German Sixth Army at Stalingrad, was undertaken in 1942, the Soviets allocated more than 13,000 artillery pieces of various types to the operation. A tremendous artillery barrage preceded the offensive and enabled infantry and armoured units to advance rapidly.

The US Army 8-inch Howitzer M1 developed a reputation for accuracy and was used with confidence to fire on enemy bunkers and strongpoints that were in close proximity to Allied troop concentrations. The 203mm (8in) shell weighed approximately 91kg (201lb) and was handled by at least four crewmembers.

The German 15cm schwere Feldhaubitze 18 was horse-drawn early in World War II; however, an improved version was towed by a halftrack, greatly increasing its mobility. The 15cm sFH 18 was successfully deployed by the German Army on all fronts and was also mounted atop a tank chassis to produce the self-propelled Hummel.

TOP: Tracks provided some short-distance mobility for the Soviet 203mm M1931 B-4 howitzer. However, relocation of any great distance required that the piece be disassembled and carried aboard several vehicles. In this photo, a tractor assists the movement of the howitzer through heavy snow.

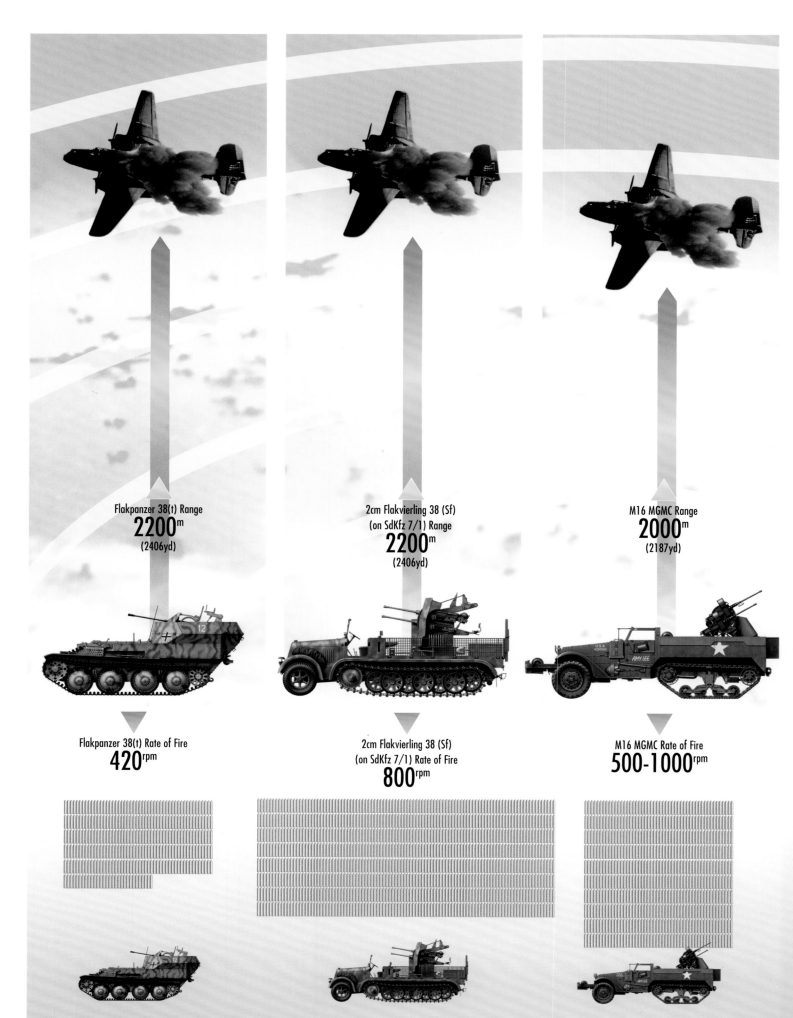

Flakpanzer 38(t) Range
2200ᵐ
(2406yd)

2cm Flakvierling 38 (Sf)
(on SdKfz 7/1) Range
2200ᵐ
(2406yd)

M16 MGMC Range
2000ᵐ
(2187yd)

Flakpanzer 38(t) Rate of Fire
420ʳᵖᵐ

2cm Flakvierling 38 (Sf)
(on SdKfz 7/1) Rate of Fire
800ʳᵖᵐ

M16 MGMC Rate of Fire
500-1000ʳᵖᵐ

Effective Range

Mobile light anti-aircraft guns were essential in defending ground targets against low-flying enemy aircraft. Most could achieve an effective range of around 2000 metres (2187 yards), and so were effective against ground attack aircraft and low-flying bombers.

2cm Flak 38 (on SdKfz 10/5) Range
2000ᵐ
(2187yd)

Crusader III AA Range
914ᵐ
(1000yd)

2cm Flak 38 (on SdKfz 10/5) Rate of Fire
280-450ʳᵖᵐ

Crusader III AA Rate of Fire
250-320ʳᵖᵐ

Rate of Fire

A high rate of fire made light anti-aircraft weapons highly effective against enemy planes. A skilled gun crew could often engage multiple targets within the span of a few minutes.

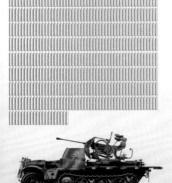

Light SP AA Guns
Effective Range and Rate of Fire

- ▶ **2cm Flakvierling 38 (Sf)**
- ▶ **2cm Flak 38**
- ▶ **M16 MGMC**
- ▶ **Crusader III AA**
- ▶ **Flakpanzer 38(t)**

With the introduction of higher-performance aircraft in the interwar years, defence against low-flying planes became a necessity. Light anti-aircraft (AA) guns were designed to protect a limited area of sky to ceilings that generally did not exceed 3000m (9843ft). Their volume of fire compounded their effectiveness.

The German 2cm Flak 38 nearly doubled the rate of fire of its predecessor, the 2cm Flak 30, when it was introduced in 1940, and the Flakvierling 38 was an adaptation from the single-barrelled 20mm (0.79in) anti-aircraft gun to four barrels firing from the same mount. Beginning in 1941, the Flakvierling 38 was routinely mounted atop the SdKfz 7 halftrack. The Flakpanzer 38(t), meanwhile, was a single-barrelled 20mm (0.79in) gun on the Czech 38(t) tank chassis.

The British Crusader III AA tank mounted twin 20mm (0.79in) Bofors anti-aircraft guns on the Crusader tank chassis. However, few of these saw action due to Allied air supremacy from 1944 on. The US M16 MGMC was an adaptation of the M3 halftrack to carry a quadruple mount of Browning 12.7mm (0.5in) machine guns. The weapon was effective against low-flying aircraft and sometimes used against ground troops as well.

BELOW: The 2cm Flakvierling 38 (Sf) provided mobile light anti-aircraft defence and was manned by a crew of six.

8.8cm Flak 41
10,675m
(35,023ft)

5cm Flak 41
9450m
(31,004ft)

40mm Bofors L/60
7200m
(23,622ft)

Effective Range

High-flying bomber formations threatened major cities during World War II, requiring that anti-aircraft guns reach altitudes of greater than 7000m (22,966ft). Their high-explosive shells damaged enemy planes not only with direct hits but also with lethal bursts of shrapnel.

Flak Guns

Range

- **8.8cm Flak 41**
- **5cm Flak 41**
- **QF 3-inch 20cwt**
- **40mm Bofors L/60**
- **3.7cm Flak 43**

Perhaps the best-known artillery piece of any type fielded during World War II was the versatile German 88mm (3.5in) series, which included the Flak 18, 37 and 41. The Flak 18 and 37 were deployed widely with the German Army and were utilized to devastating effect as anti-tank guns as well as anti-aircraft weapons. The '88' was so widely respected that to Allied soldiers virtually every shell fired at them had come from one.

The German armed forces' inventory also included a 5cm Flak 41, which covered the belt of altitude between the larger guns and the 37mm (1.5in) weapons. However, the design was not a success and only 60 were produced. The 3.7cm Flak 43, of which more than 7000 were made to 1945, fired up to 150 rounds per minute and was fielded as a self-propelled or towed weapon.

Britain's QF 3-inch 20cwt had entered service during World War I and was steadily improved during the 1920s and 1930s. Many gun crews preferred it to the newer QF 3.7-inch AA gun. The 40mm Bofors L/60 AA gun was designed by the Swedish firm and exported to both Allied and Axis countries. Chrysler Corporation built nearly 60,000 under licence for the US armed forces.

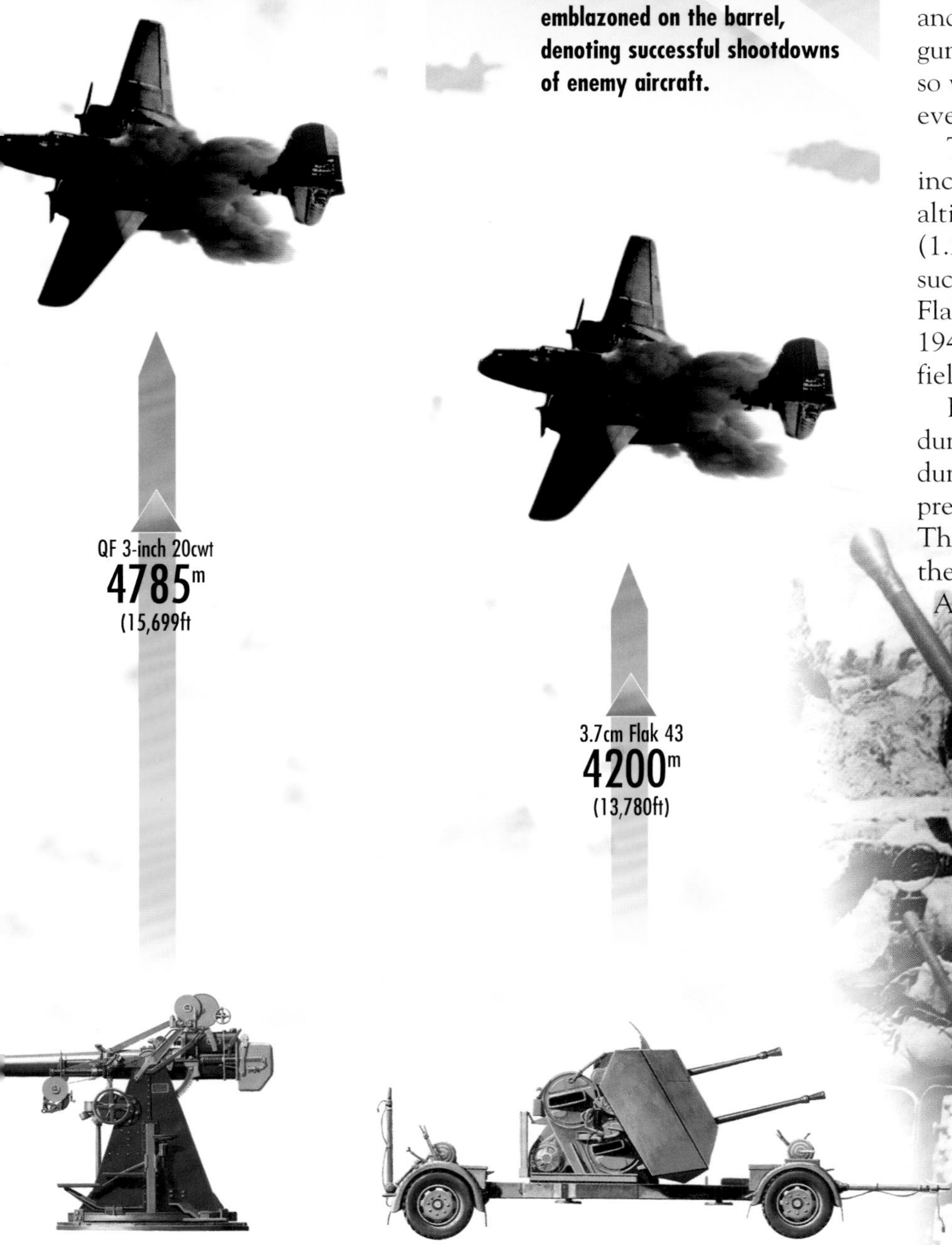

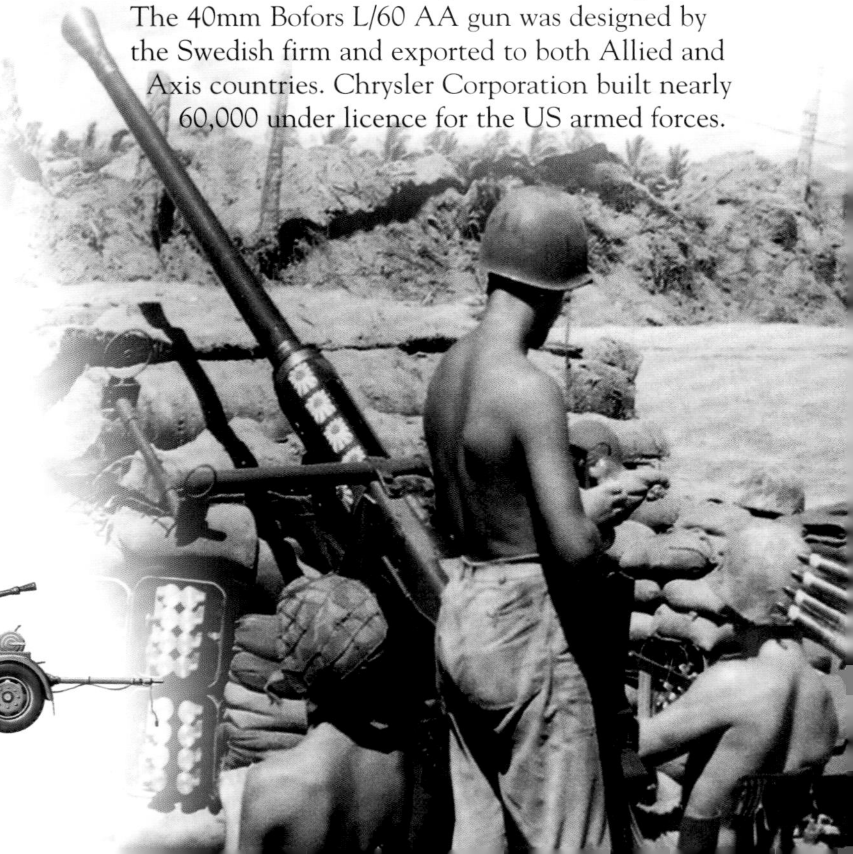

QF 3-inch 20cwt
4785m
(15,699ft)
3.7cm Flak 43
4200m
(13,780ft)

BELOW: An American gun crew in the Pacific stack ammunition and ready their 40mm (1.57in) Bofors anti-aircraft weapon for action. Note the Japanese flags emblazoned on the barrel, denoting successful shootdowns of enemy aircraft.

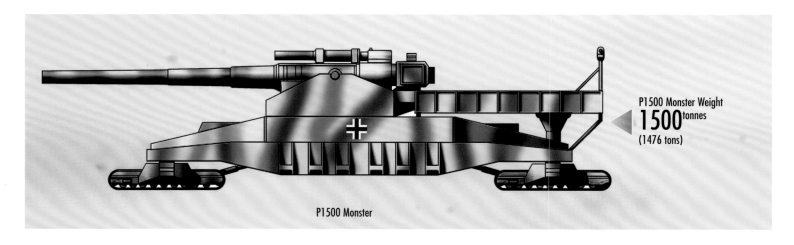

P1500 Monster

P1500 Monster Weight
1500tonnes
(1476 tons)

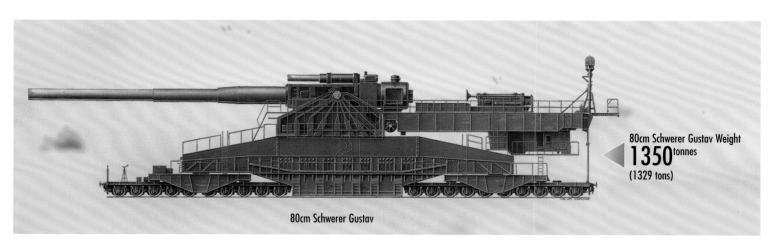

80cm Schwerer Gustav

80cm Schwerer Gustav Weight
1350tonnes
(1329 tons)

Weight

The tremendous weight of the barrels and carriages of the super guns required that many of them be transported by rail, which diminished their mobility and effectiveness. Therefore, they were deployed in static situations such as siege operations or in long-term defensive positions.

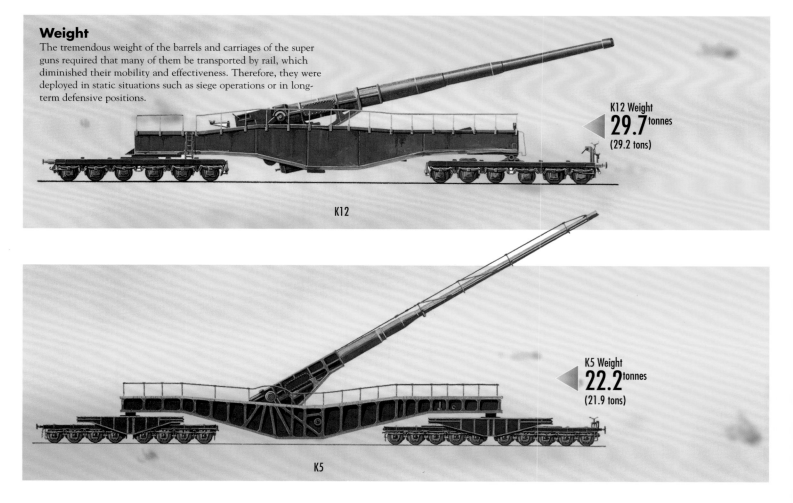

K12

K12 Weight
29.7tonnes
(29.2 tons)

K5

K5 Weight
22.2tonnes
(21.9 tons)

Super Guns 1

Weight and Calibre

▶ **80cm Schwerer Gustav**
▶ **K12**
▶ **K5**
▶ **P1500 Monster**

Calibre
Among the heaviest-calibre guns ever fired in anger, the super guns of World War II were immense, and their shells required complicated systems for transport and loading. Their rail carriages absorbed some of the tremendous recoil generated when the weapons discharged.

P1500 Monster Calibre
800mm
(31.5in)

80cm Schwerer Gustav Calibre
800mm
(31.5in)

K12 Calibre
211mm
(8.3in)

K5 Calibre
283mm
(11.1in)

Late in World War II, German engineers were continuing to work on a prototype tank that would dwarf any other armoured vehicle. The P1500 Monster never reached operational status; however, it was to have weighed 1500 tonnes (1476 tons) and mounted the 80cm Schwerer Gustav cannon developed by Krupp. The Gustav itself, however, did enter service with German forces at the siege of Sevastopol in the Crimea. During the siege, Gustav fired 48 shells and wore out its original barrel.

The Germans deployed a pair of 211mm (8.3in) K12 railway guns, and these were assigned to Artillery Battery 701 on the coast of the English Channel. Reportedly, some shells were fired at targets in southern England. The guns carried their own T-shaped section of track for use in siting the weapons prior to target acquisition. Their shells weighed 107.5kg (237lb).

The 283mm (11.1in) K5 railway gun was produced by the Germans in greater numbers than any other such weapon. More than 20 were manufactured, and two of the guns, Robert and Leopold, shelled the Anzio beachhead in Italy in the spring of 1944. Three others were stationed along the coast of the English Channel to fire on British shipping in the narrow waterway.

BELOW: The massive Schwerer Gustav and its sister, Dora, were originally conceived as weapons capable of destroying the fixed fortifications of the French Maginot Line. At 800mm (31.5in), the type was the largest-calibre weapon in history to actually participate in combat and fired armour-piercing shells weighing 7100kg (15,653lb).

Super Guns 2

Maximum Range

▶ **80cm Schwerer Gustav**
▶ **K12**
▶ **K5**
▶ **P1500 Monster**

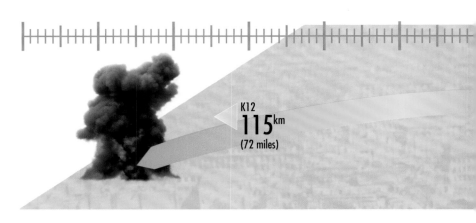

K12
115^{km}
(72 miles)

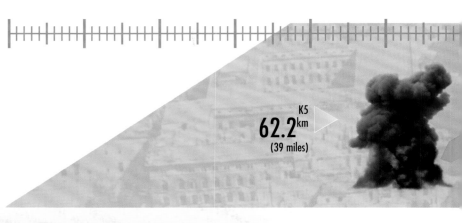

K5
62.2^{km}
(39 miles)

80cm Schwerer Gustav
38^{km}
(23.6 miles)

Harking back to the power of the fabled Paris Gun of World War I, the Germans invested in an array of heavy railway guns in World War II. These were fearsome, if somewhat impractical, weapons of destruction and demoralization. Although they fired a relative few rounds during the war, rumours of their presence raised the anxiety levels among Allied troops.

The 80cm Schwerer Gustav and its sister, Dora, were deployed to the battlefield on the Eastern Front, and the K5 railway guns were in action in Italy. Generally restricted to available rail lines and requiring crews of dozens of soldiers to service them, the heavy German guns were also permanently placed along the French coastline to menace Allied ships. These included the 211mm (8.3in) K12, as well as some 283mm (11.1in) K5s. Susceptible to enemy air attack, the guns were ringed with anti-aircraft weapons during firing operations. Most of the guns were destroyed in the last days of the war; however, examples do survive. Of these, some are constructed of salvaged components from more than a single weapon.

LEFT: A K5 railway gun emerges from a hidden location and fires towards Allied positions. A pair of K5 weapons terrorized the Allied beachhead at Anzio, Italy, firing heavy shells that reminded the British and American soldiers of the sound of an oncoming freight train.

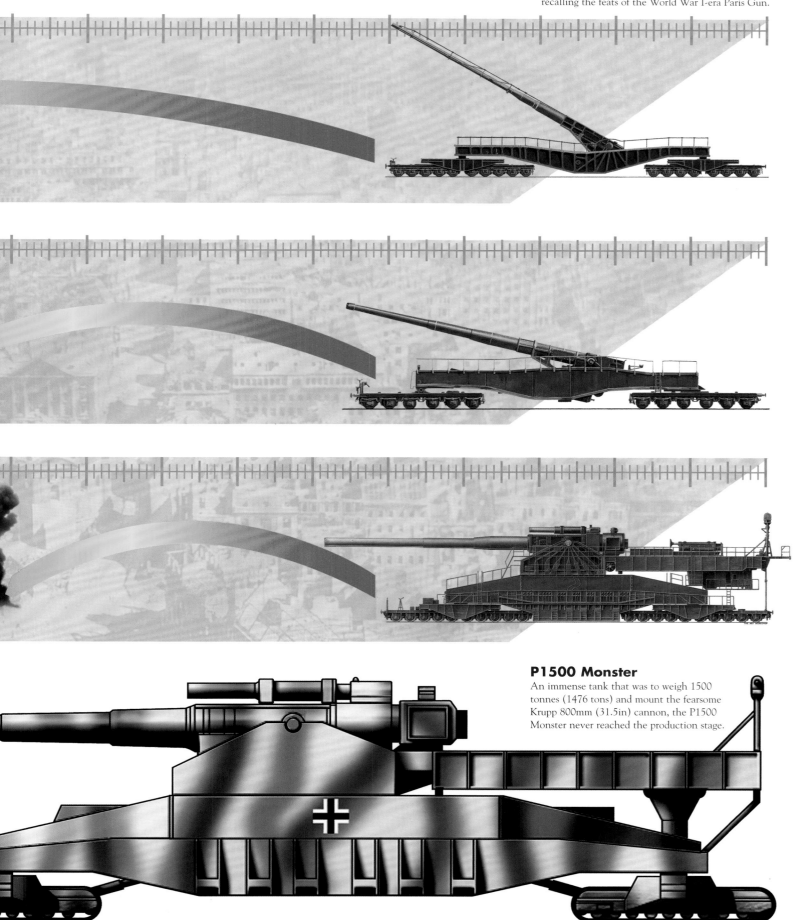

Maximum Range

The heavy-calibre German railway guns of World War II were capable of hurling large shells many tens of kilometres, recalling the feats of the World War I-era Paris Gun.

P1500 Monster

An immense tank that was to weigh 1500 tonnes (1476 tons) and mount the fearsome Krupp 800mm (31.5in) cannon, the P1500 Monster never reached the production stage.

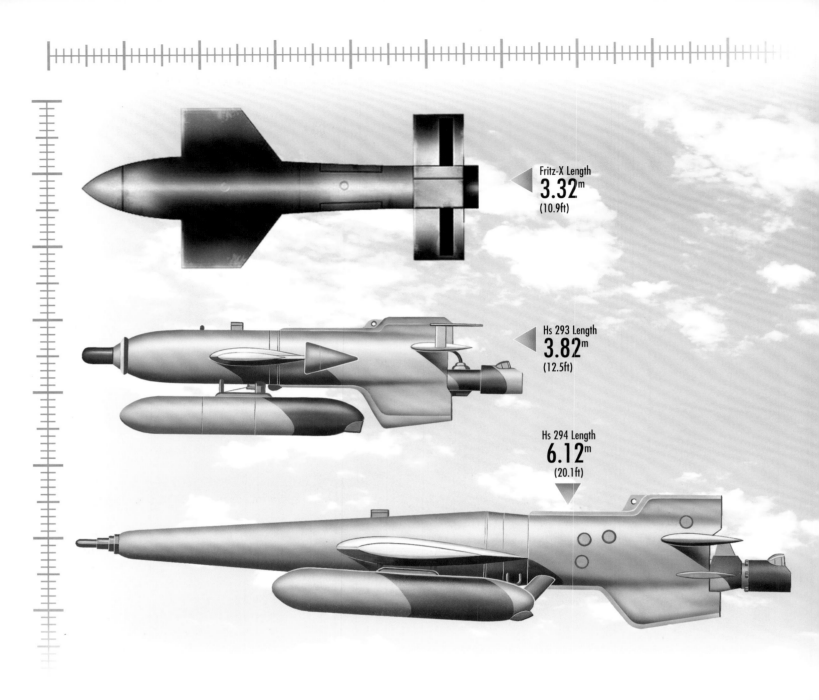

Fritz-X Length
3.32m
(10.9ft)

Hs 293 Length
3.82m
(12.5ft)

Hs 294 Length
6.12m
(20.1ft)

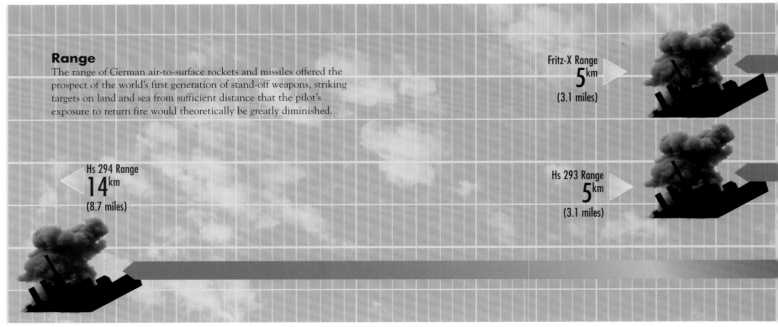

Range

The range of German air-to-surface rockets and missiles offered the prospect of the world's first generation of stand-off weapons, striking targets on land and sea from sufficient distance that the pilot's exposure to return fire would theoretically be greatly diminished.

Fritz-X Range
5km
(3.1 miles)

Hs 293 Range
5km
(3.1 miles)

Hs 294 Range
14km
(8.7 miles)

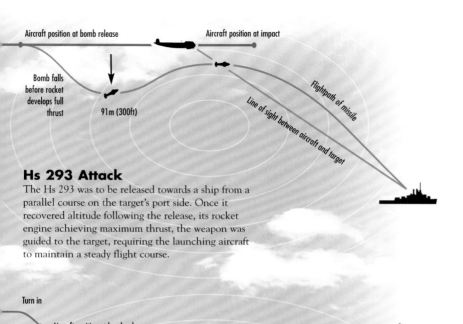

Aircraft position at bomb release

Aircraft position at impact

Bomb falls before rocket develops full thrust

91m (300ft)

Flightpath of missile

Line of sight between aircraft and target

Hs 293 Attack

The Hs 293 was to be released towards a ship from a parallel course on the target's port side. Once it recovered altitude following the release, its rocket engine achieving maximum thrust, the weapon was guided to the target, requiring the launching aircraft to maintain a steady flight course.

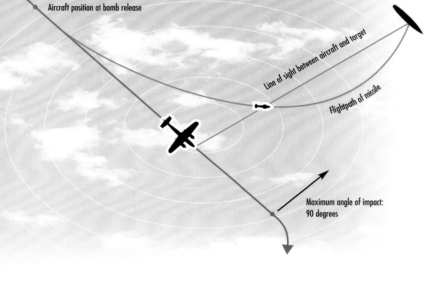

Turn in

Aircraft position at bomb release

Line of sight between aircraft and target

Flightpath of missile

Maximum angle of impact: 90 degrees

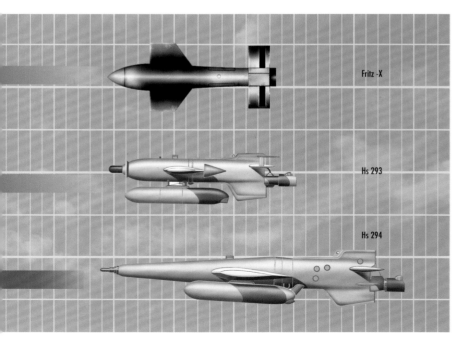

Fritz -X

Hs 293

Hs 294

Air-to-Surface Rockets and Missiles

Range and Length

▶ **Fritz-X**
▶ **Henschel Hs 293**
▶ **Henschel Hs 294**

The first weapons of their kind to see actual combat, the air-to-surface rockets and missiles developed by Germany during World War II were harbingers of a generation of smart weaponry that revolutionized modern warfare later in the twentieth century. Theoretically, the weapons could be released from an aircraft at a safe distance that might minimize exposure to return fire. However, the opposite was actually true. The radio-guided systems of weapons such as the Fritz-X and the Henschel Hs 293 and Hs 294 required the launching aircraft to maintain a straight flight line, in effect exposing it to greater enemy fire.

The Fritz-X was a freefall bomb controlled by electromagnetic spoilers guided by radio signals. The weapon was tested in 1942, and in September 1943 damaged the Italian battleship *Italia* and sank the battleship *Roma* as the two warships steamed to surrender to the Allies. The battleship HMS *Warspite* and the cruiser USS *Savannah* were also damaged by the Fritz-X, and more than 60 examples of the weapon were produced each month in Germany. High losses among the launching aircraft stymied the programme.

Powered by rocket engines, the Hs 293 and the more streamlined Hs 294 were also launched by aircraft. Controlled from the starboard side of the aircraft, the Hs 293 was launched against the port side of the target and guided by radio to impact while a flare in the missile's rear assisted the aimer in maintaining course. The Hs 293 was credited with sinking or damaging numerous Allied vessels, including the troop transport *Rohna*, which went down with the loss of more than 1000 lives. The Hs 294 actually functioned as a guided torpedo, launched from a distance of more than 19,000m (20,779yd) and slamming into the water approximately 400m (437yd) from its target, the tail and wings falling away on impact.

After the war, German technology was applied to numerous projects in the United States, Great Britain and the Soviet Union, and a new generation of sophisticated weapons emerged.

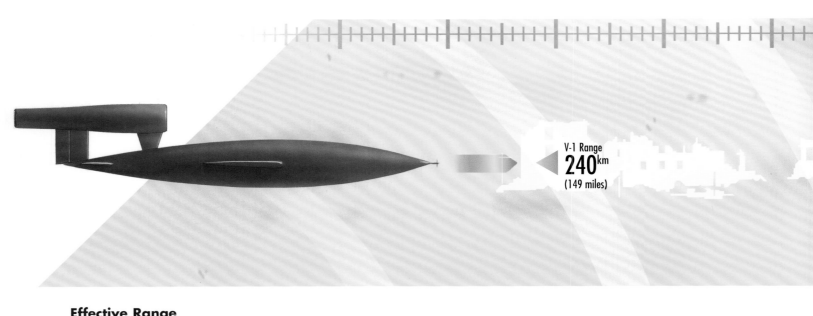

V-1 Range
240km
(149 miles)

Effective Range

The range of the vengeance weapons was sufficient to reach the major cities of Great Britain and other European Allied countries; therefore, the capture of V-1 and V-2 launch sites on the European continent became a priority for Allied troops.

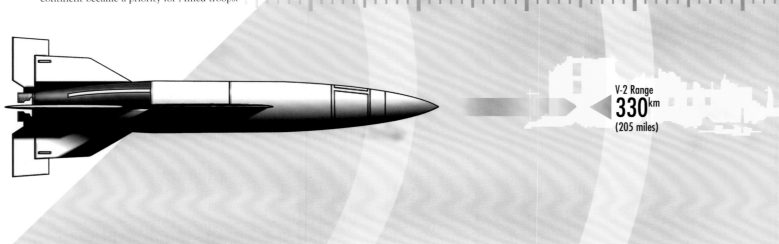

V-2 Range
330km
(205 miles)

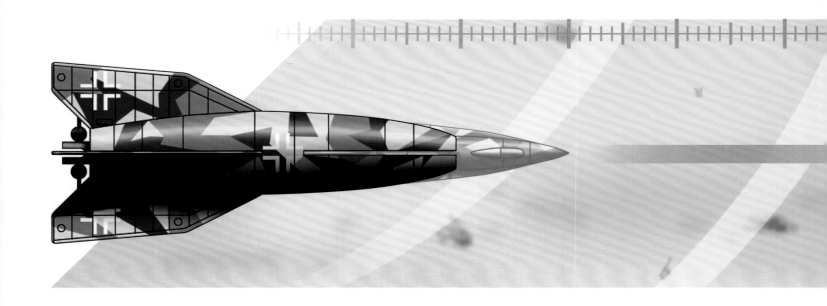

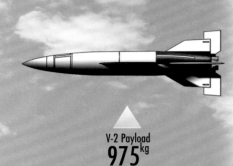

V-1 Payload
830^{kg}
(1830lb)

Revenge Weapons

Effective Range and Payload

▶ **V-1**
▶ **V-2**
▶ **A-9/A-10**

Payload

The explosive warheads carried by Hitler's V-1, V-2 and A-9/A-10 vengeance weapons were sufficient to inflict significant damage on the cities targeted. These advanced weapons were available in too few numbers to effect a change in the course of the war; however, they caused serious loss of life and a great deal of concern among Allied leaders.

V-2 Payload
975^{kg}
(2150lb)

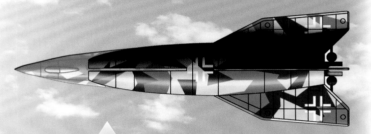

A-9/A-10 Payload
1000^{kg}
(2205lb)

BELOW: A V-2 rocket sits on a mobile launcher following its capture by Allied forces. After the war, thousands of V-2 components were shipped to the United States along with more than 100 German scientists who had worked on the advanced programme.

As the fortunes of war turned against Nazi Germany, the use of rocket- and jet-powered surface-to-surface missiles was seen by Hitler as a means of exacting vengeance against the Allies for heavy bombing raids on German cities. In 1944, the pulse-jet V-1 flying bomb, popularly known as the Doodle Bug, became operational. Subsequently, nearly 10,000 were launched against Britain and 2500 against the Belgian port of Antwerp. As the V-1 ran out of fuel, the silence indicated that impact would come shortly.

The V-2 rocket was the world's first ballistic missile and the forerunner of modern rockets. More than 3000 were launched against London, Antwerp and other cities during the waning months of the war in Europe, reportedly inflicting more than 7500 casualties. Propelled by a mixture of ethanol and liquid oxygen, the V-2, technically called the A-4 by the Germans, was powered by a rocket engine that pushed the missile to a height of approximately 80km (50 miles). When the fuel was consumed, the warhead would freefall to impact. A larger, longer-range version of the V-2, the A-9, was engineered with wings that stabilized the rocket and contributed to its extended range. The A-10 designation referred to a booster to allow the rocket to strike the United States.

A-9/A-10 Range
5000^{km}
(3107 miles)

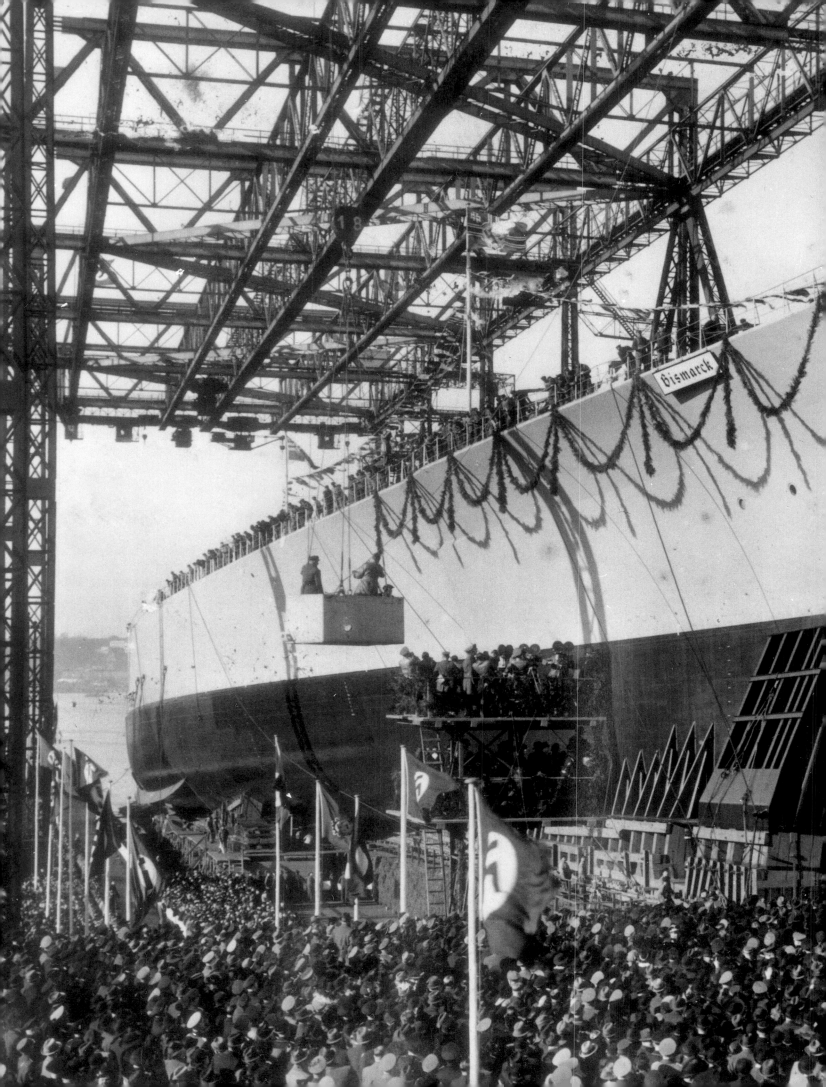

Naval Power

During World War II, control of the world's oceans and sea lanes proved central to the Allied victory. British Prime Minister Winston Churchill once remarked that the only aspect of the war against Nazi Germany that truly caused his anxiety to appreciably heighten was the Battle of the Atlantic and the continuing Royal Navy and US Navy effort to defeat the Nazi U-boat wolfpacks intent on severing the lifeline of supplies and war materiel from the Western Hemisphere to the British Isles and the Soviet Union.

While warships and merchantmen of every description took part in the naval war, the era of the capital ship waned as battleships engaged in few surface actions with their heavy guns and the prospect of a decisive Jutland-style battle faded away. In the battleship's place, the aircraft carrier emerged as the primary weapon of the world's great navies, projecting air power across great distances and demonstrating that surface ships were highly vulnerable to enemy aircraft in the absence of their own protective air umbrella.

LEFT: The German battleship *Bismarck* was launched in 1939 amidst great fanfare. It was one of only two ships in its class, the other being *Tirpitz*. The two battleships were the largest warships built by the German Navy and the heaviest capital ships ever completed in Europe.

Battle of the River Plate

Armour Thickness and Ship Length

- ▶ **Admiral Graf Spee**
- ▶ **HMS Exeter**
- ▶ **HMS Ajax**
- ▶ **HMS Achilles**

Limited at least nominally by the terms of the Versailles Treaty to capital ships displacing a maximum of 10,000 tons (10,160 tonnes), the German Navy developed an ingenious class of warships in the early 1930s that were officially classified as *Panzerschiffe*, or armoured ships. To the Allies, these sleek vessels mounting a 280mm (11in) main armament and exceeding the Versailles limitation by at least 2000 tons (2032 tonnes) came to be known as 'pocket battleships'.

The innovative construction of the three vessels – *Admiral Graf Spee*, *Admiral Scheer* and *Lützow* (originally named *Deutschland*) – included electric welding instead of riveting, which saved as much as 15 per cent of each ship's weight and allowed for its redistribution to armour protection and heavier armament, as well as eight efficient diesel engines that drove a pair of propeller shafts and provided economical fuel consumption.

The most familiar of the pocket battleships, *Graf Spee* was the subject of an extended hunt by warships of the Royal Navy, and its demise at the hands of its own crew resulted from a spirited engagement with the British cruisers *Exeter*, *Ajax* and *Achilles* on 13 December 1939. During the clash, the Battle of the River Plate, off the coast of South America, *Exeter*, a heavy cruiser with a main armament of 203mm (8in) guns, was heavily damaged, and *Graf Spee* managed to score hits on both *Ajax* and *Achilles*, Leander-class light cruisers mounting 152mm (6in) main batteries.

Graf Spee was hit no fewer than 70 times during the running battle and retired up the Plate estuary to the port of Montevideo, capital of neutral Uruguay. Allowed to remain in harbour for just 72 hours and erroneously believing that a large British naval force awaited him at sea, Hans Langsdorff (1894–1939), *Graf Spee*'s captain, sailed on 17 December and scuttled his ship, rather than risk internment or further loss of life among his crew. Three days later, Langsdorff committed suicide.

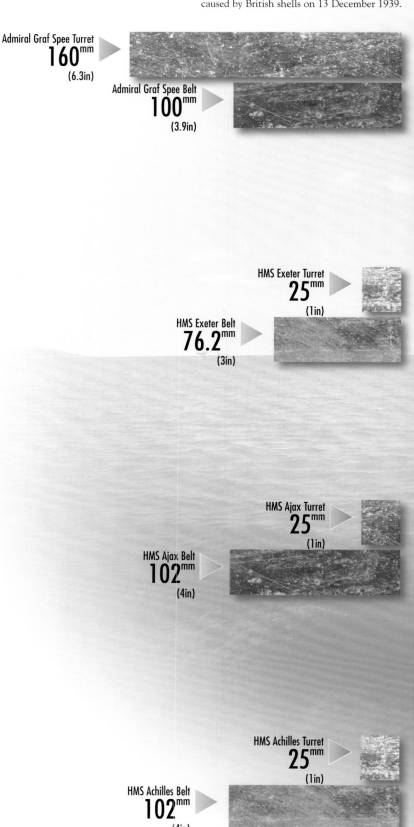

Armour Thickness
The thick armour plating of *Graf Spee* was substantially greater than that of the British cruisers that the pocket battleship faced during the Battle of the River Plate. Electric welding rather than riveting in the German ship allowed the allotment of more tonnage to armour protection, minimizing the damage caused by British shells on 13 December 1939.

Admiral Graf Spee Turret
160mm
(6.3in)

Admiral Graf Spee Belt
100mm
(3.9in)

HMS Exeter Turret
25mm
(1in)

HMS Exeter Belt
76.2mm
(3in)

HMS Ajax Turret
25mm
(1in)

HMS Ajax Belt
102mm
(4in)

HMS Achilles Turret
25mm
(1in)

HMS Achilles Belt
102mm
(4in)

Admiral Graf Spee

Constructed as a commerce raider, the 'pocket battleship' *Graf Spee* was heavily armed with a powerful 280mm (11in) main battery and a secondary armament of 150mm (5.9in) and 105mm (4.1in) weapons along with torpedo tubes.

Admiral Graf Spee Length
186ᵐ
(610ft)

HMS Exeter

The heavy cruiser HMS *Exeter* was outgunned by *Graf Spee* at the Battle of the River Plate and suffered extensive damage.

HMS Exeter Length
175ᵐ
(574ft)

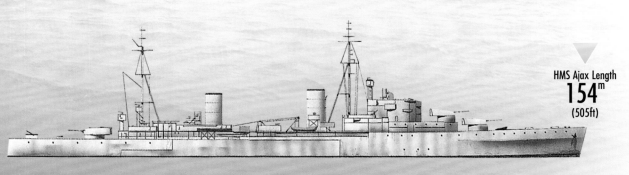

HMS Ajax

Launched 1 March 1934, the cruiser displaced 7375 tonnes (7259 tons). *Ajax* survived the war and was scrapped in 1949.

HMS Ajax Length
154ᵐ
(505ft)

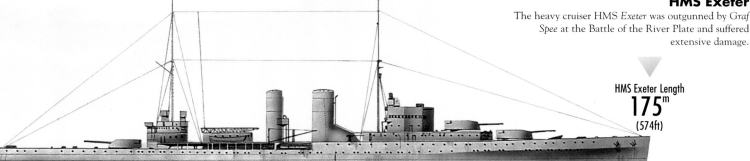

HMS Achilles

The 152mm (6in) guns of the Leander-class light cruiser HMS *Achilles* were far outranged by the main armament of *Graf Spee*. Nevertheless, the German vessel was hit by numerous 152mm (6in) shells from *Achilles* and its sister, *Ajax*.

HMS Achilles Length
154ᵐ
(505ft)

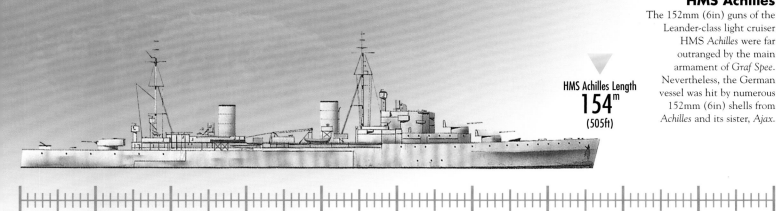

Chasing the Bismarck 1

Main Gun Calibre and Ship Length

▶ **Bismarck**
▶ **HMS Hood**

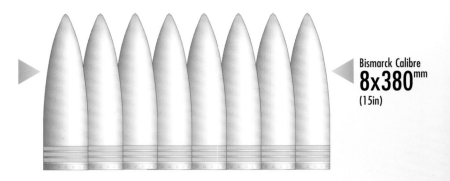

Bismarck Calibre
8x380mm
(15in)

Launched in February 1939, *Bismarck* was emblematic of the rise of the armed might of Nazi Germany. Mounting eight 380mm (15in) guns and capable of a top speed of 52.2km/h (29 knots), the ship was designed to raid Allied merchant convoys and defend itself against any warship then in service with the Royal Navy. Displacing 41,660 tonnes (41,000 tons), *Bismarck* carried a secondary armament of 150mm (5.9in) and 105mm (4.1in) guns, while the battleship was protected by armour up to 355mm (14in) thick.

Bismarck departed Gotenhafen on 19 May 1941, effected a rendezvous with the heavy cruiser *Prinz Eugen* and headed for the open sea through the Denmark Strait. The British Admiralty had been warned that the German warships were at sea and recognized the threat posed by a freely ranging *Bismarck*. British cruisers guarded the avenues of approach to the Atlantic.

Among the British warships sent against *Bismarck* were the new battleship HMS *Prince of Wales* and the venerable battlecruiser HMS *Hood*, launched in 1918. Something of an anachronism by 1941, *Hood* had been built on the premise that heavy armament and speed were a winning combination in naval warfare. Thus it mounted 381mm (15in) main guns, but in order to achieve an original maximum speed of 55.8km/h (31 knots) the battlecruiser sacrificed a measure of armour protection. Displacing tonnage roughly equivalent to that of *Bismarck*, *Hood* was believed by some to be the only Royal Navy warship that could engage in single combat with it and win.

In the predawn hours of 24 May, the British ships spotted *Bismarck* and *Prinz Eugen* in the Denmark Strait and engaged them. The 203mm (8in) guns of *Prinz Eugen* hit *Hood* first, starting a large fire. Then, *Bismarck*'s fifth salvo scored a fatal hit that penetrated to an ammunition magazine, resulting in a catastrophic explosion, and the battlecruiser sank within minutes. Only three members of a crew of more than 1400 survived. *Prince of Wales* was also damaged in the battle, and *Bismarck* suffered a hit that ruptured a fuel bunker and left a telltale oil slick.

Main Gun Calibre

The German battleship *Bismarck* and the British battlecruiser HMS *Hood* carried a similar main armament. A full broadside from either warship placed a massive weight of explosive armour-piercing shells into the air. During the Battle of the Denmark Strait, fire from the *Bismarck* was highly accurate.

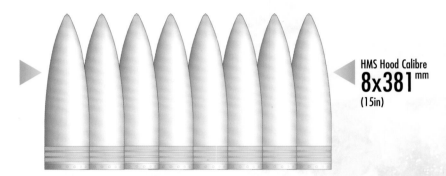

HMS Hood Calibre
8x381mm
(15in)

Bismarck

The sleek, modern German battleship *Bismarck* took several hits from British shells during the Battle of the Denmark Strait but exhibited outstanding fire control in sinking the battlecruiser HMS *Hood* and damaging the battleship HMS *Prince of Wales*.

HMS Hood

A World War I-era warship constructed with relatively light armour protection atop its turrets and main deck, the battlecruiser HMS *Hood* suffered a catastrophic explosion after being hit by a 380mm (15in) shell from *Bismarck* in the Denmark Strait.

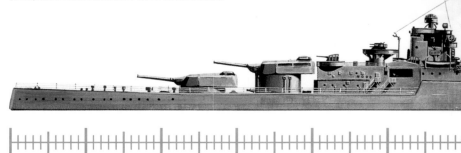

The Deck of the Bismarck
A vessel of massive proportions, the modern German battleship *Bismarck* was 36m (118ft) wide at the beam, and its eight 380mm (15in) guns were arranged in four turrets. Nearly 2200 officers and sailors served as its crew, and the warship was large enough to carry two Arado floatplanes for reconnaissance.

The Deck of HMS Hood
With a beam of 31.8m (104ft), the battlecruiser HMS *Hood* was nearly as broad as *Bismarck*. Launched in 1918 and commissioned two years later, *Hood* was the pride of the Royal Navy for more than two decades. The vessel's Achilles' heel, however, was a lack of armour protection on upper surfaces.

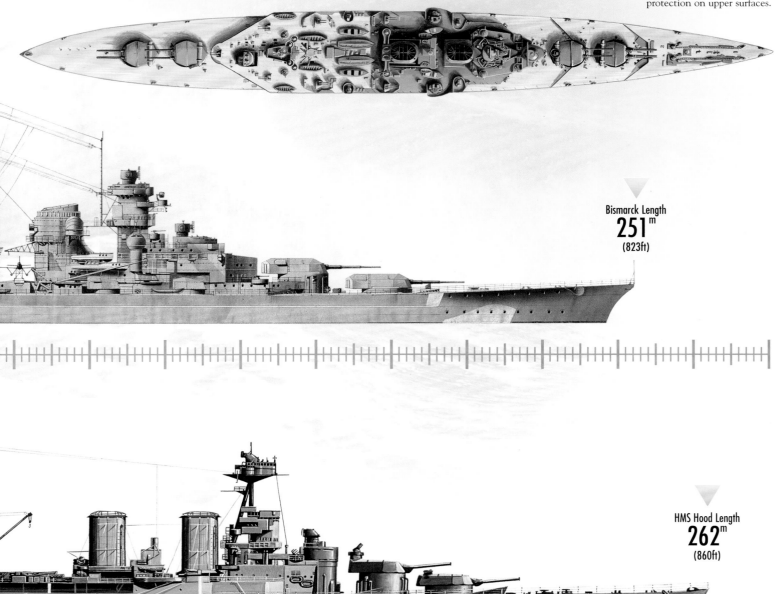

Bismarck Length
251m
(823ft)

HMS Hood Length
262m
(860ft)

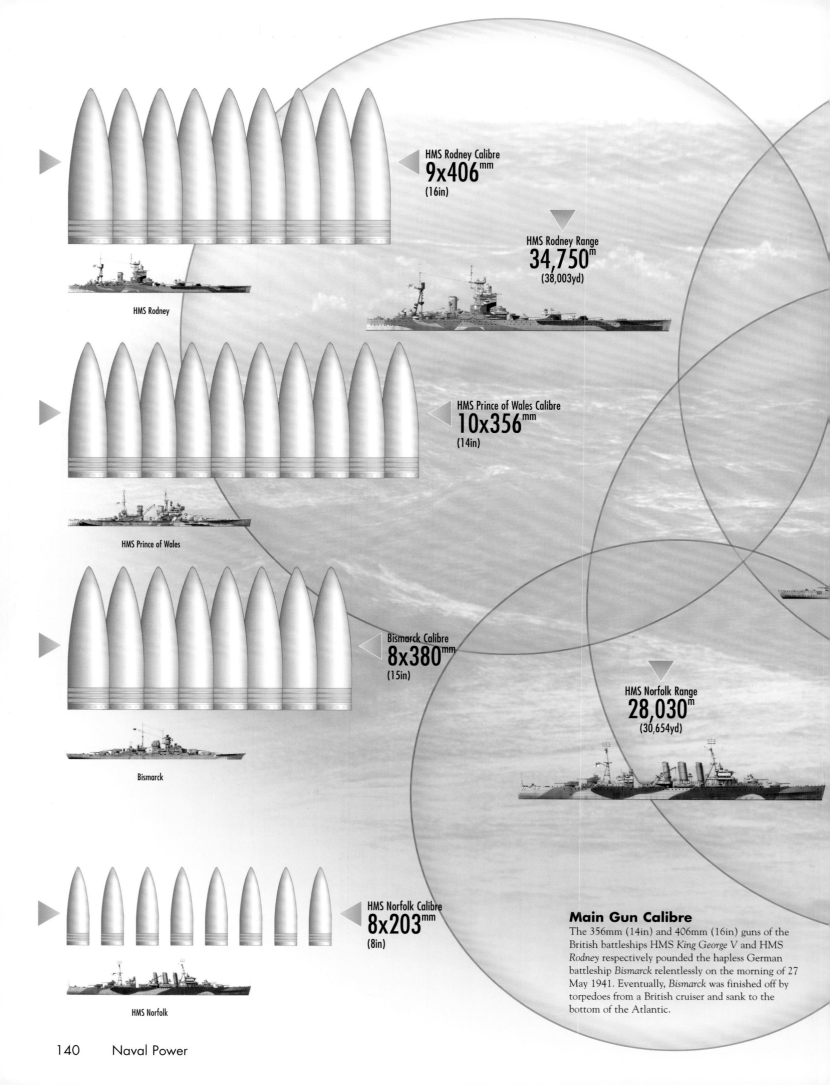

HMS Rodney Calibre
9x406mm
(16in)

HMS Rodney Range
34,750m
(38,003yd)

HMS Rodney

HMS Prince of Wales Calibre
10x356mm
(14in)

HMS Prince of Wales

Bismarck Calibre
8x380mm
(15in)

Bismarck

HMS Norfolk Range
28,030m
(30,654yd)

HMS Norfolk Calibre
8x203mm
(8in)

HMS Norfolk

Main Gun Calibre

The 356mm (14in) and 406mm (16in) guns of the British battleships HMS *King George V* and HMS *Rodney* respectively pounded the hapless German battleship *Bismarck* relentlessly on the morning of 27 May 1941. Eventually, *Bismarck* was finished off by torpedoes from a British cruiser and sank to the bottom of the Atlantic.

Main Gun Effective Range

The 356mm (14in) guns carried by the British battleships HMS *King George V* and HMS *Prince of Wales* were outranged by the 380mm (15in) main armament of *Bismarck*. However, by the morning of 27 May 1941, *Bismarck*'s steering had been crippled by a British torpedo hit and the ship was unable to manoeuvre effectively against overwhelming enemy gunfire.

HMS Prince of Wales Range
29,720^m
(32,502yd)

Bismarck Range
36,520^m
(39,939yd)

Chasing the Bismarck 2

Main Gun Calibre and Effective Range

▶ **HMS Rodney**
▶ **HMS Prince of Wales**
▶ **Bismarck**
▶ **HMS Norfolk**

Following a game of cat and mouse during which British cruisers such as the County-class HMS *Norfolk* and HMS *Suffolk*, mounting 203mm (8in) guns, had shadowed the great German battleship *Bismarck*, the heavy surface units of the Royal Navy brought the enemy to heel on the morning of 27 May 1941. The guns of the battleships HMS *King George V* and HMS *Rodney* scored repeated hits on the German warship, starting raging fires. When the stubborn *Bismarck* refused to sink, the cruiser HMS *Dorsetshire* slammed torpedoes into the blackened hulk, finally sending *Bismarck* to the bottom.

The battleship's demise was made possible through a strike by obsolete Fairey Swordfish torpedo planes launched from British aircraft carriers. The lumbering Swordfish biplane was constructed of wood and canvas, but heroic pilots pressed home their attacks and finally produced a single damaging hit on the German battleship, jamming its steering and causing *Bismarck* to turn in a circle. Although the ship was protected by 320mm (12.6in) of armour at the waterline, the torpedo struck home at its most vulnerable spot.

Two classes of British battleships were represented in the sinking of *Bismarck*. *Prince of Wales*, damaged in the Battle of the Denmark Strait, had been completed only two months before the epic chase and displaced 38,610 tonnes (38,000 tons), as did its sister ship, the class leader *King George V*. *Rodney* was the second of the Nelson-class battleships, launched in 1925 and displacing 34,500 tonnes (33,950 tons). Unusually, all three of its 406mm (16in) gun turrets sat forward of the bridge and main superstructure.

A frontal view of *Bismarck*, showing its two forward 380mm (15in) gun turrets, named 'Anton' and 'Bruno'.

Battle of Midway 1

Number of Aircraft

▶ **USS Yorktown**

▶ **Kaga**

▶ **Akagi**

▶ **Hiryu**

The Japanese Carrier Striking Force that sortied from Hashirajima in the home islands at the end of May 1942 to provide the air power to crush American defences prior to the occupation of Midway atoll included four powerful aircraft carriers, *Akagi*, *Kaga*, *Soryu* and *Hiryu*. Between them, the complement of aircraft topped 250 in number and included dive-bombers, torpedo planes and fighters. *Akagi*, which had originally been laid down as a battleship, and *Kaga*, constructed on the hull of a battlecruiser, were considerably larger than the others, with *Hiryu* and *Soryu* each carrying roughly the same numbers of planes as one another.

Opposing the Japanese were three American aircraft carriers of the Yorktown class, each carrying nearly 100 planes. Although the American carriers, *Yorktown*, *Enterprise* and *Hornet*, were only slightly more than half the size of *Akagi* and *Kaga* and roughly equivalent to *Soryu* and *Hiryu*, the American ships were planned as carriers from the keel up and stored aircraft more efficiently than their larger Japanese counterparts.

Sailing from Pearl Harbor, the American carrier commanders were warned of Japanese intentions by outstanding codebreaking personnel. Grouped into two task forces, the Americans waited for the Japanese to arrive within striking distance, and though their torpedo planes were ravaged by Japanese fighters, US dive-bombers destroyed all four Japanese carriers. The US Navy lost the *Yorktown* during a battle that proved to be the turning point of the Pacific War.

Yorktown

Kaga

Akagi

Akagi
66 airc

Hiryu

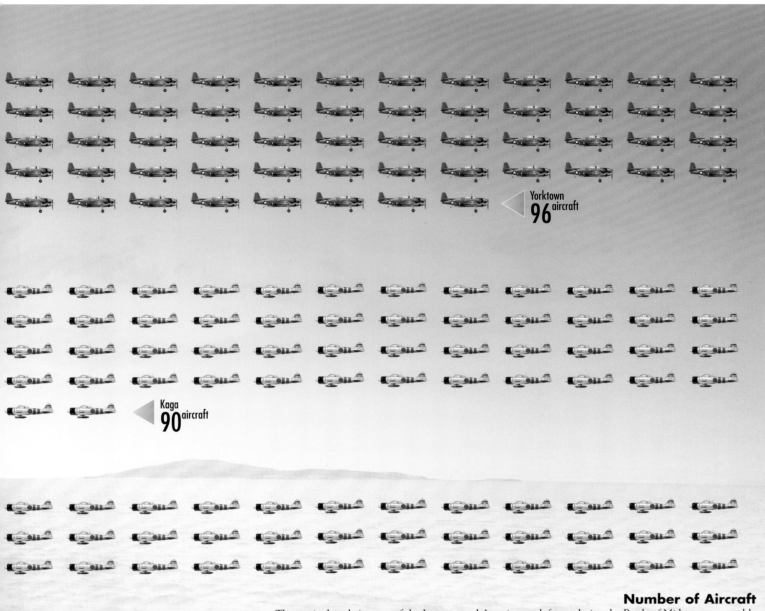

Yorktown
96 aircraft

Kaga
90 aircraft

Number of Aircraft

The carrier-based air assets of the Japanese and American task forces during the Battle of Midway were roughly equivalent in number. However, Japanese striking power was divided between the land targets of Midway atoll and the American warships, each requiring specialized armament to inflict maximum damage. When the Japanese planes were caught aboard their carriers during rearmament, American dive-bombers wrought devastation.

Hiryu
54 aircraft

LEFT: The 37,100-tonne (36,500-ton) carrier *Akagi* served as the flagship of the Japanese Carrier Striking Force at Midway, under Admiral Chuichi Nagumo (1887–1944).

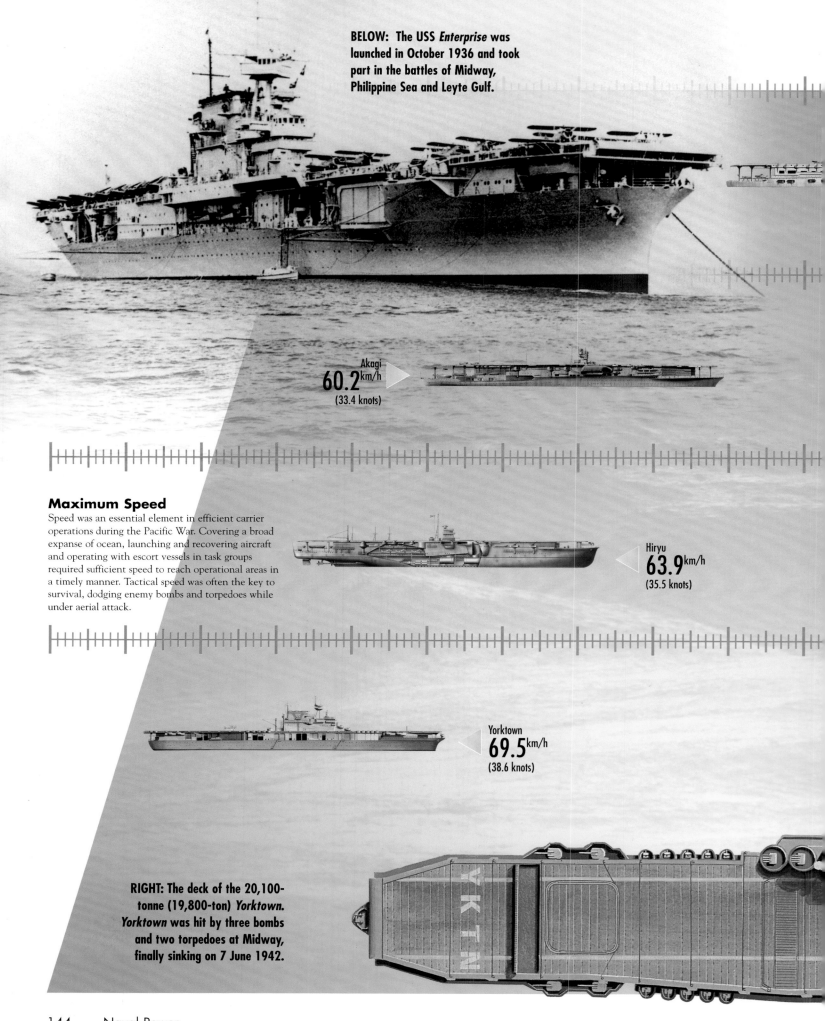

BELOW: The USS *Enterprise* was launched in October 1936 and took part in the battles of Midway, Philippine Sea and Leyte Gulf.

Akagi
60.2km/h
(33.4 knots)

Maximum Speed

Speed was an essential element in efficient carrier operations during the Pacific War. Covering a broad expanse of ocean, launching and recovering aircraft and operating with escort vessels in task groups required sufficient speed to reach operational areas in a timely manner. Tactical speed was often the key to survival, dodging enemy bombs and torpedoes while under aerial attack.

Hiryu
63.9km/h
(35.5 knots)

Yorktown
69.5km/h
(38.6 knots)

RIGHT: The deck of the 20,100-tonne (19,800-ton) *Yorktown*. *Yorktown* was hit by three bombs and two torpedoes at Midway, finally sinking on 7 June 1942.

Battle of Midway 2

Maximum Speed

▶ **USS Yorktown**
▶ **Kaga**
▶ **Akagi**
▶ **Hiryu**

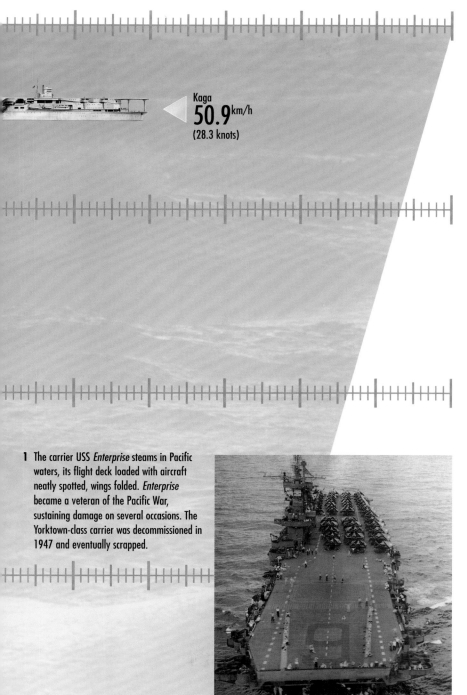

Kaga
50.9km/h
(28.3 knots)

1 The carrier USS *Enterprise* steams in Pacific waters, its flight deck loaded with aircraft neatly spotted, wings folded. *Enterprise* became a veteran of the Pacific War, sustaining damage on several occasions. The Yorktown-class carrier was decommissioned in 1947 and eventually scrapped.

Employing their considerable speed, the American aircraft carriers of Task Forces 16 and 17 arrived at their rendezvous at Point Luck, 523km (325 miles) northeast of Midway atoll, on 2 June 1942, two days prior to the series of air engagements that changed the course of the war in the Pacific. US commanders were without battleships just six months after the devastating Japanese attack on Pearl Harbor in December 1941; however, it is likely that the slower battleships would not have sortied from Hawaiian waters with the carriers had they been available.

The speed and timing of the deployment of the American carriers *Yorktown*, *Enterprise* and *Hornet* also allowed them to avoid detection by a cordon of Japanese submarines that arrived on station too late to notify Japanese commanders that elements of the US Navy were already at sea. Preserving the element of surprise, the Americans launched airstrikes against the heart of the Imperial Japanese Navy and shattered four aircraft carriers during the Battle of Midway. Following the triumph, Admiral Raymond A. Spruance (1886–1969) again utilized the speed of his carriers to temporarily retire eastwards, away from the threat of a night engagement with superior Japanese surface warships.

The large Japanese carriers *Kaga* and *Akagi*, laid down during the 1920s initially as other warship types, were somewhat slower than their American counterparts. *Hiryu*, commissioned in 1939, was purpose-built as a modified carrier of the Soryu class, and was a little quicker than its compatriots.

Main Gun Calibre

At the Battle of North Cape, the German battleship *Scharnhorst*, mounting nine 280mm (11in) guns, was pounded by the heavier British battleship HMS *Duke of York*, with its complement of 10 356mm (14in) weapons that could hurl a full broadside of ordnance more than 22,000m (24,060yd). Ten 356mm (14in) shells from the British battleship crashed into *Scharnhorst*, some fired from only 9500m (10,389yd).

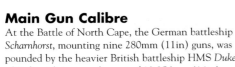

HMS Duke of York Calibre
10x356mm
(14in)

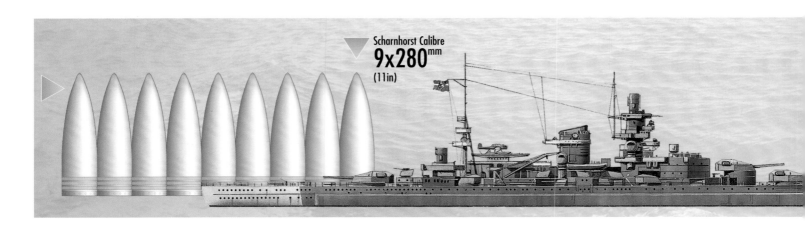

Scharnhorst Calibre
9x280mm
(11in)

HMS Norfolk Calibre
8x203mm
(8in)

Battle of North Cape

Main Gun Calibre and Armour Thickness

▶ **HMS Duke of York**
▶ **Scharnhorst**
▶ **HMS Norfolk**

With a main armament of 10 x 356mm (14in) guns, the British battleship HMS *Duke of York* ended the quite active career of the German battleship *Scharnhorst* during the Battle of North Cape on 26 December 1943. The swift *Scharnhorst* had moved into Arctic waters in search of Allied merchant shipping en route to the Soviet Union, and *Duke of York*, a King George V-class battleship displacing 42,800 tonnes (42,076 tons) at full load, hunted the raider in company with several cruisers and destroyers, finally making contact off the coast of Norway.

As the British County-class heavy cruiser HMS *Norfolk*, mounting 203mm (8in) guns, shadowed *Scharnhorst*, the German warship fired its 280mm (11in) guns, scoring a hit that damaged a gun turret and rendered the cruiser's radar inoperable. Late in the afternoon of 26 December, another British cruiser, HMS *Belfast*, illuminated *Scharnhorst* with starshells. Surprised, the German commander attempted to turn away as HMS *Duke of York* opened fire, hitting the forward turret and then destroying the aircraft hangar. British cruisers blocked the potential escape route. Nevertheless, *Scharnhorst* opened the range with its top speed of 55.8km/h (31 knots) and gained a brief respite from the onslaught.

At 1820, a 356mm (14in) shell scored a damaging hit on *Scharnhorst*, penetrating its armour belt at the waterline and flooding a boiler room. Slowed, the German warship was then struck by four torpedoes from British destroyers. *Duke of York* and the accompanying cruisers had so damaged the *Scharnhorst* that they ceased firing sometime after 2100. Subsequently, the German battleship endured a further fusillade of British torpedoes, capsized and sank in the frigid water. A total of 1932 German and 11 British sailors were killed in the action.

TOP: A cutaway view of the German battleship *Scharnhorst* reveals the inner compartments of the warship. At North Cape, *Scharnhorst* sustained tremendous damage from British 203mm (8in) and 356mm (14in) shells as well as taking numerous torpedo hits. *Scharnhorst* now rests in 290m (951ft) of water 66 miles (106km) off North Cape.

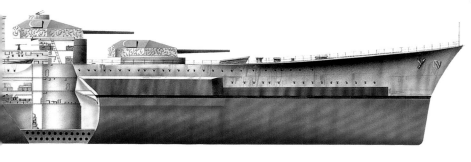

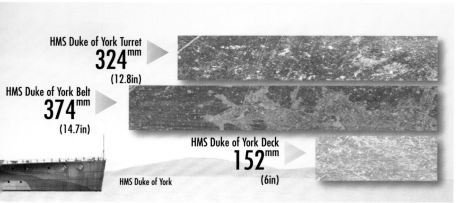

HMS Duke of York Turret
324mm
(12.8in)

HMS Duke of York Belt
374mm
(14.7in)

HMS Duke of York Deck
152mm
(6in)

HMS Duke of York

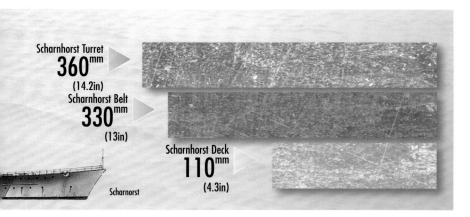

Scharnhorst Turret
360mm
(14.2in)

Scharnhorst Belt
330mm
(13in)

Scharnhorst Deck
110mm
(4.3in)

Scharnorst

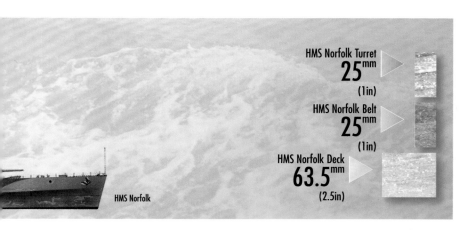

HMS Norfolk Turret
25mm
(1in)

HMS Norfolk Belt
25mm
(1in)

HMS Norfolk Deck
63.5mm
(2.5in)

HMS Norfolk

USS Essex

HMS Eagle

USS Essex
100 aircraft

HMS Eagle
80 aircraft

HMS Indomitable

USS Independence

HMS Indomitable
45 aircraft

USS Independence
45 aircraft

Number of Aircraft

Allied aircraft carriers evolved to greater aircraft capacity and operating efficiency due to improved designs as World War II progressed, and aircraft capacity was further increased with aircraft types whose wings could be folded for easier storage and movement from hangar to flight deck.

RIGHT: This cutaway view of the Essex-class USS *Lexington* illustrates the ship's intricate compartmentalization along with the spacious hangar deck where the carrier's complement of approximately 100 aircraft were armed and serviced.

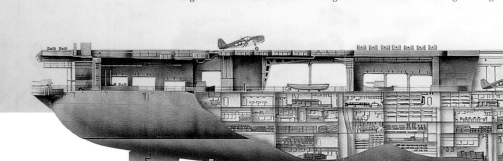

USS Wasp

USS Wasp
76 aircraft

Allied Carriers Compared

Number of Aircraft

- ▶ **USS Essex**
- ▶ **HMS Eagle**
- ▶ **USS Wasp**
- ▶ **HMS Indomitable**
- ▶ **USS Independence**
- ▶ **HMS Formidable**

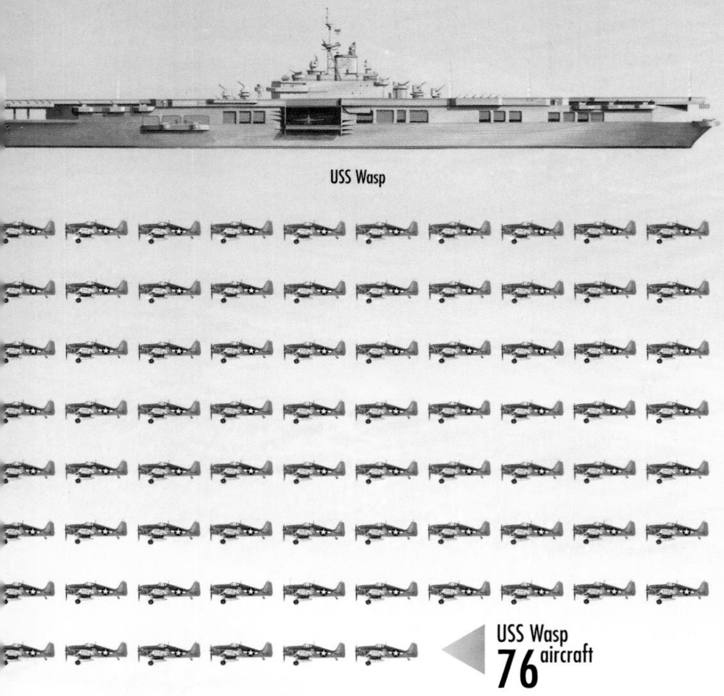

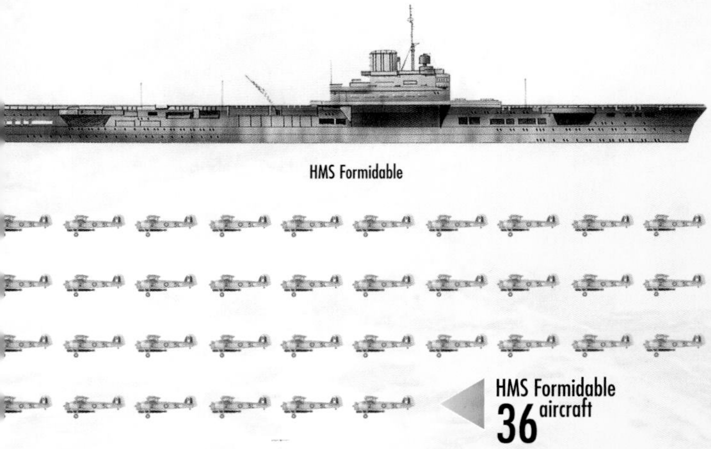

Early Allied aircraft carriers had significant aircraft capacity in several cases due to their sheer size. An example was the British carrier HMS *Eagle*, laid down as a battleship in 1913. The later British Illustrious class, including the 23,370-tonne (23,000-ton) *Indomitable* and *Formidable*, were designed with heavy anti-aircraft capabilities and armoured flight decks. Their aircraft complement, however, was considerably lower than that of their US fleet carrier counterparts due to the extensive armour and the fact that the Americans routinely carried aircraft atop their flight decks as well as in their hangars.

The light carrier *Wasp*, at 14,900 tonnes (14,700 tons), was built under Washington Naval Treaty tonnage restrictions, while *Independence*, displacing 10,830 tonnes (10,660 tons), was constructed from the converted hull of a cruiser and was the lead ship of a carrier class that entered service in early 1943. The Essex-class fleet carriers entered service in late 1942, and 24 of the 27,430-tonne (27,000-ton) ships were eventually built. With a top speed of 59.4km/h (33 knots), none of these was lost to enemy action during World War II despite the fact that their flight decks were primarily of wood. Although the lighter construction allowed for greater aircraft capacity, it also made the carriers vulnerable to Japanese bombs or kamikaze suicide planes.

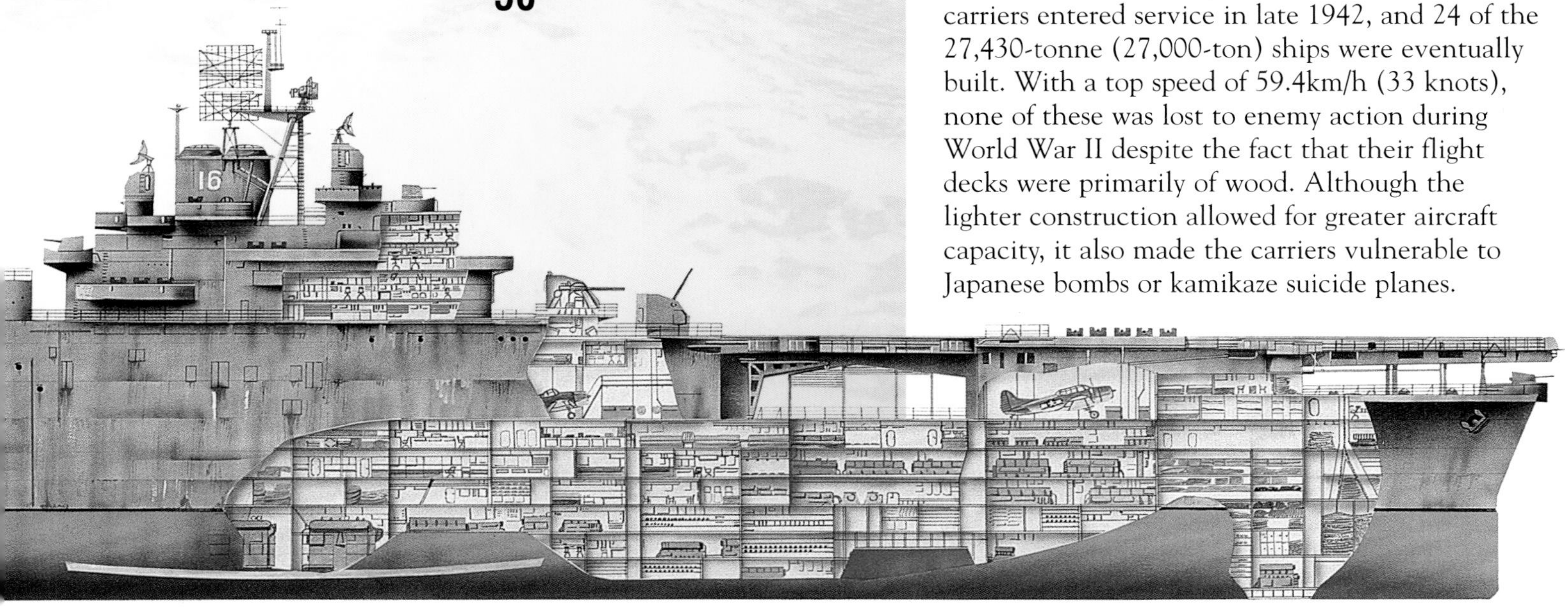

HMS Formidable

HMS Formidable
36 aircraft

Mediterranean Fleets Compared

Full-load Displacement

- ▶ **HMS Arethusa**
- ▶ **Gloire**
- ▶ **Conte di Cavour**
- ▶ **HMS Barham**
- ▶ **HMS Warspite**
- ▶ **Littorio**

Numerous Allied and Axis warships plied the waters of the Mediterranean Sea during World War II, ranging in displacement from small, sleek destroyers to light cruisers such as the British HMS *Arethusa*, struck by an Italian torpedo in 1942 and put out of action for months, the elderly battleship HMS *Barham*, sunk by three torpedoes from the German submarine *U-331* on 25 November 1941, and *Barham*'s sister, the battleship HMS *Warspite*, which survived the fight for control of the Mediterranean and was sold for scrap in 1946. The French light cruiser *Gloire* served in the Atlantic and the Mediterranean, supporting the Allied landings at Anzio, Italy, and Operation Dragoon, the invasion of southern France.

The brand new Italian battleship *Littorio* was one of the largest warships to see action in the Mediterranean theatre. Along with its sister, *Vittorio Veneto*, and the older battleship *Conte di Cavour*, *Littorio* was at Taranto during the daring 11 November 1940 air raid by British torpedo planes flying from the carrier HMS *Illustrious*. *Littorio* sustained three torpedo hits during the raid, while *Vittorio Veneto* escaped damage. A single torpedo sank the elderly *Conte di Cavour* in the shallow waters of Taranto harbour.

ABOVE: An aerial view of the decks of HMS Warspite.

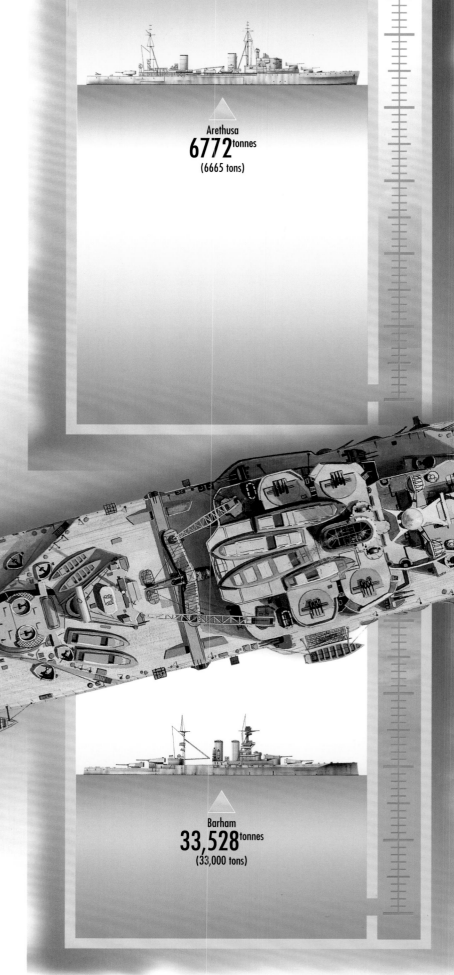

Arethusa
6772 tonnes
(6665 tons)

Barham
33,528 tonnes
(33,000 tons)

Full-load Displacement

Displacement is the weight of a warship expressed in terms of the tonnage of water it displaces. Standard displacement is the weight of a ship fully equipped for war, but without fuel and water for its boilers. Full-load displacement includes everything.

Gloire
9266 tonnes
(9120 tons)

Conte di Cavour
29,566 tonnes
(29,100 tons)

Warspite
33,945 tonnes
(33,410 tons)

Littorio
45,961 tonnes
(45,237 tons)

Destroyers 1

Maximum Speed

- ▶ **Akitsuki**
- ▶ **Hamakaze**
- ▶ **HMS Cossack**
- ▶ **Artigliere**
- ▶ **Z30**
- ▶ **L'Indomptable**

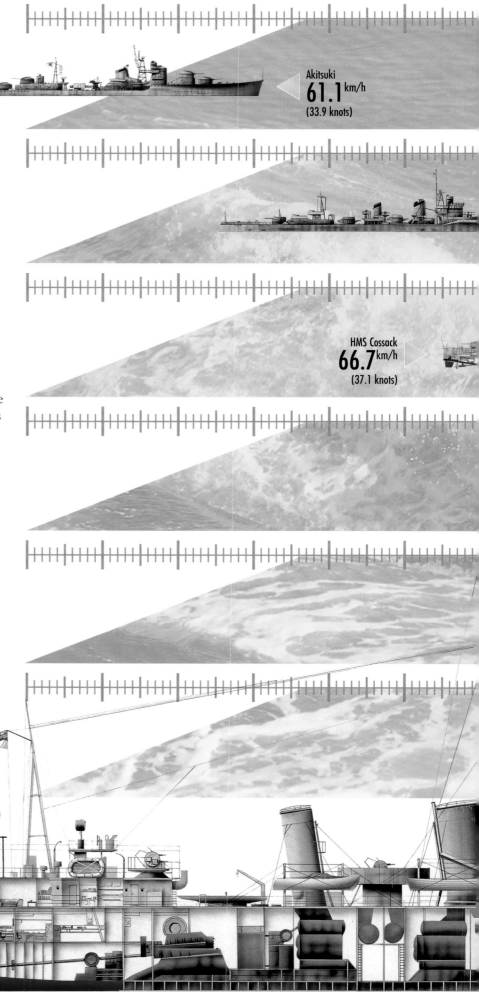

Akitsuki
61.1 km/h
(33.9 knots)

HMS Cossack
66.7 km/h
(37.1 knots)

Sleek, heavily armed and built for speed, the destroyers of the world's navies during the World War II era demonstrated their versatility in a variety of roles, including anti-submarine warfare, early-warning and screening duties, air-sea rescue, convoy escort, anti-aircraft work, shore bombardment and reconnaissance. The destroyers of the Imperial Japanese Navy distinguished themselves early in the war, particularly with their prowess in night combat. The Kagero-class destroyer *Hamakaze*, launched in 1940, displaced 2066 tonnes (2033 tons) standard, escorted the super-battleship *Yamato* on its final combat sortie in April 1945 and was sunk by US planes. The *Akitsuki* led a class of Japanese destroyers displacing 2745 tonnes (2700 tons). The Akitsuki-class destroyers were the largest vessels of their kind produced by the Japanese.

The German destroyer Z30, one of the nine warships of the Type 1936A, or Narvik class, which displaced 2600 tonnes (2559 tons), patrolled Scandinavian waters and was turned over to the British at the end of the war, while the Italian *Artigliere*, a Soldati-class destroyer launched in 1937, displaced 1645 tonnes (1620 tons) and was sunk by the British heavy cruiser HMS *York* on 13 October 1940. The French Fantasque-class destroyer *L'Indomptable* displaced 2570 tonnes (2530 tons) and served in five navies, both Allied and Axis, during the war. Britain's Tribal-class HMS *Cossack* displaced 1900 tonnes (1870 tons) and was lost to a German submarine in October 1941.

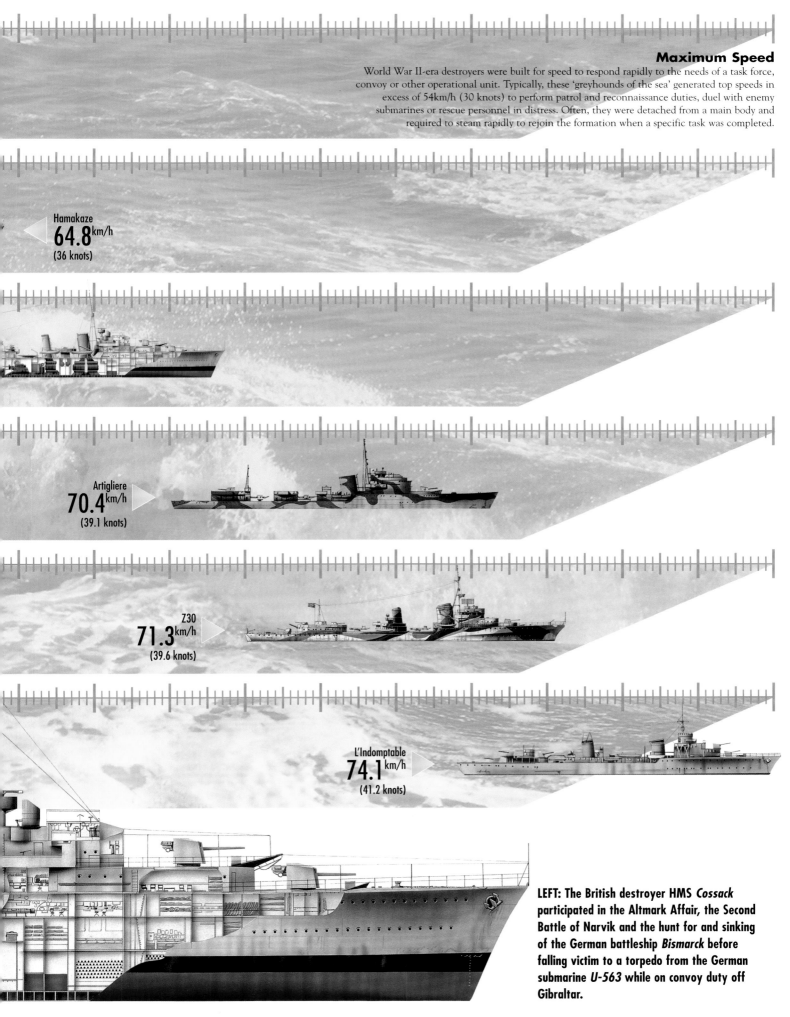

Maximum Speed

World War II-era destroyers were built for speed to respond rapidly to the needs of a task force, convoy or other operational unit. Typically, these 'greyhounds of the sea' generated top speeds in excess of 54km/h (30 knots) to perform patrol and reconnaissance duties, duel with enemy submarines or rescue personnel in distress. Often, they were detached from a main body and required to steam rapidly to rejoin the formation when a specific task was completed.

Hamakaze
64.8km/h
(36 knots)

Artigliere
70.4km/h
(39.1 knots)

Z30
71.3km/h
(39.6 knots)

L'Indomptable
74.1km/h
(41.2 knots)

LEFT: The British destroyer HMS _Cossack_ participated in the Altmark Affair, the Second Battle of Narvik and the hunt for and sinking of the German battleship _Bismarck_ before falling victim to a torpedo from the German submarine _U-563_ while on convoy duty off Gibraltar.

Fletcher Calibre
5x127ᵐᵐ
(5in)

Armament

Based on tonnage, destroyers were among the most heavily armed naval vessels of World War II. Equipped with a variety of weapons, including torpedoes, naval cannon, depth charges and anti-aircraft guns, destroyers performed both offensive and defensive fire-support missions against land, sea and air targets.

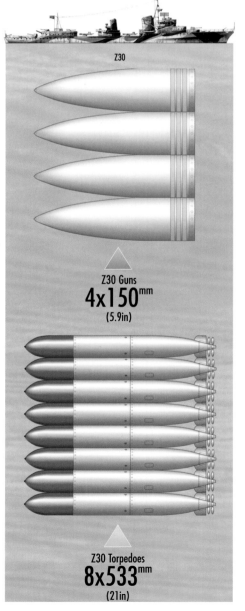

Z30

Z30 Guns
4x150ᵐᵐ
(5.9in)

Z30 Torpedoes
8x533ᵐᵐ
(21in)

Hamakaze

Hamakaze Torpedoes
8x610ᵐᵐ
(24in)

Hamakaze Guns
6x127ᵐᵐ
(5in)

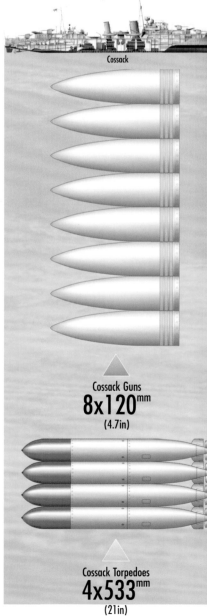

Cossack

Cossack Guns
8x120ᵐᵐ
(4.7in)

Cossack Torpedoes
4x533ᵐᵐ
(21in)

Fletcher Calibre
10x533mm
(21in)

Destroyers 2

Armament

▶ **Akitsuki**
▶ **Hamakaze**
▶ **HMS Cossack**
▶ **Z30**
▶ **L'Indomptable**
▶ **USS Fletcher**

Akitsuki

L'Indomptable

Akitsuki Guns
8x100mm
(3.9in)

Akitsuki Torpedoes
4x610mm
(24in)

L'Indomptable Guns
5x138mm
(5.4in)

L'Indomptable Torpedoes
9x533mm
(21in)

Armed with the formidable Type 93 Long Lance torpedo, destroyers of the Imperial Japanese Navy gained notoriety during operations in the vicinity of the Solomon Islands during 1942, including the delivery of reinforcements and supplies to the embattled island of Guadalcanal where they earned the nickname of the 'Tokyo Express'. The large Akitsuki-class destroyers, armed with four twin 100mm (3.9in) guns, a pair of twin 25mm (1in) anti-aircraft positions and a quadruple 610mm (24in) torpedo-tube mounting, were originally intended primarily for air defence. The smaller *Hamakaze* mounted three twin 127mm (5in) gun turrets, a pair of twin 25mm (1in) anti-aircraft mounts and two quadruple 610mm (24in) torpedo tubes.

The German destroyer *Z30*, well suited to coastal operations, carried four 150mm (5.9in) guns in single turrets, five single 20mm (0.79in) and two twin 37mm (1.5in) anti-aircraft mounts, two quadruple 533mm (21in) torpedo-tube mountings and up to 60 mines. The French *L'Indomptable* was equipped with five 138mm (5.4in) main guns, numerous anti-aircraft guns and up to 40 mines.

Britain's famed *Cossack* was armed with eight 120mm (4.7in) guns in twin turrets, 2-pounder and 12.7mm (0.5in) anti-aircraft guns, depth charges and a quadruple torpedo tube. The US destroyers of the Fletcher class were workhorses during the two-ocean war; however, they served primarily in the Pacific Theatre, proving adept at covering the broad expanse of the great ocean. The Fletcher-class destroyers carried five 127mm (5in) guns in single turrets, up to 10 40mm (1.57in) Bofors and 10 20mm (0.79in) Oerlikon anti-aircraft guns, 10 torpedo tubes and depth charges.

TOP: Fitted with heavy anti-aircraft weaponry, a total of 175 Fletcher-class ships were built for the US Navy from 1942 to 1944, and a number of them served into the 1960s.

Cruisers

Armour Thickness

▶ **HMS Belfast**

▶ **Mogami**

▶ **USS Indianapolis**

▶ **Kirov**

▶ **De Ruyter**

HMS Belfast

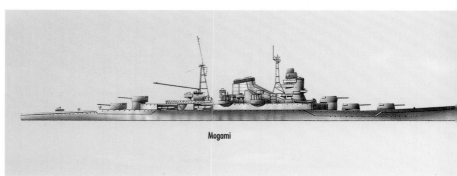

Mogami

The 9960-tonne (9800-ton) Portland-class heavy cruiser USS *Indianapolis* gained lasting fame during its tragic final mission. Following the delivery of atomic-bomb components to Tinian in the Marianas, *Indianapolis* was hit by torpedoes from the Japanese submarine *I-58* on 30 July 1945, sinking in 12 minutes. More than 800 men drifted for days on the open sea and suffered from exposure and shark attacks. Only 317 survived.

The British Town-class light cruiser *Belfast* participated in the Battle of North Cape and in the Normandy invasion on 6 June 1944. Launched in 1938, *Belfast* later served with the Royal Navy during the Korean War and became a floating museum in London. Launched in 1935, the Dutch light cruiser *de Ruyter* was sunk by a single Japanese torpedo during the Battle of the Java Sea in February 1942. The cruiser *Kirov* led the first class of large Soviet warships to be constructed from scratch following the Russian Civil War. *Kirov* was launched in 1936 and wasn't decommissioned until 1974.

The Japanese cruiser *Mogami* led a class of four warships originally intended as light cruisers; however, by 1937 these were upgraded to heavy cruisers. *Mogami* was launched in 1934 and displaced 13,900 tonnes (13,670 tons) following its final refit with 203mm (8in) main guns. *Mogami* and its sister, *Mikuma*, were involved in a collision during the Battle of Midway. Repaired, *Mogami* was sunk in October 1944 during the Battle of Leyte Gulf.

RIGHT: The Dutch light cruiser *de Ruyter* was the product of difficult economic times in the Netherlands that had restricted its original displacement to 5080 tonnes (5000 tons).

Indianapolis

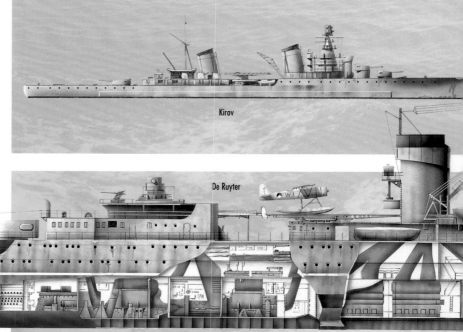

Kirov

De Ruyter

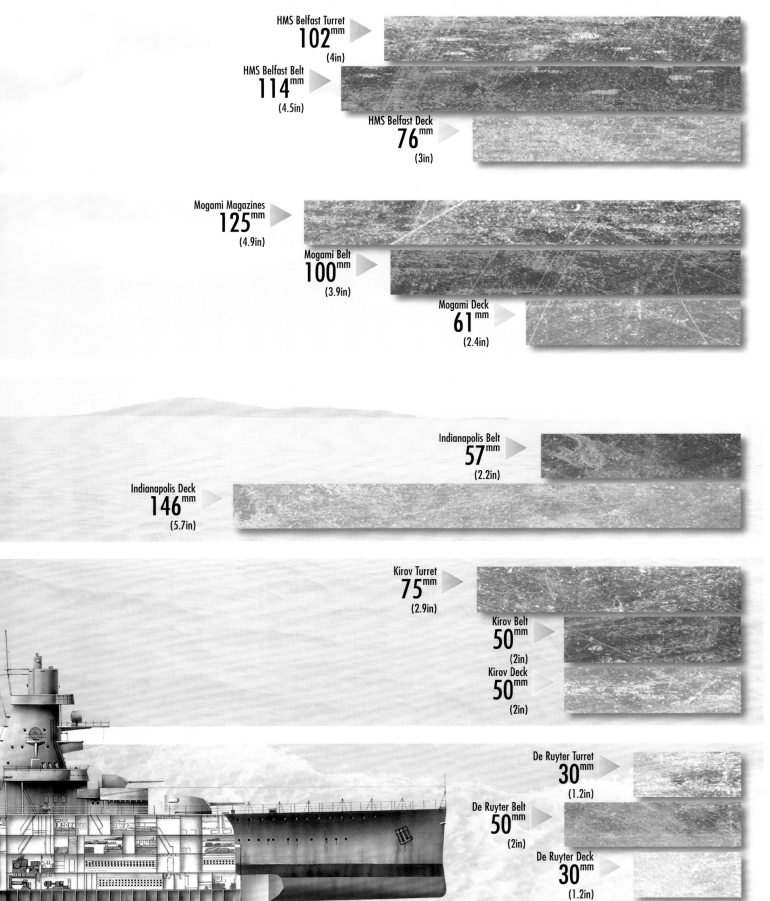

Armour Thickness

Although armour thickness limited the top speeds of Allied and Axis cruisers during World War II, the realities of naval warfare were significant enough that ship designers and builders attempted to achieve a balance between speed and protection. Even then, well-placed torpedoes or bombs often heavily damaged or sank the warships.

HMS Belfast Turret
102mm
(4in)

HMS Belfast Belt
114mm
(4.5in)

HMS Belfast Deck
76mm
(3in)

Mogami Magazines
125mm
(4.9in)

Mogami Belt
100mm
(3.9in)

Mogami Deck
61mm
(2.4in)

Indianapolis Belt
57mm
(2.2in)

Indianapolis Deck
146mm
(5.7in)

Kirov Turret
75mm
(2.9in)

Kirov Belt
50mm
(2in)

Kirov Deck
50mm
(2in)

De Ruyter Turret
30mm
(1.2in)

De Ruyter Belt
50mm
(2in)

De Ruyter Deck
30mm
(1.2in)

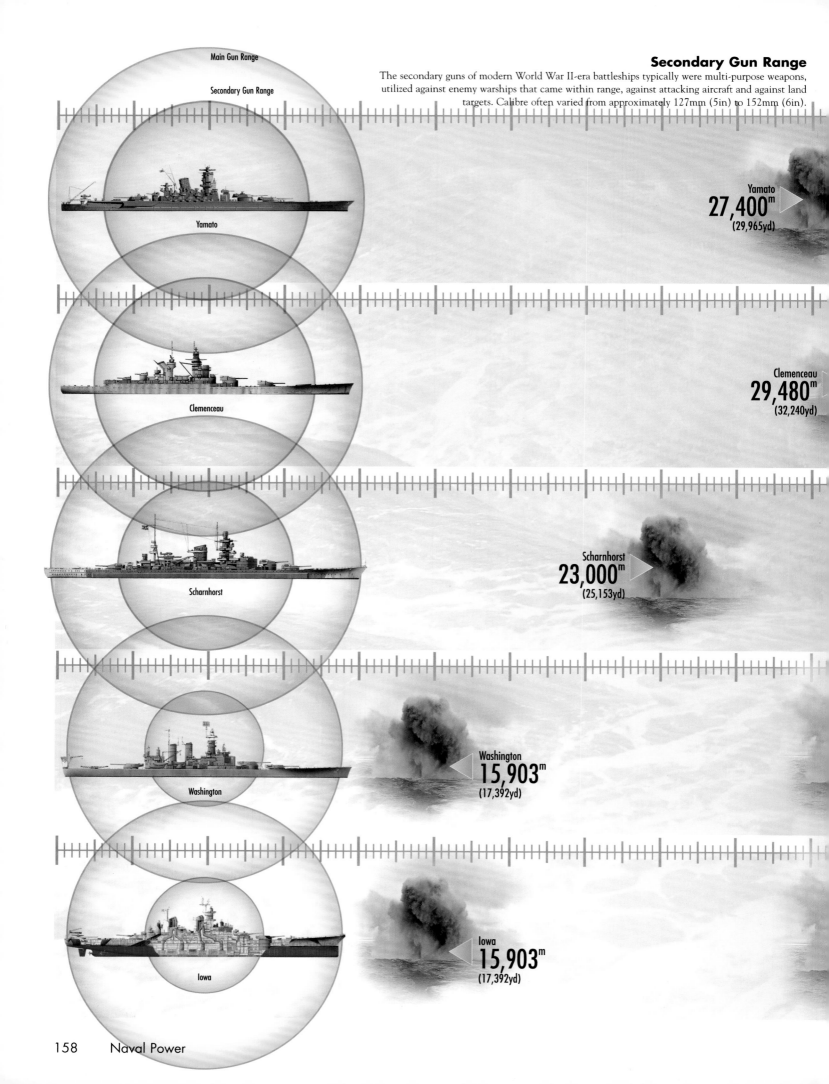

Main Gun Range

Secondary Gun Range

Yamato

Clemenceau

Scharnhorst

Washington

Iowa

Secondary Gun Range

The secondary guns of modern World War II-era battleships typically were multi-purpose weapons, utilized against enemy warships that came within range, against attacking aircraft and against land targets. Calibre often varied from approximately 127mm (5in) to 152mm (6in).

Yamato
27,400ᵐ
(29,965yd)

Clemenceau
29,480ᵐ
(32,240yd)

Scharnhorst
23,000ᵐ
(25,153yd)

Washington
15,903ᵐ
(17,392yd)

Iowa
15,903ᵐ
(17,392yd)

Main Gun Range

Firing heavy shells great distances, the main guns of battleships were capable of huge displays of firepower, a full broadside hurling tonnes of explosive and armour-piercing ordnance towards an unseen enemy detected only by radar.

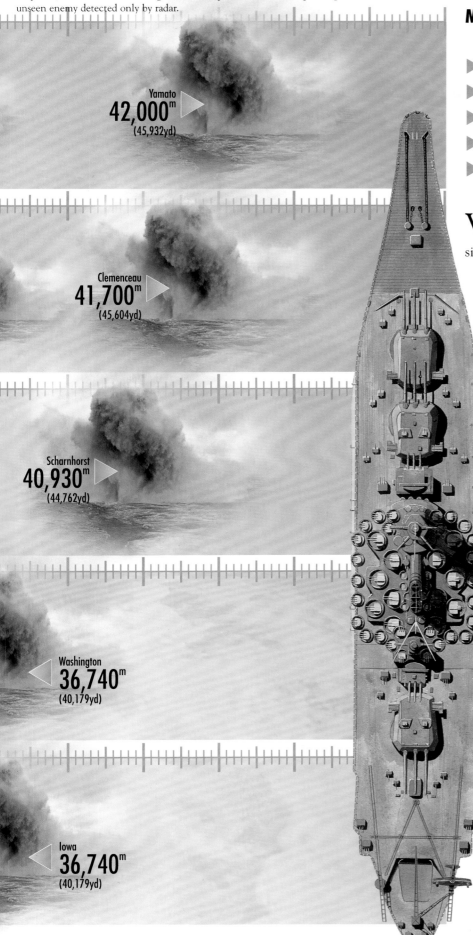

Yamato
42,000ᵐ
(45,932yd)

Clemenceau
41,700ᵐ
(45,604yd)

Scharnhorst
40,930ᵐ
(44,762yd)

Washington
36,740ᵐ
(40,179yd)

Iowa
36,740ᵐ
(40,179yd)

Battleships 1

Main and Secondary Gun Range

▶ **Yamato**
▶ **Clemenceau**
▶ **Scharnhorst**
▶ **USS Washington**
▶ **USS Iowa**

With 460mm (18.1in) main batteries, the Japanese super-battleship *Yamato* and its sister, *Musashi*, mounted the heaviest naval guns of World War II. Launched in August 1940, *Yamato* displaced 65,025 tonnes (64,000 tons) but fired its main armament against enemy surface vessels only once, during the Battle of Leyte Gulf on 25 October 1944. In April 1945, *Yamato* undertook a suicide mission against US forces at Okinawa, took massive punishment from American aircraft and sank.

On the night of 14 November 1942, off Guadalcanal, the North Carolina-class battleship USS *Washington*, armed with 406mm (16in) main guns, sank the Japanese battleship *Kirishima* and damaged two heavy cruisers. Commissioned the following year, USS *Iowa* led a class of four fast battleships mounting 406mm (16in) main batteries. All four were refitted with modern equipment in the 1980s, and two, *Wisconsin* and *Missouri*, saw action during the 1991 Gulf War.

With main batteries of 380mm (15in) guns, the French battleship *Clemenceau* was authorized as part of a programme to counter growing Italian naval strength in the Mediterranean. It was never completed, the unfinished hull being sunk by Allied planes during operations to capture Brest in 1944.

Germany's *Scharnhorst* was armed with 280mm (11in) guns, and with its sister, *Gneisenau*, posed a significant threat to Allied merchant convoys but lacked the firepower to take on the modern battleships of the Royal Navy.

LEFT: *Yamato*, displacing 65,025 tonnes (64,000 tons), was the pride of the Imperial Japanese Navy. Mounting 460mm (18.1in) main guns, the battleship also carried a dozen 155mm (6.1in) secondary weapons and 12 127mm (5in) anti-aircraft cannon. On 7 April 1945, *Yamato* was struck by at least 11 torpedoes and six bombs from US carrier-based planes before sinking.

Iowa

The battleship USS *Iowa*, commissioned in 1943, was the lead ship of a class of four such warships intended to provide heavy fire support while maintaining speed with the fast aircraft carriers of the Essex class.

Iowa Length
270 m
(886ft)

Yamato

The product of Japanese intent during the 1930s to design a battleship with heavier armament than any other in the world, *Yamato*, launched in 1940, exceeded established tonnage restrictions significantly.

Yamato Length
263 m
(863ft)

Tirpitz

Displacing nearly 43,000 tonnes (42,325 tons), the German battleship *Tirpitz* was slightly larger than its more famous sister, *Bismarck*. *Tirpitz* was launched in spring 1939 and became operational in September 1941.

Tirpitz Length
251 m
(823ft)

Battleships 2

Weight of Fire and Ship Length

▶ **USS Iowa**

▶ **Yamato**

▶ **Tirpitz**

Iowa Calibre
9x406mm
(16in)

Yamato Calibre
9x460mm
(18.1in)

Weight of Fire

The heavy broadside armament of a battleship was devastating. Although such main weapons were deployed in anticipation of a major surface engagement with enemy battleships, these encounters were extremely rare during Wolrd War II, which was dominated by carrier-based aircraft.

Tirpitz Calibre
8x380mm
(15in)

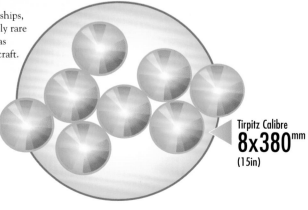

Even as they were designed, laid down, launched and commissioned, the great battleships of World War II were anachronistic. Displacing tremendous tonnages, from 42,875 tonnes (42,200 tons) for *Tirpitz* to the 45,720 tonnes (45,000 tons) of *Iowa* and the massive 65,025 tonnes (64,000 tons) of *Yamato*, these naval behemoths were initially conceived to engage the battleships of enemy nations in a Jutland-style surface battle that would decide pre-eminence on the world's oceans. While the 460mm (18.1in) guns of *Yamato* were the highest-calibre weapons mounted aboard warships of the period, the main 406mm (16in) guns of *Iowa* and the 380mm (15in) batteries of *Tirpitz* were nothing less than imposing.

However, the role that each was to play in World War II was modified from the original purpose of the prewar capital ship. *Tirpitz* posed a real threat to Allied merchant convoys operating in the Atlantic. Therefore, the British Admiralty made it a priority to neutralize the German battleship. This was not accomplished until the vessel was damaged by British midget submarines and later hit by Royal Air Force 5.4-tonne (5.3-ton) Tallboy bombs.

The super-battleship *Yamato* fired its guns at US surface targets only once during the Pacific War, at the Battle of Leyte Gulf, and was sunk after taking hits from at least 11 American torpedoes and six bombs during a one-way suicide mission to attack US naval forces operating off the coast of Okinawa in the spring of 1945. Its sister, *Musashi*, was sunk by US carrier-based aircraft during the Battle of the Philippine Sea in 1944.

The Iowa-class battleships, *Iowa*, *Missouri*, *Wisconsin* and *New Jersey*, were active with the fast carrier task forces of the US Navy during World War II. *Iowa* later conducted shore-bombardment assignments during the Korean War, and in the 1980s all four vessels were renovated to carry modern weaponry and redeployed. The ships retained their main armament, and in the 1991 Gulf War the big guns of *Missouri* and *Wisconsin* fired again almost five decades after the ships' original commissioning.

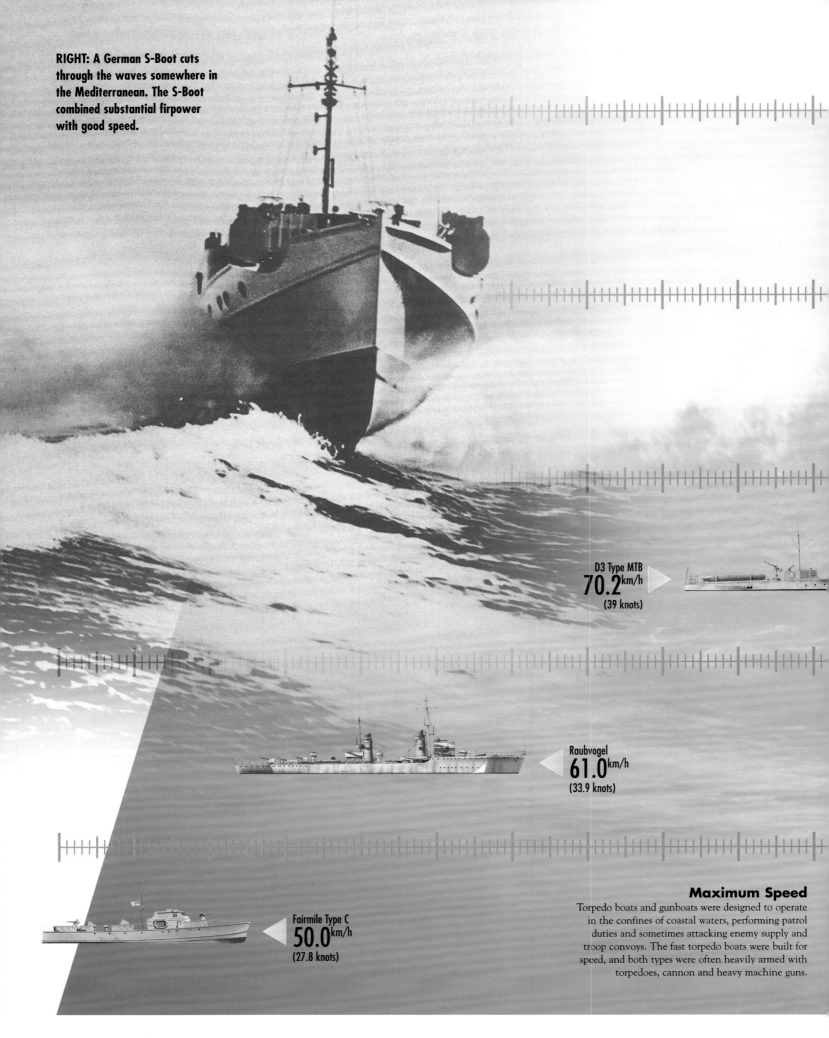

RIGHT: A German S-Boot cuts through the waves somewhere in the Mediterranean. The S-Boot combined substantial firpower with good speed.

D3 Type MTB
70.2km/h
(39 knots)

Raubvogel
61.0km/h
(33.9 knots)

Fairmile Type C
50.0km/h
(27.8 knots)

Maximum Speed

Torpedo boats and gunboats were designed to operate in the confines of coastal waters, performing patrol duties and sometimes attacking enemy supply and troop convoys. The fast torpedo boats were built for speed, and both types were often heavily armed with torpedoes, cannon and heavy machine guns.

Gunboats and Torpedo Boats

Maximum Speed

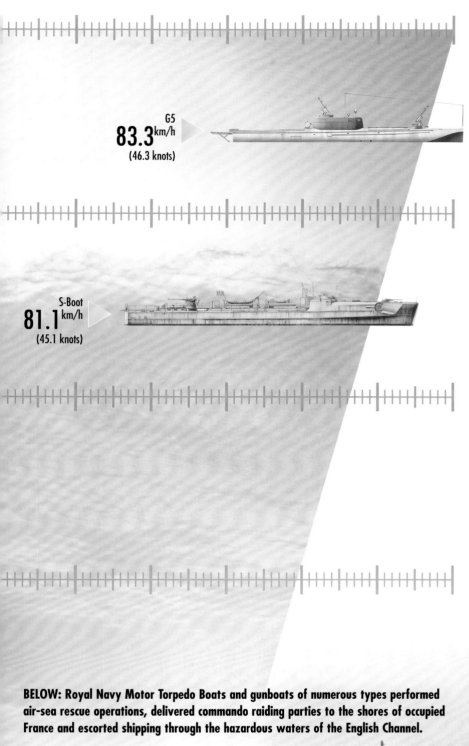

83.3 km/h G5
(46.3 knots)

81.1 km/h S-Boot
(45.1 knots)

▶ **G5**
▶ **Schnellboot (S-Boot)**
▶ **D3 Type MTB**
▶ **Raubvogel**
▶ **Fairmile Type C**

The waters of the English Channel were alive with torpedo-boat and gunboat activity during World War II as the Royal Navy prepared for a potential Nazi invasion early in the conflict and then turned to active raiding against occupied France. The British Fairmile Type C was a modification of the familiar Type A that was intended to fend off German landing craft and support-ships in the event of an invasion. With supercharged engines, the Type C was faster, and it was armed with twin 2-pounder guns and heavy 12.7mm (0.5in) machine guns. The swift, 80.3-tonne (79-ton) German S-Boot, known to the Allies as the E-boat, was armed with 533mm (21in) torpedo tubes and 20mm (0.79in) cannon. In early 1944, the S-Boot inflicted heavy casualties on Allied landing craft and troops who were conducting exercises at Slapton Sands prior to the Normandy invasion. The larger German Raubvogel torpedo boats patrolled coastal waters and were heavily armed with 105mm (4.1in) cannon, 20mm (0.79in) flak guns and torpedoes. The Soviet D3 Type MTB (Motor Torpedo Boat) carried a crew of up to 14. Its armament consisted of two 533mm (21in) torpedo tubes plus cannon or machine guns. The Soviet Navy's nimble G5 was armed with two 533mm (21in) torpedoes plus machine guns.

BELOW: Royal Navy Motor Torpedo Boats and gunboats of numerous types performed air-sea rescue operations, delivered commando raiding parties to the shores of occupied France and escorted shipping through the hazardous waters of the English Channel.

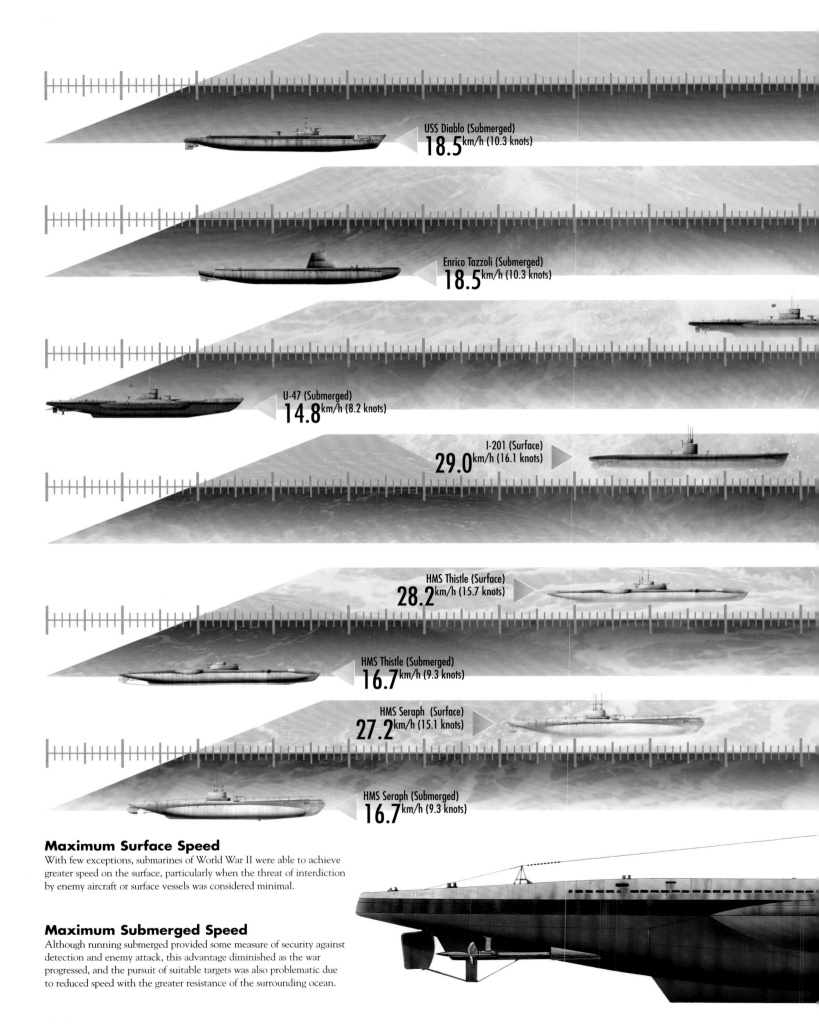

USS Diablo (Submerged)
18.5km/h (10.3 knots)

Enrico Tazzoli (Submerged)
18.5km/h (10.3 knots)

U-47 (Submerged)
14.8km/h (8.2 knots)

I-201 (Surface)
29.0km/h (16.1 knots)

HMS Thistle (Surface)
28.2km/h (15.7 knots)

HMS Thistle (Submerged)
16.7km/h (9.3 knots)

HMS Seraph (Surface)
27.2km/h (15.1 knots)

HMS Seraph (Submerged)
16.7km/h (9.3 knots)

Maximum Surface Speed

With few exceptions, submarines of World War II were able to achieve greater speed on the surface, particularly when the threat of interdiction by enemy aircraft or surface vessels was considered minimal.

Maximum Submerged Speed

Although running submerged provided some measure of security against detection and enemy attack, this advantage diminished as the war progressed, and the pursuit of suitable targets was also problematic due to reduced speed with the greater resistance of the surrounding ocean.

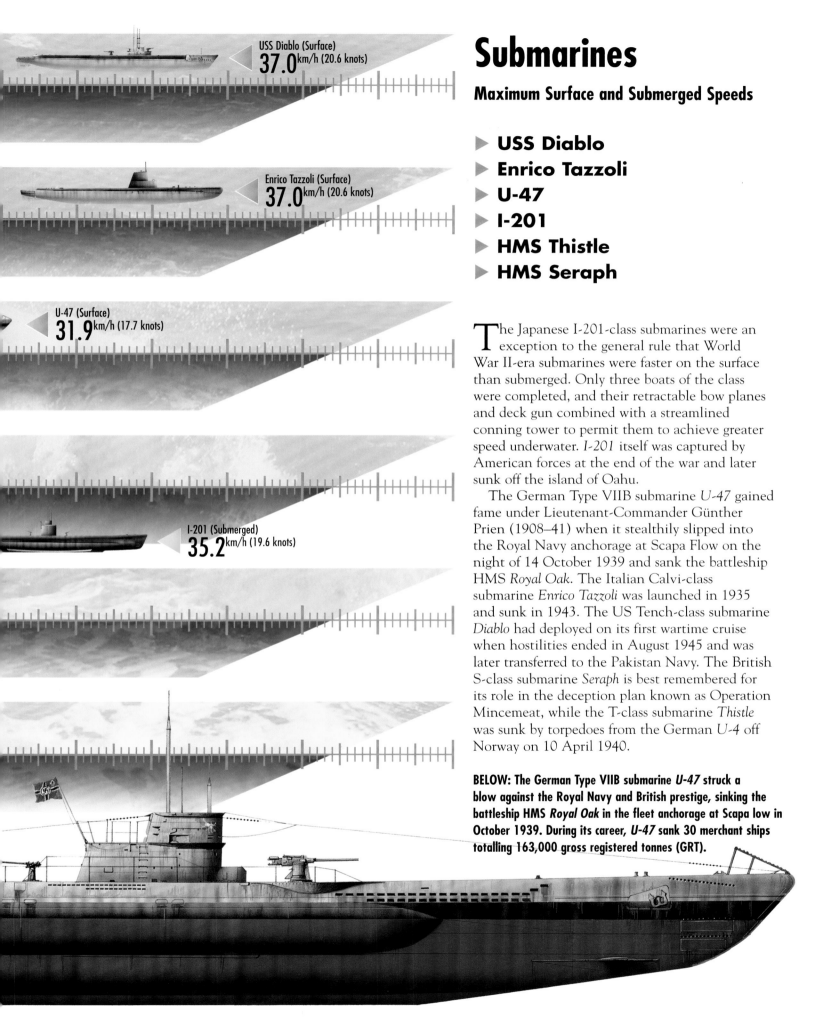

USS Diablo (Surface)
37.0km/h (20.6 knots)

Enrico Tazzoli (Surface)
37.0km/h (20.6 knots)

U-47 (Surface)
31.9km/h (17.7 knots)

I-201 (Submerged)
35.2km/h (19.6 knots)

Submarines

Maximum Surface and Submerged Speeds

▶ **USS Diablo**
▶ **Enrico Tazzoli**
▶ **U-47**
▶ **I-201**
▶ **HMS Thistle**
▶ **HMS Seraph**

The Japanese I-201-class submarines were an exception to the general rule that World War II-era submarines were faster on the surface than submerged. Only three boats of the class were completed, and their retractable bow planes and deck gun combined with a streamlined conning tower to permit them to achieve greater speed underwater. *I-201* itself was captured by American forces at the end of the war and later sunk off the island of Oahu.

The German Type VIIB submarine *U-47* gained fame under Lieutenant-Commander Günther Prien (1908–41) when it stealthily slipped into the Royal Navy anchorage at Scapa Flow on the night of 14 October 1939 and sank the battleship HMS *Royal Oak*. The Italian Calvi-class submarine *Enrico Tazzoli* was launched in 1935 and sunk in 1943. The US Tench-class submarine *Diablo* had deployed on its first wartime cruise when hostilities ended in August 1945 and was later transferred to the Pakistan Navy. The British S-class submarine *Seraph* is best remembered for its role in the deception plan known as Operation Mincemeat, while the T-class submarine *Thistle* was sunk by torpedoes from the German *U-4* off Norway on 10 April 1940.

BELOW: The German Type VIIB submarine *U-47* struck a blow against the Royal Navy and British prestige, sinking the battleship HMS *Royal Oak* in the fleet anchorage at Scapa low in October 1939. During its career, *U-47* sank 30 merchant ships totalling 163,000 gross registered tonnes (GRT).

U-Boats 1

Maximum Submerged Range

- ▶ **Type VIIC**
- ▶ **Type VIIC/41**
- ▶ **Type IXC**
- ▶ **Type XXIII**
- ▶ **Type XXI**

Continuing development in U-boat technology allowed German submarines to lengthen their submerged range substantially during World War II, providing some measure of defence against detection as Allied anti-submarine vigilance and weapons systems improved rapidly. The Type VIIC, the most familiar of the series that has become symbolic of the German U-boat offensive in the Atlantic, was a stretched version of the original Type VIIA, increasing internal spaces and providing room for larger diesel engines. The modified Type VIIC/41 was equipped with a stronger pressure hull and lighter equipment, allowing the boat to dive deeper.

By 1943, the Type VIIC and Type IXC U-boats had been fitted with a device called a snorkel that allowed the submarines to take in air from the outside while remaining submerged, therefore lengthening submerged range. On the Type VII and Type IX U-boats, the snorkel folded, while on the later Type XXI and Type XXIII boats the snorkel projected from a telescoping mast that rose from the conning tower.

The Type IX U-boats were developed for extended operations, with lengthened hulls and storage for 22 torpedoes, twice the capacity of the Type VII boats. Along with some Type VIIC boats, the Type IX brought the U-boat war to the western hemisphere, attacking shipping off the coast of the United States and in the Caribbean Sea in 1942.

The Type XXI U-boat included such innovations as air conditioning and better respiration equipment for crew comfort, and the boat was designed to extend the entire duration of its cruise under water with the snorkel in use primarily to charge batteries. A total of 118 Type XXI U-boats were constructed from 1943 to the end of the war. The Type XXIII U-boat was also intended to operate submerged, primarily in shallow water near the arrival ports of Allied merchant shipping. The Type XXIII was a small U-boat with space for only two torpedoes.

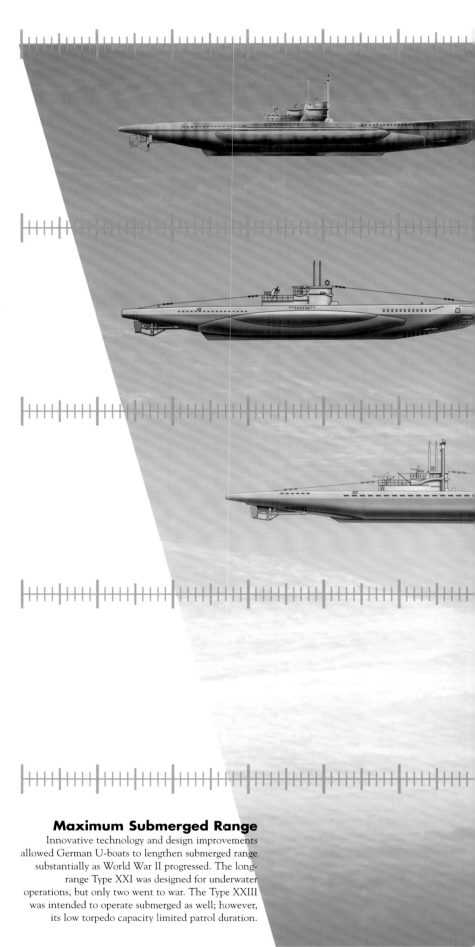

Maximum Submerged Range
Innovative technology and design improvements allowed German U-boats to lengthen submerged range substantially as World War II progressed. The long-range Type XXI was designed for underwater operations, but only two went to war. The Type XXIII was intended to operate submerged as well; however, its low torpedo capacity limited patrol duration.

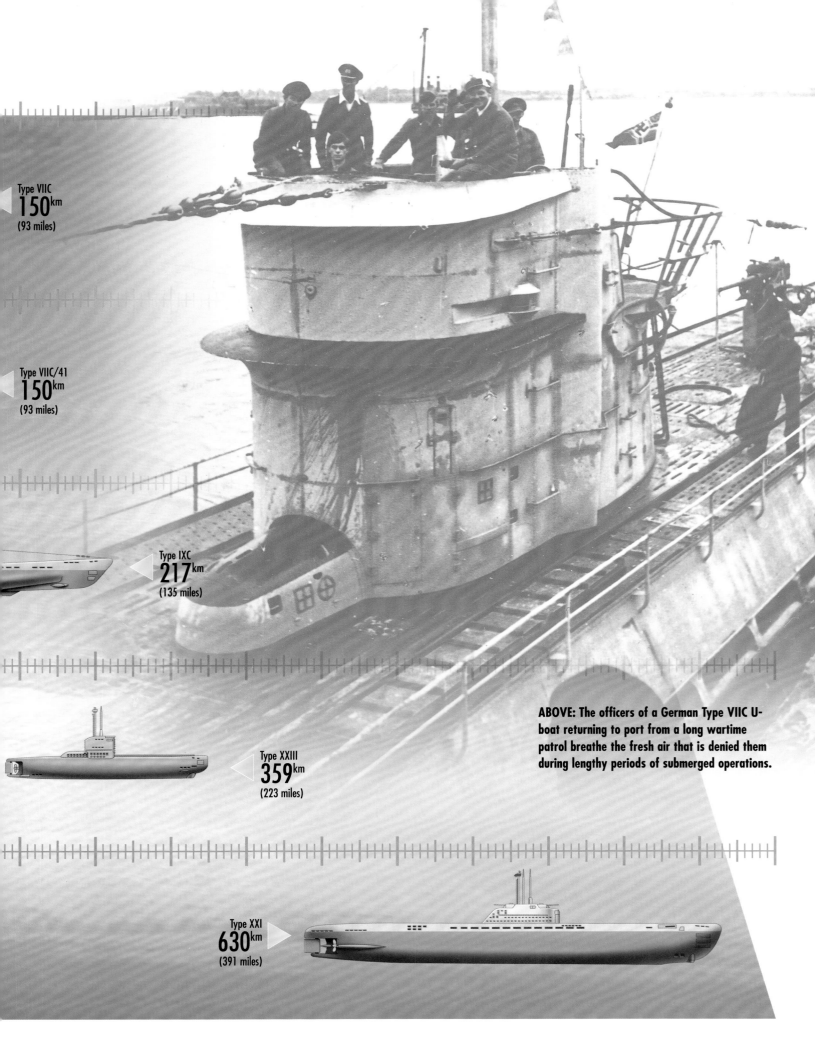

Type VIIC
150km
(93 miles)

Type VIIC/41
150km
(93 miles)

Type IXC
217km
(135 miles)

Type XXIII
359km
(223 miles)

ABOVE: The officers of a German Type VIIC U-boat returning to port from a long wartime patrol breathe the fresh air that is denied them during lengthy periods of submerged operations.

Type XXI
630km
(391 miles)

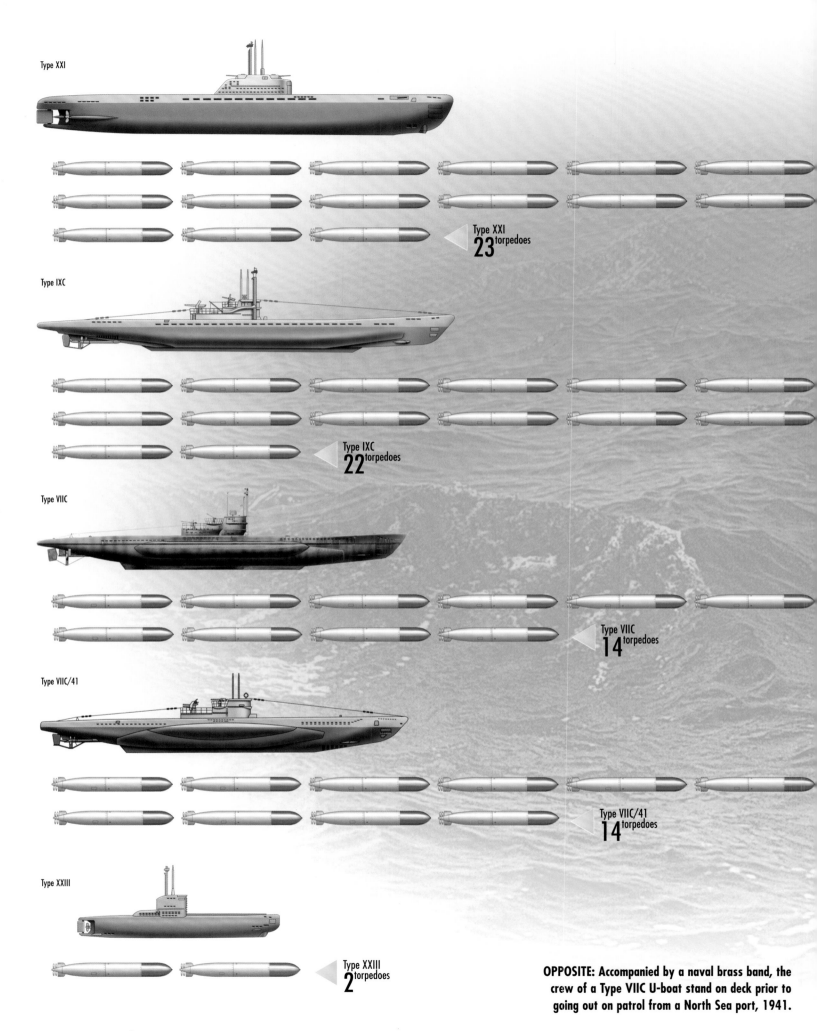

Type XXI

**Type XXI
23** torpedoes

Type IXC

**Type IXC
22** torpedoes

Type VIIC

**Type VIIC
14** torpedoes

Type VIIC/41

**Type VIIC/41
14** torpedoes

Type XXIII

**Type XXIII
2** torpedoes

**OPPOSITE: Accompanied by a naval brass band, the
crew of a Type VIIC U-boat stand on deck prior to
going out on patrol from a North Sea port, 1941.**

Number of Torpedoes

For U-boat commanders during the Battle of the Atlantic, the torpedo was a precious commodity. Lengthy patrols required that they be fired only against high-value targets. The resupply of torpedoes from one of the few available Type XIV 'Milk Cow' submarines during a wartime patrol was a hazardous and time-consuming task.

U-Boats 2

Number of Torpedoes

▶ **Type VIIC**
▶ **Type VIIC/41**
▶ **Type IXC**
▶ **Type XXIII**
▶ **Type XXI**

In order for the new generation of long-range German U-boats that were developed during the war years to be effective, their torpedo-carrying capacity had to be augmented along with other enhancements to the submarines' performance. The Type VII series ranged into the Atlantic and participated in Operation Drumbeat along the coast of the United States in 1942.

The Type IX submarine was designed for long-range operations in the western and southern Atlantic. The Type IX also carried a substantially greater number of torpedoes than the Type VII. Still, it was important for the U-boats to expend their torpedoes on a selective basis, and early in the war – prior to aggressive patrolling by Allied anti-submarine aircraft and naval vessels – it was preferred to halt a merchant ship on the high seas, remove the crew and sink the vessel with the more economical deck gun.

Although the Type XXIII submarine carried only two torpedoes, it was capable of operating submerged for extended periods and was intended for use against merchant shipping that approached Allied ports of entry. Armed with 23 torpedoes, the Type XXI was designed to operate fully submerged for its entire patrol, using the snorkel device to charge batteries.

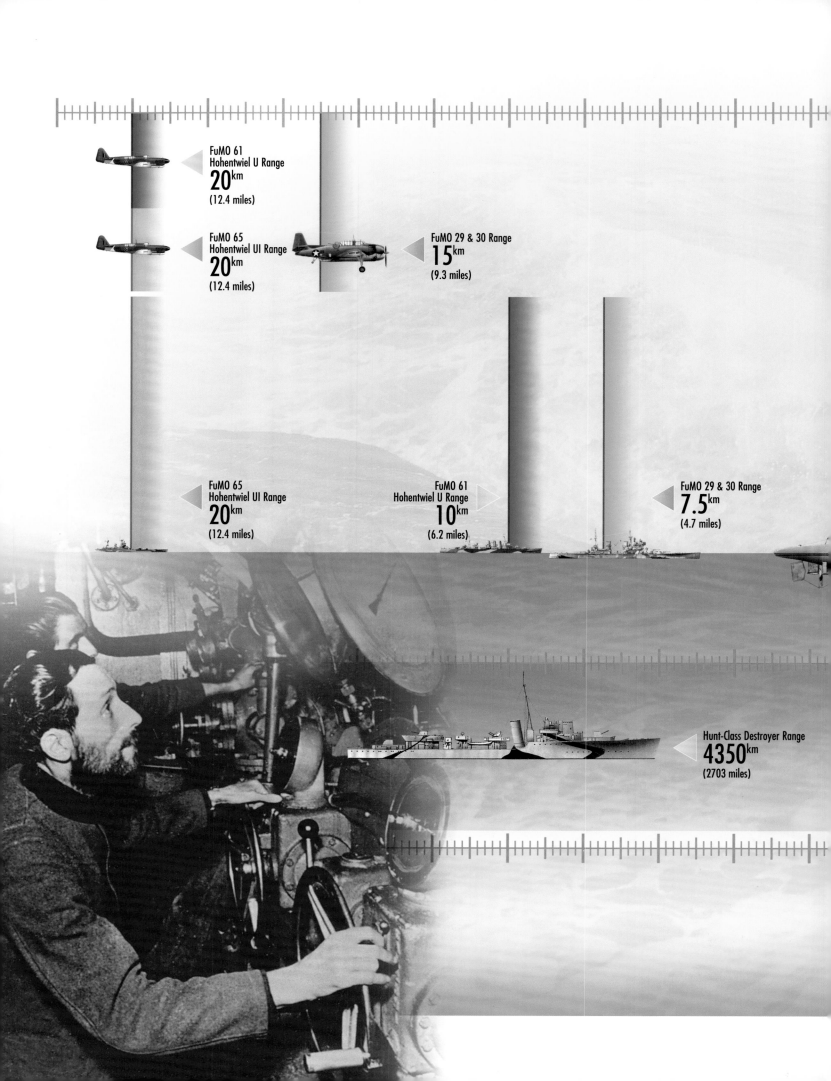

FuMO 61
Hohentwiel U Range
20km
(12.4 miles)

FuMO 65
Hohentwiel UI Range
20km
(12.4 miles)

FuMO 29 & 30 Range
15km
(9.3 miles)

FuMO 65
Hohentwiel UI Range
20km
(12.4 miles)

FuMO 61
Hohentwiel U Range
10km
(6.2 miles)

FuMO 29 & 30 Range
7.5km
(4.7 miles)

Hunt-Class Destroyer Range
4350km
(2703 miles)

U-Boat Radar Detection

Maximum Radar Range – Surface and Air; Maximum Surface Range of Vessels

► **Type VIIC U-Boat**
► **Hunt-Class Destroyer**

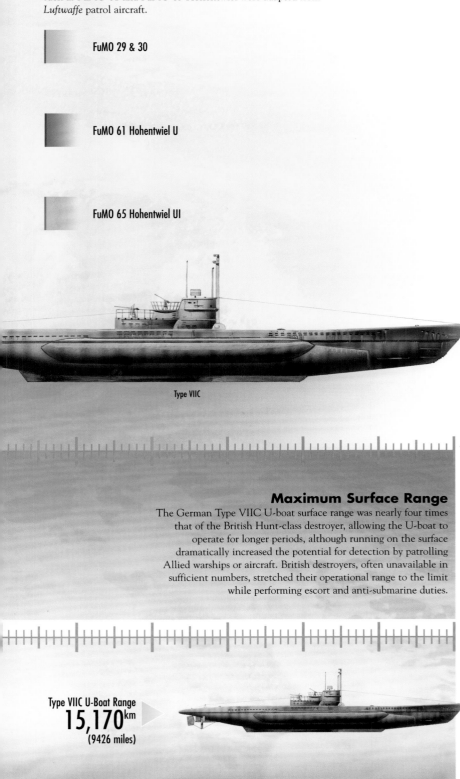

Radar Detection Equipment

During the 1930s, the German Navy began to evaluate the installation of radar aboard surface ships, and soon the development of radar compact enough to function aboard a U-boat followed. From the rather primitive FuMO 29, more sophisticated radar structures such as FuMO 61 and FuMO 65 Hohentwiel were adapted from *Luftwaffe* patrol aircraft.

FuMO 29 & 30

FuMO 61 Hohentwiel U

FuMO 65 Hohentwiel UI

Type VIIC

Maximum Surface Range

The German Type VIIC U-boat surface range was nearly four times that of the British Hunt-class destroyer, allowing the U-boat to operate for longer periods, although running on the surface dramatically increased the potential for detection by patrolling Allied warships or aircraft. British destroyers, often unavailable in sufficient numbers, stretched their operational range to the limit while performing escort and anti-submarine duties.

Type VIIC U-Boat Range
15,170km
(9426 miles)

Early detection of Allied aircraft and surface warships often spelled the difference between life and death for a U-boat crew. Allied radar was more advanced than its German counterpart and provided a definite edge in the Battle of the Atlantic as it came into widespread use. However, as early as the mid-1930s senior *Kriegsmarine* commanders recognized the importance of fitting U-boats with operational radar.

At least two attempts to install suitable radar aboard U-boats failed, and it was not until 1942 that a few Type VII and Type IX U-boats were equipped with FuMO 29, which had a narrow detection range. FuMO 30 was introduced shortly thereafter with its rotating antenna turned by hand from the radio room. It was necessary to remove the antenna for submersion.

In the spring of 1944, FuMO 61 Hohentwiel, adapted from the airborne radar carried aboard the Focke-Wulf Fw-200 Condor coastal-patrol aircraft of the *Luftwaffe*, was installed on Type VII and Type IX U-boats. Placing the radar aboard a U-boat restricted the size of the antenna and the height of the mast, decreasing its range to about half that aboard a surface ship. FuMO 65 combined the separate screens showing range and azimuth into a single display and proved satisfactory, although it was only fitted on Type XXI U-boats, of which just two went on war patrols.

The U-boat did maintain a significant advantage in surface range over many Allied ships that engaged in anti-submarine and convoy-escort operations. This advantage, however, sharply diminished with stepped-up Allied coastal aircraft patrols and more aggressive deployment of Royal Navy and US Navy hunter-killer groups, combining surface ships and carrier-based aircraft, which actively sought out U-boats.

OPPOSITE: An alert bow-planesman, whose station was on the starboard side of his U-boat's control room, glances up at the depth meter and awaits orders from his captain.

Wartime Submarine Construction

Major Naval Powers

▶ **Germany**
▶ **USA**
▶ **UK**
▶ **Japan**
▶ **Italy**

Although Nazi Germany far outpaced the combined submarine construction of the Allied powers, Admiral Karl Dönitz, commander of the U-boat force of the *Kriegsmarine*, never received the number of operational boats he believed were necessary to win the Battle of the Atlantic, particularly given the rising number of losses sustained as the war progressed.

Among the various types of U-boats built during the war, the Type VII was produced in the greatest quantity, with more than 700 completed. By the time the long-range Type XXI programme was approved, an unrealistic schedule of three per week was mandated in the hope of producing 1500. Only 118 were finished in yet another example of outstanding German technology that became operational too late and in too few numbers to change the outcome of the war. With the Type XXI, the Type XXIII exhibited advanced technology that would influence postwar submarine designs into the atomic age, but only 61 were completed. U-boat losses were horrendous, approaching 800 by 1945, and their crews suffered a casualty rate of more than 70 per cent.

In sharp contrast to German U-boat numbers, the Royal Navy topped its production of a single type with 62 units of the S-class. Many of the 49 U-class and 22 V-class boats patrolled the Mediterranean and the North Sea. The best-known submarines of the US Navy were those of the Gato class, with 122 completed. The majority of these were deployed to the Pacific and ravaged Japanese merchant shipping, effectively strangling the island nation.

Japanese submarines in the Pacific ranged from two-man midget submersibles armed with a pair of torpedoes to large, ocean-going submarines with deck hangars for aircraft. Japan's largest wartime series was the B1 class. Twenty were completed, and only a single boat survived to surrender.

Germany

United States

United Kingdom

Japan

Italy

Italy
28 submarines

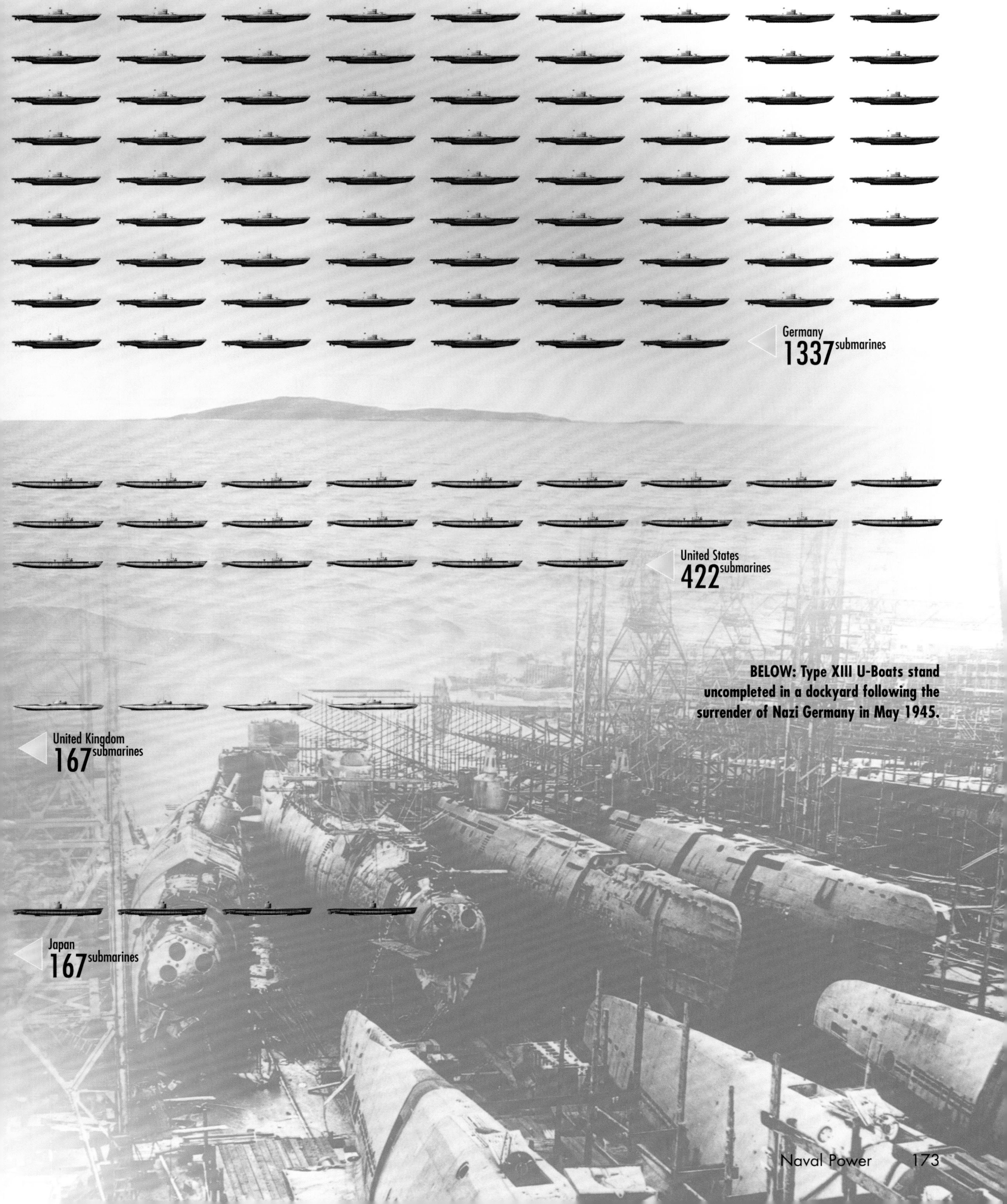

Germany
1337 submarines

United States
422 submarines

United Kingdom
167 submarines

Japan
167 submarines

BELOW: Type XIII U-Boats stand uncompleted in a dockyard following the surrender of Nazi Germany in May 1945.

Landing Craft

Capacity and Maximum Speed

▶ **LCI(S)**
▶ **LCI(L)**
▶ **LSI(M)**
▶ **LCT(1)**

During the course of World War II, the Allies designed and manufactured a variety of landing craft for amphibious operations in both the European and Pacific theatres. Capable of carrying significant numbers of troops or combinations of troops, tanks, trucks and other war materiel, the larger landing craft were operational on the open sea and some were designed to beach on the shore, while smaller craft were designed to deliver assault troops directly to hostile beaches. A number of the landing craft deployed during World War II were the products of American–British cooperation.

The LCI(L), or Landing Craft Infantry, Large, could carry up to 210 troops and undertake a sea voyage of 48 hours' duration. It was built in the United States to British specifications and intended initially for raiding operations. Powered by eight diesel engines, the LCI(L) was not configured to carry vehicles, and its bow was more ship-like than other craft. The LCI(S) Landing Craft Infantry, Small, was one of several types also intended for raiding Axis-held territory that was built by the British Fairmile company.

The LSI(M), or Landing Ship Infantry, Medium, was one of a number of ocean-going transport vessels in use by the Allies in cross-Channel operations. Specifically, LSI(M)s were converted from packet ships that were relatively swift but had short range. Two of the most prominent, HMS *Princess Beatrix* and HMS *Queen Emma*, were converted Dutch vessels. The LSI(M) could carry personnel plus smaller landing craft. The type took part in the abortive raid on the French port of Dieppe in 1942.

The LCT(1) was essentially the prototype of later Landing Craft Tank models. Following the evacuation of the British Expeditionary Force from Dunkirk in 1940, the need for such a vessel was recognized. The LCT(1) was designed to accommodate three tanks and offload them directly onto a beach in water of up to one meter (39in). Only 30 examples of the LCT(1) were constructed before the LCT(2) was in production.

LCI(S)

LCI(L)

LSI(M)

Capacity

The size of Allied landing craft varied greatly, and they could carry infantry, as well as tanks, trucks, artillery and smaller landing craft. These vessels combined shallow draft with adequate capacity, while their design facilitated offloading. The coming of war accelerated the development of landing craft, and the majority of the designs proved quite successful.

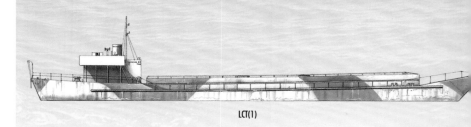

LCT(1)

Maximum Speed

Landing-craft speed was considered a tremendous asset, particularly in combat conditions, and a number of Allied designs were well suited for rapid runs across the Channel to the European continent. In the Pacific, converted destroyers provided capacity along with speed. Small infantry assault craft were generally capable of top speeds of under 18km/h (10 knots).

LCT(1) Speed
18.5km/h
(10.3 knots) ▶

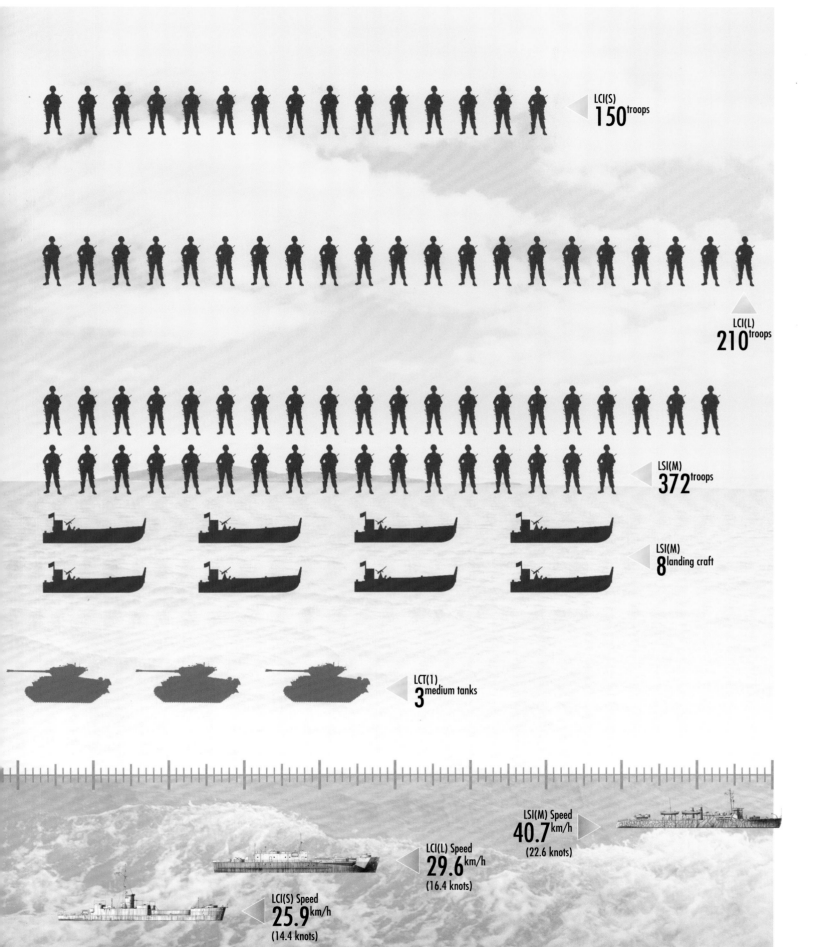

LCI(S)
150troops

LCI(L)
210troops

LSI(M)
372troops

LSI(M)
8landing craft

LCT(1)
3medium tanks

LSI(M) Speed
40.7km/h
(22.6 knots)

LCI(L) Speed
29.6km/h
(16.4 knots)

LCI(S) Speed
25.9km/h
(14.4 knots)

Small Arms

During World War II, as throughout the history of warfare, the individual soldier depended on his personal weapon for protection and to inflict damage upon the enemy. Small arms remained the backbone of attack, defence and the infantryman's responsibilities to defeat the enemy, take and hold territory. Numerous small arms achieved lasting fame during the war and remain iconic to this day, including the British Lee-Enfield, American M1 Garand and German Mauser K98k rifles.

The firepower of the individual soldier increased substantially with the introduction of light and heavy machine guns, submachine guns, semiautomatic rifles and automatic weapons. The M1 Garand was the first semiautomatic rifle to become standard issue to any army. Late in the war, the Germans fielded the Sturmgewehr 44, the first modern assault rifle to see combat. Additionally, infantrymen were supplied with some measure of defence against enemy armour, which had become common on the battlefield. The American Bazooka, British PIAT and German Panzerfaust gave soldiers a fighting option in situations in which they would once have been overwhelmed or compelled to withdraw.

LEFT: A US Marine pauses to aim his 'Tommy Gun' during fighting for the Pacific island of Okinawa, 1945.

Side Arms 1

Calibre and Magazine Capacity

▶ **Browning Hi-Power**
▶ **Pistole Parabellum 1908**
▶ **Walther P38**
▶ **Tokarev TT-33**
▶ **Enfield No. 2 Mk I**

An iconic weapon of the world wars, the German Pistole Parabellum 1908, or Luger (after its designer), is highly prized by collectors. Originally chambered for a 7.65mm (0.301in) cartridge, the Luger was later reconfigured and popularized the 9mm (0.35in) Parabellum round. A favourite of German officers during a production run that stretched from 1900 to 1945, the Luger operated with a toggle-locking system rather than a slide. The capable Walther P38 was introduced with the German armed forces in the 1930s and was intended to replace the Luger. Although it was never available in large numbers during World War II, the P38 and other pistols of the Walther family remain among the world's finest weapons of their kind.

The Browning Hi-Power 9mm (0.35in) pistol derived its name from its 13-round magazine, providing a decided edge in rate of fire during close combat.

The basic design was put forth by American arms engineer John Browning (1855–1926), who died before it was perfected by Belgian manufacturers. One of the most successful pistols of all time, the Hi-Power remains in use today. Britain's Enfield No. 2 Mk I revolver was a standard British side arm of World War II. A top-break revolver with double-action trigger, it could be reloaded rapidly and fire up to 30 rounds per minute. The Soviet Tokarev TT-33 introduced an improved trigger, frame and barrel to the design of the TT-30, of which more than two million were produced during the war.

Calibre

Sometimes employed as the last line of defence, the side arm is required to fire a cartridge substantial enough to immobilize an attacker at a reasonable distance. During the interwar years, prototype pistols were sometimes reconfigured to provide more stopping power.

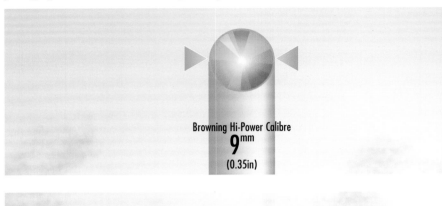

Browning Hi-Power Calibre
9mm
(0.35in)

Parabellum 1908 Calibre
9mm
(0.35in)

BELOW: The semiautomatic P38 was the first locked-breech pistol to employ a traditional double-action trigger.

Walther P38 Calibre
9mm
(0.35in)

Tokarev TT-33 Calibre
7.62mm
(0.3in)

Enfield No. 2 Mk I Calibre
9.6mm
(0.38in)

Magazine Capacity

One of the primary functions of the side arm is to provide sustained fire in close combat.
Prominent side arms of World War II met this demand through magazine capacities of, typically,
six to eight rounds. A notable exception, the Browning Hi-Power boasted a 13-round magazine.

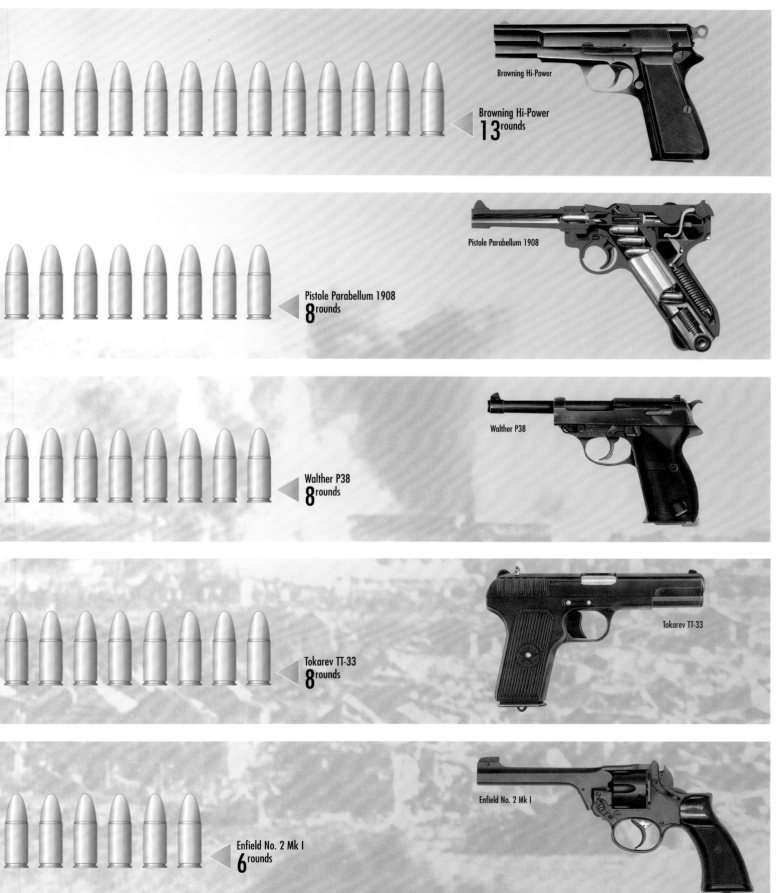

Browning Hi-Power

Browning Hi-Power
13 rounds

Pistole Parabellum 1908

Pistole Parabellum 1908
8 rounds

Walther P38

Walther P38
8 rounds

Tokarev TT-33

Tokarev TT-33
8 rounds

Enfield No. 2 Mk I

Enfield No. 2 Mk I
6 rounds

Muzzle Velocity

The speed of a projectile as it leaves the barrel, muzzle velocity is a function of barrel length, projectile weight and the quality and quantity of the propellant used. Higher muzzle velocity resists the force of gravity more efficiently, resulting in better accuracy, and delivers greater energy on impact with the target.

415m/sec
(1362ft/sec)

351 m/sec
(1152ft/sec)

350m/sec
(1148ft/sec)

335m/sec
(1099ft/sec)

189m/sec
(620ft/sec)

Tokarev TT-33

Pistole Parabellum 1908

Walther P38

Browning Hi-Power

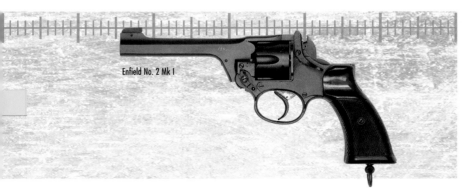

Enfield No. 2 Mk I

Side Arms 2

Muzzle Velocity

▶ **Browning Hi-Power**
▶ **Pistole Parabellum 1908**
▶ **Walther P38**
▶ **Tokarev TT-33**
▶ **Enfield No. 2 Mk I**

Designed by Georg Luger and patented in 1898, the Pistole Parabellum 1908 is easily recognized with its distinctive profile and was widely used as a side arm by the German Army in both world wars. One of the first semi-automatic pistols to see widespread use, it fired 9mm (0.35in) ammunition fed from an eight-round magazine carried within the stock. The Walther P38 was purpose built as a military pistol but also proved a commercial success. When the German Army was reconstituted during the Cold War, the P38 became the standard side arm for officers.

The 13-round Browning Hi-Power pistol was a recoil-operated, locked-breech weapon. It was actually a collaborative design by American inventor John Browning (1855–1926) and the Belgian manufacturer Fabrique Nationale. During World War II, the Hi-Power served with both Allied and Axis forces, the Germans placing a number of Brownings in service after their capture in occupied Belgium.

The Enfield No. 2 Mk I revolver served alongside the Webley Mk IV and the Smith & Wesson Victory as a standard side arm of the British armed forces during World War II. With its double-action trigger and top-break reloading system, the 9.6mm (0.38in) Mk I was effective up to 13m (43ft), although lighter and of smaller calibre than its Enfield predecessor.

The Soviet Tokarev TT-33 improved on its predecessor, the TT-30. Similar to the earlier Browning FN Model 1903 blowback pistol and also incorporating elements of Browning's famed Model 1911 pistol, the TT-33 was in widespread use by the outbreak of World War II.

OPPOSITE: The Browning Hi-Power was originally adopted by the Belgian Army in 1935. Its 13-round detachable box magazine provided a substantial advantage during close-quarter fighting. Its single-action trigger required the pistol to be cocked by hand before the first shot was fired.

Bolt-action Rifles 1

Effective Range

▶ **Springfield M1903**
▶ **Mosin-Nagant Model 1891**
▶ **Lee-Enfield No. 4**
▶ **Arisaka 38th Year Rifle**
▶ **Mauser Karabiner 98k**

Numerous bolt-action rifles of World War II shared a common lineage, tracing their ancestry to the Mauser Gewehr 98, which entered service with the German armed forces around the turn of the twentieth century. In 1935, the German Army formally adopted the Mauser Karabiner 98 Kurz, also known as the K98k, Kar 98k or K98, and nearly 15 million were manufactured during a decade-long production run that ended in 1945. The K98k earned a reputation as a sturdy and reliable shoulder arm.

Also based on the original Mauser Gewehr 98 design, the US Springfield M1903 was slated for replacement with the M1 Garand by 1937; however, the weapon had proved so popular in the field that it remained in use throughout World War II, particularly in its sniper variant, the M1903A4. The M1903 entered service with the US Army in 1905, and more than 800,000 were produced during World War I.

A third weapon to exhibit strong influence of the German Mauser design was the Japanese Arisaka 38th Year, or Type 38, Rifle. Firing a 6.5mm (0.256in) round, it was named for the 38th year of the Meiji period and remained in service with the Imperial Japanese Army throughout World War II, supplemented by the later Type 99.

Britain's Lee-Enfield No. 4 was introduced in 1941 as an improvement in design and manufacturing processes over the earlier standard-issue Mk III SMLE. The No. 4 was distinguished from its predecessor by a barrel that protruded prominently from the stock and modifications to the bolt action.

The Mosin-Nagant Model 1891, or M1891, rifle served as the standard-issue shoulder arm of the Soviet Red Army throughout the war, modifications having taken place in 1936 to improve speed of production. The Model 1891/31, a sniper variant, was the weapon of choice for the famed Vasily Zaitsev (1915–91), who recorded more than 225 kills on the Eastern Front.

Springfield M1903
The M1903 was still in widespread use at the outbreak of World War II. Its sniper variant entered service in 1942 and is still employed today.

Mosin-Nagant Model 1891
As World War II progressed, the Soviets stepped up production of the Mosin-Nagant, and later weapons were crudely finished due to the exigencies of war.

Lee-Enfield No. 4
Accepted for service with the British Army by 1941, the Lee-Enfield No. 4 served alongside its predecessor, the Mk III SMLE (Short Magazine Lee-Enfield).

Arisaka 38th Year Rifle
Slightly inferior in firepower to Western rifles, the Arisaka 38th Year Rifle was also unwieldy in combat for some Japanese soldiers due to its length.

Mauser Karabiner 98k
The K98k was a durable weapon, and copied or licence-built by many other countries.

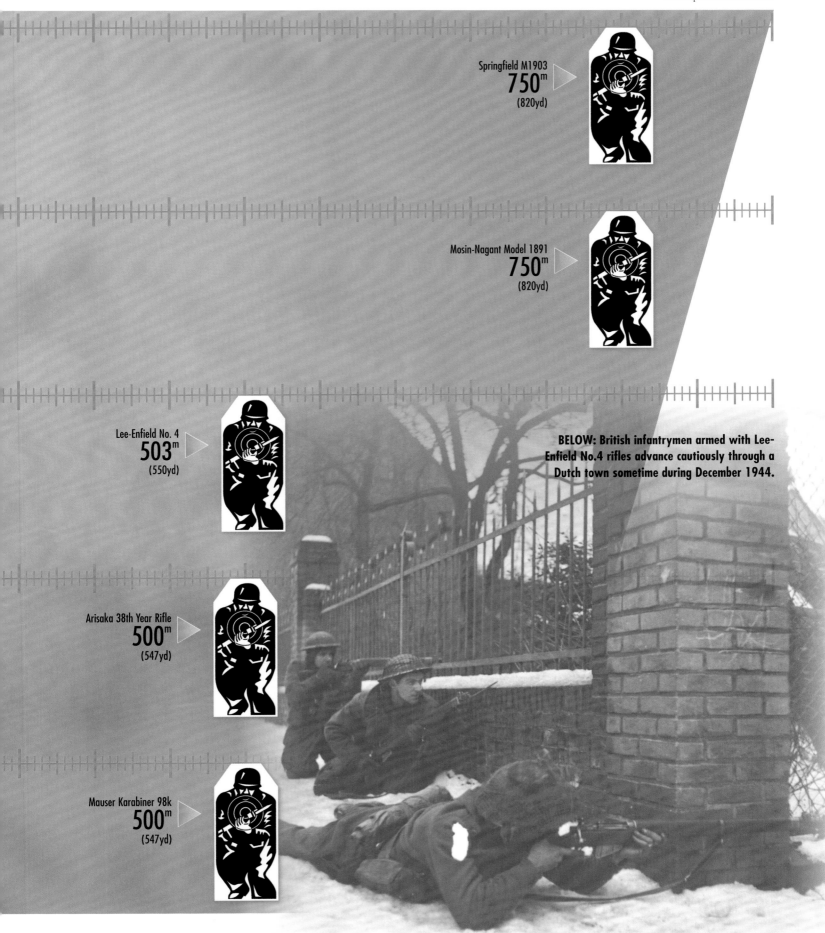

Bolt-action rifles of the World War II era were deadly at great distances and extremely accurate in the hands of an accomplished marksman.

Springfield M1903
750ᵐ
(820yd)

Mosin-Nagant Model 1891
750ᵐ
(820yd)

Lee-Enfield No. 4
503ᵐ
(550yd)

BELOW: British infantrymen armed with Lee-Enfield No.4 rifles advance cautiously through a Dutch town sometime during December 1944.

Arisaka 38th Year Rifle
500ᵐ
(547yd)

Mauser Karabiner 98k
500ᵐ
(547yd)

Bolt-action Rifles 2

Weight and Rifle-vs-Pistol Range

▶ **Springfield M1903**
▶ **Mosin-Nagant Model 1891**
▶ **Lee Enfield No. 4**
▶ **Arisaka 38th Year Rifle**
▶ **Mauser Karabiner 98k**

The standard shoulder arms of World War II were remarkable precision weapons, each exhibiting the characteristics of an engineering evolution that had begun a century earlier. Continual refinement introduced modifications, and the process was accelerated during wartime.

The predecessor of the K98k, the Gewehr 98, was widely respected by the time the latest of the line entered service with the German Army in the 1930s, and numerous countries fielded rifles that were heavily influenced by the Mauser design. Among these rifles, the US Springfield M1903, the Japanese Arisaka 38th Year Rifle and the Russian/Soviet Mosin-Nagant Model 1891 became iconic weapons in their own right. Mauser once filed a suit against Springfield for patent infringement and was awarded royalties for use of K98k design elements in the M1903.

The K98k was introduced as an improvement to the Gewehr 98, with a shorter length, lighter overall weight, better placement of the iron sights and a turndown bolt action, rather than a straight action, to facilitate the operation of the weapon in combat. The K98k and the three Mauser-inspired weapons were all fed by five-round internal magazines and stripper clips. The British Lee-Enfield No. 4, on the other hand, carried twice the number of rounds in a detachable box magazine.

RIGHT: A US Marine carries an M1903A4 sniper version of the venerable Springfield rifle.

M1903 Weight
3.9kg
(8.6lb)

K98k Weight
3.9kg
(8.6lb)

M1903 Weight: 3.9kg (8.6lb)

K98k Weight: 3.9kg (8.6lb)

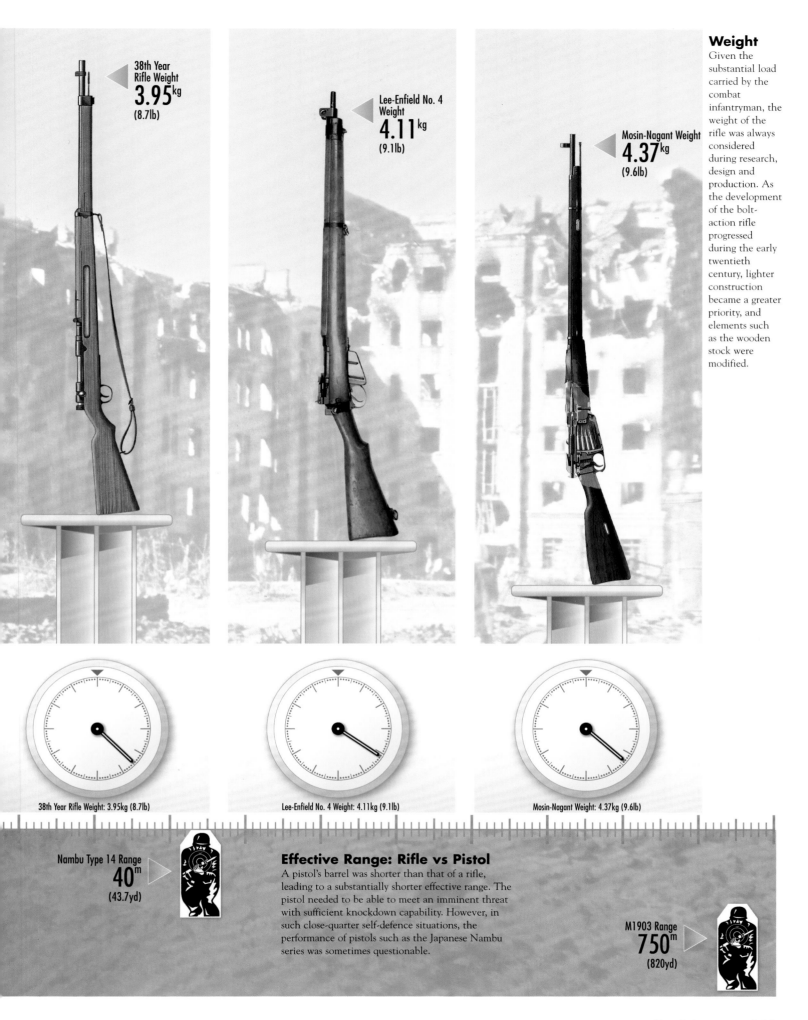

38th Year
Rifle Weight
3.95kg
(8.7lb)

Lee-Enfield No. 4
Weight
4.11kg
(9.1lb)

Mosin-Nagant Weight
4.37kg
(9.6lb)

Weight
Given the substantial load carried by the combat infantryman, the weight of the rifle was always considered during research, design and production. As the development of the bolt-action rifle progressed during the early twentieth century, lighter construction became a greater priority, and elements such as the wooden stock were modified.

38th Year Rifle Weight: 3.95kg (8.7lb)

Lee-Enfield No. 4 Weight: 4.11kg (9.1lb)

Mosin-Nagant Weight: 4.37kg (9.6lb)

Nambu Type 14 Range
40m
(43.7yd)

Effective Range: Rifle vs Pistol
A pistol's barrel was shorter than that of a rifle, leading to a substantially shorter effective range. The pistol needed to be able to meet an imminent threat with sufficient knockdown capability. However, in such close-quarter self-defence situations, the performance of pistols such as the Japanese Nambu series was sometimes questionable.

M1903 Range
750m
(820yd)

Effective Range

In some cases, semiautomatic rifles sacrificed a degree of effective range for a substantially increased rate of fire. As the weapons were introduced, the firepower of the standard infantry squad was greatly augmented.

M1 Carbine Range
300ᵐ
(328yd)

RSC M1917 Range
300ᵐ
(328yd)

Type 44 Range
400ᵐ
(437yd)

Magazine Capacity

Capable of a higher sustained rate of fire than the bolt-action rifle, a semi-automatic weapon was designed for ease of reloading and accuracy at a reasonable distance. Although its magazine capacity was often equivalent to a contemporary bolt-action, there were notable exceptions such as the short-range M1 Carbine.

5 x 8mm (0.314in) rounds

5 x 6.5mm (0.256in) rounds

30 x 7.62mm (0.3in) rounds

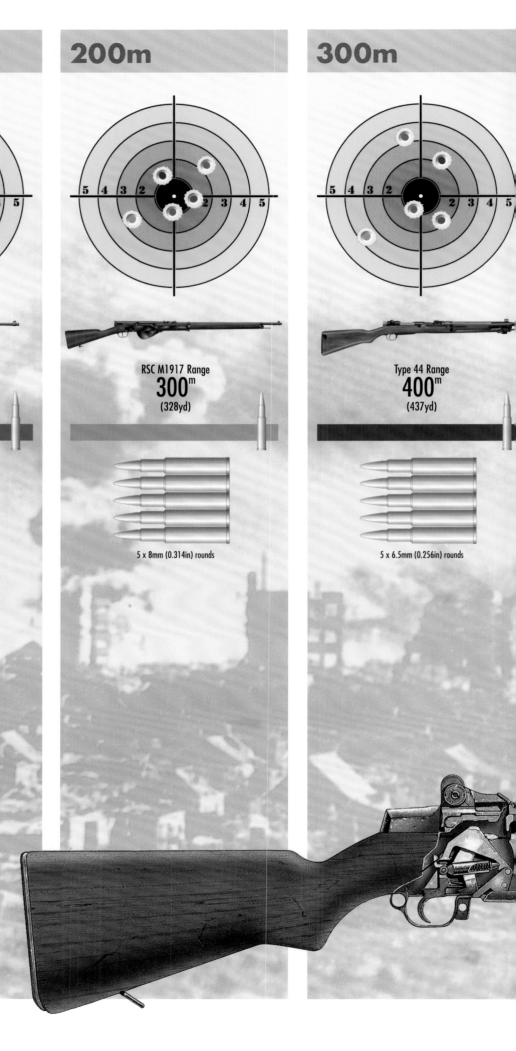

M1 Garand Range
400ᵐ
(437yd)

8 x 7.62mm (0.3in) rounds

SVT-38 Range
500ᵐ
(547yd)

10 x 7.62mm (0.3in) rounds

Semi-automatic Rifles

Effective Range and Magazine Capacity

▶ **M1 Carbine**
▶ **RSC M1917**
▶ **Type 44**
▶ **M1 Garand**
▶ **SVT-38**

Issued to US troops in 1936, the M1 Garand was the first semiautomatic rifle to become standard issue with any army in the world. Designed by the Canadian-born engineer John C. Garand (1888–1974), the weapon featured a gas-operated rotating bolt and fired a 7.62mm (0.3in) cartridge. Particularly in the Pacific Theatre, the US infantryman possessed a telling firepower advantage over his adversary with the capability of firing up to 50 accurate rounds per minute.

Contrary to popular belief, the M1 Carbine was largely a separate design from the M1 Garand and not an identical but smaller version of the standard infantry rifle. Fed by a 15- or 30-round external box magazine, the M1 Carbine was often issued to airborne troops or officers and remained in service with the US Army from mid-1942 until the 1970s. In contrast, the standard Japanese carbine of World War II remained an outmoded bolt-action weapon. The Type 44 carried only five rounds in an internal magazine, and it fired the standard but lightweight 6.5mm (0.256in) round.

The Soviet SVT-38 and its successor, the SVT-40, were gas-operated rifles designed by Fedor Tokarev (1871–1968). Both fired a 7.62mm (0.3in) cartridge from a 10-round detachable

ABOVE: The American M1 Garand rifle (above) remained in service with the US armed forces from 1936 into the 1960s before it was partially replaced with the select-fire M14. The M1 provided the highest rate of fire of any standard-issue rifle in World War II.

box magazine. The French RSC M1917 was an early attempt to improve the firepower of troops fighting in the trenches of World War I. Intended to replace the bolt-action Lebel rifle, it fired an 8mm (0.314in) cartridge from a five-round clip; however, its substantial 1331mm (52.4in) length made it unpopular with French soldiers.

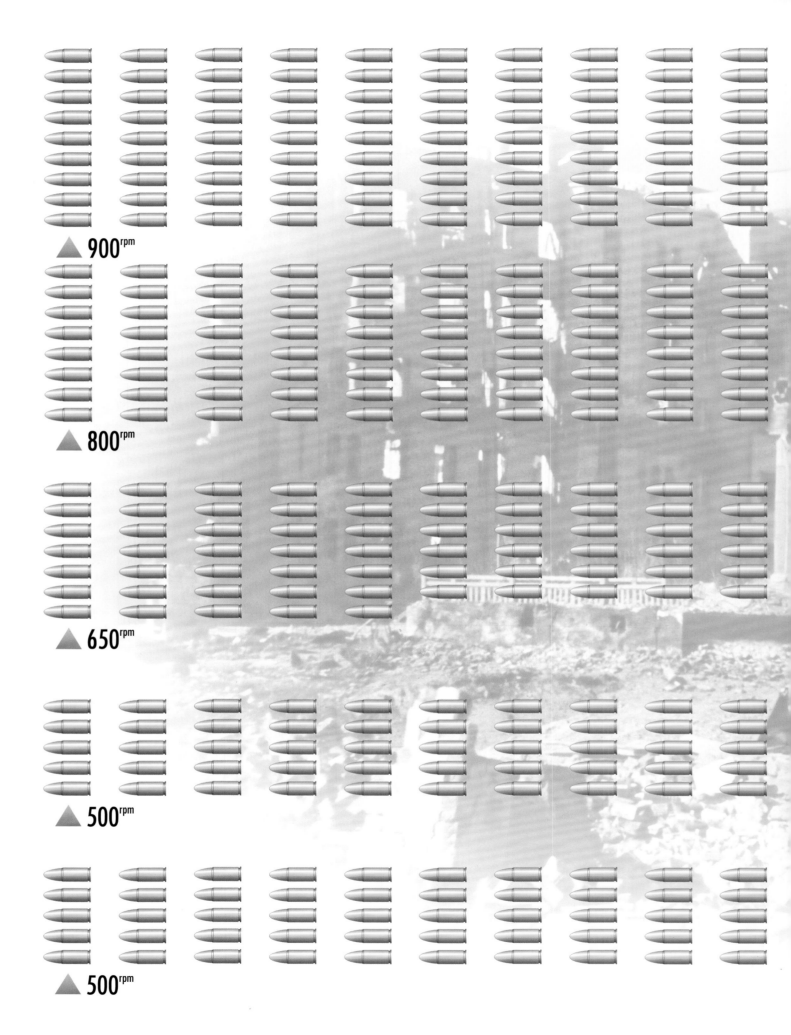

▲ 900^{rpm}

▲ 800^{rpm}

▲ 650^{rpm}

▲ 500^{rpm}

▲ 500^{rpm}

PPSh-41

Combining efficient manufacturing processes with a high rate of fire, the Soviet PPSh-41 was deployed in great numbers on the Eastern Front.

PPD-1934/38

An early Soviet submachine gun, the PPD-1934/38 was a virtual copy of the German Bergmann MP 28. Expensive to produce, it entered Red Army service in 1935.

PPS-42

Even more cost-effective than the PPSh-41, the PPS-42 was notable among Soviet submachine guns with its stamped metal stock and was deployed initially in 1943.

MP 41

A select-fire variant of the MP 40, the MP 41 was otherwise identical to the earlier weapon. Although it was intended for infantry use, it remained in limited deployment.

MP 40

Despite its relatively inexpensive cost, the MP 40 was remarkably durable in harsh conditions. It remains an icon of the bitter struggle on the Eastern Front.

Eastern Front Submachine Guns

Rate of Fire

▶ **PPSh-41**
▶ **PPD-1934/38**
▶ **PPS-42**
▶ **MP 41**
▶ **MP 40**

The emergence of the submachine gun (SMG) revolutionized the firepower of the individual infantryman, and the years of combat on the Eastern Front offered a proving ground for a generation of such weapons, capable of startling sustained rates of fire. Among the best-known submachine guns of World War II was the German Maschinenpistole 40, better known simply as the MP 40, the latest in a line of German automatic weapons that had been in development for two decades prior to the invasion of the Soviet Union. The MP 40 fired only in automatic mode, utilizing the 9mm (0.35in) Parabellum cartridge in a 32-round detachable box magazine. The MP 40 followed the earlier MP 38 as the need for rapid manufacture with primarily stamped parts arose during the war. The MP 41, with a wooden stock, was essentially the same as the MP 40 with a select-fire option.

During the 1930s, the Soviets recognized the potential of the submachine gun on the battlefield and quickly borrowed from early German designs, particularly the Bergmann MP 28. The PPD-1934/38 was nearly an exact copy of the German weapon and fired the Soviet 7.62mm (0.3in) cartridge. Its 25-round box magazine was also a copy – in this case from Finland. Even as the PPD-1934/38 was issued, its successor, the PPSh-41, was nearing production. Entering service in 1941, the PPSh-41 was much more economical to produce than its predecessor. More than six million were completed during the war. Still in service today, the PPSh-41 offers semiautomatic or automatic firing modes, and at the peak of Soviet production more than 3000 per day were being finished. By 1943, the PPS-42, even cheaper to produce than the PPSh-41, was issued to Red Army troops. It fired the same 7.62mm (0.3in) cartridge, and by the end of the year production exceeded 350,000 per month.

Street Fighting in Stalingrad

Magazine Capacity and Effective Range

- ▶ **Mosin-Nagant Model 1891**
- ▶ **Mauser Karabiner 98k**
- ▶ **AVT-40**
- ▶ **PPSh-41**
- ▶ **MP 40**

Often fighting in such close quarters that their positions were only paces apart, German and Soviet soldiers struggled to the death for months in the rubble-strewn streets of Stalingrad, the industrial city on the River Volga where Nazi dreams of conquest in the East were dashed.

The cramped nature of urban warfare at Stalingrad, with fighting taking place street-to-street, house-to-house and sometimes in the sewers, diminished the requirements for distant range and accuracy with one notable exception: that of the sniper, who plied his craft with M1891/31 and ZF39 telescopic-sight-equipped sniper variants of the standard Soviet Mosin-Nagant M1891 and German K98k rifles respectively, dealing death at a distance. Literally millions of examples of Model 1891 and K98k infantry rifles were manufactured during the war years, and each earned a reputation for reliability, although the finished quality on later weapons was markedly reduced.

Submachine guns came into their own at Stalingrad. The PPSh-41 was a favourite of Red Army soldiers, particularly due to the durability of its chrome-lined barrel and a drum magazine that held up to 71 rounds. The German MP 40 proved an exceptional performer, even in the sub-zero winter weather of the Eastern Front. At Stalingrad, it was a superb automatic weapon with up to 64 rounds available in a dual magazine.

The MP 40, however, was in relatively short supply and issued mainly to German squad and platoon leaders, while the PPSh-41 sometimes equipped entire Red Army platoons, tipping the balance of firepower in favour of the Red Army during a prolonged fight. The Soviet AVT-40 was a fully automatic version of the SVT-40, though its combat efficiency was limited due to a box magazine that held only 10 rounds of 7.62mm (0.3in) ammunition.

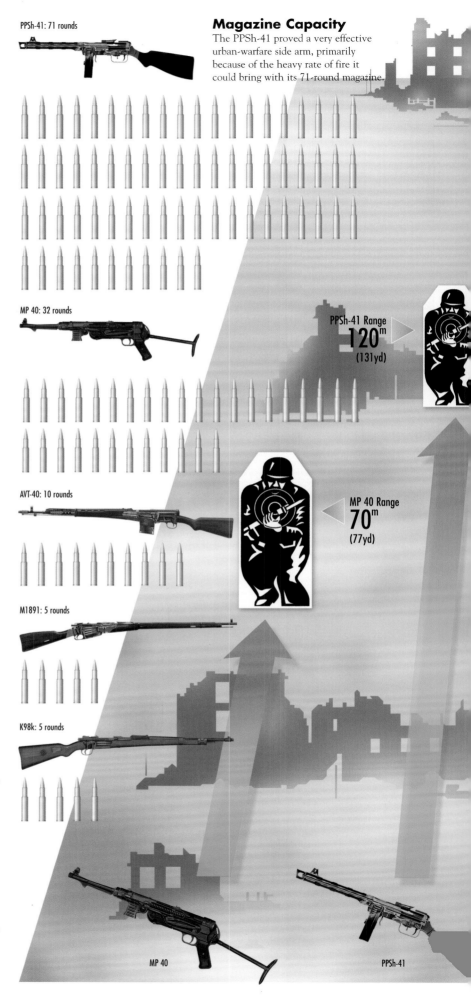

PPSh-41: 71 rounds

Magazine Capacity
The PPSh-41 proved a very effective urban-warfare side arm, primarily because of the heavy rate of fire it could bring with its 71-round magazine.

MP 40: 32 rounds

AVT-40: 10 rounds

M1891: 5 rounds

K98k: 5 rounds

PPSh-41 Range
120^m
(131yd)

MP 40 Range
70^m
(77yd)

MP 40

PPSh-41

M1891 Range
750ᵐ
(820yd)

Effective Range

Although their rates of fire were substantially higher than those of bolt-action rifles, the submachine guns fielded at Stalingrad were effective only at greatly reduced ranges. Therefore, the standard bolt-action Mosin-Nagant M1891 and Mauser K98k rifles remained viable weapons in rapidly evolving arsenals.

AVT-40 Range
500ᵐ
(547yd)

K98k Range
500ᵐ
(547yd)

AVT-40

Mauser Karabiner 98k

Mosin-Nagant Model 1891

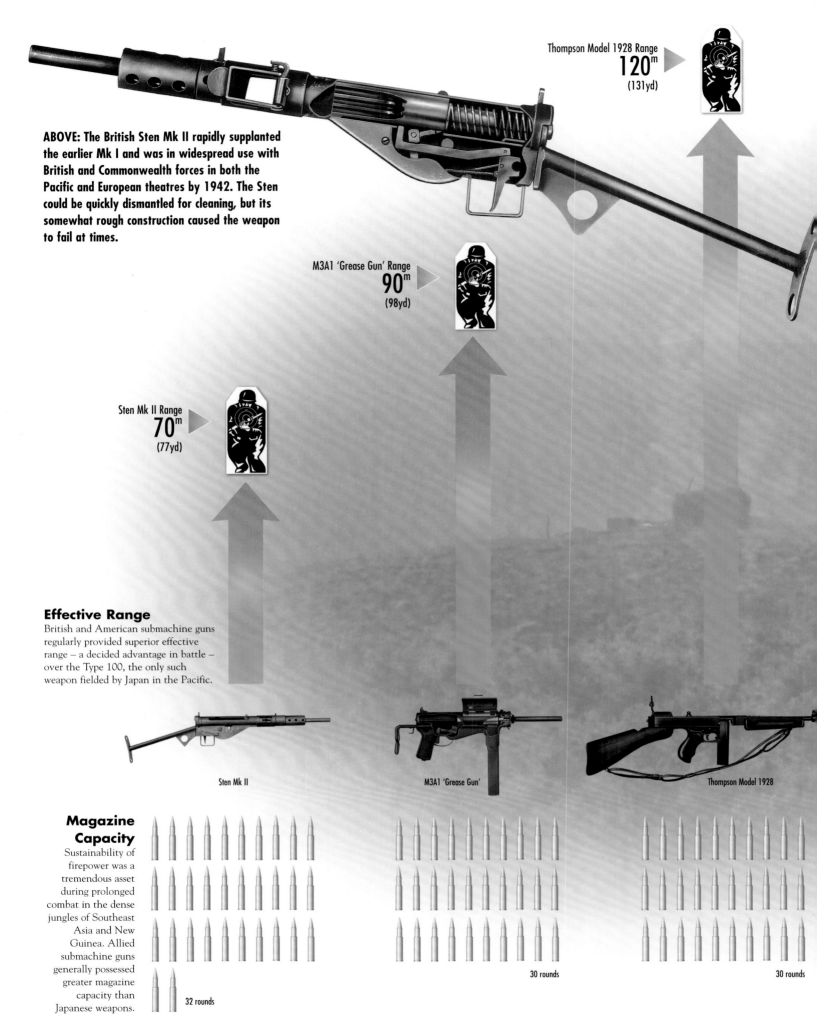

ABOVE: The British Sten Mk II rapidly supplanted the earlier Mk I and was in widespread use with British and Commonwealth forces in both the Pacific and European theatres by 1942. The Sten could be quickly dismantled for cleaning, but its somewhat rough construction caused the weapon to fail at times.

Thompson Model 1928 Range
120ᵐ
(131yd)

M3A1 'Grease Gun' Range
90ᵐ
(98yd)

Sten Mk II Range
70ᵐ
(77yd)

Effective Range
British and American submachine guns regularly provided superior effective range – a decided advantage in battle – over the Type 100, the only such weapon fielded by Japan in the Pacific.

Sten Mk II

M3A1 'Grease Gun'

Thompson Model 1928

Magazine Capacity
Sustainability of firepower was a tremendous asset during prolonged combat in the dense jungles of Southeast Asia and New Guinea. Allied submachine guns generally possessed greater magazine capacity than Japanese weapons.

32 rounds

30 rounds

30 rounds

Reising Model 55 Range
120ᵐ
(131yd)

1 A US Marine fires a Thompson SMG during fighting in the Pacific.

Type 100 Range
70ᵐ
(77yd)

Reising Model 55

Type 100

25 rounds

30 rounds

Pacific War Submachine Guns

Effective Range and Magazine Capacity

▶ **Sten Mk II**
▶ **M3A1 'Grease Gun'**
▶ **Thompson Model 1928**
▶ **Reising Model 55**
▶ **Type 100**

In the face of a fanatical Japanese banzai charge on a remote Pacific island, there was no more effective weapon for the American Marine or soldier than the submachine gun. The most famous of these US weapons was the Thompson Model 1928, adopted by the US military in 1938 after the gun had already achieved a measure of fame with gangsters and law-enforcement agencies during the Prohibition Era in the United States.

The Thompson fired an 11.4mm (0.45in) cartridge from 18-, 20-, or 30-round detachable magazines. It was expensive to produce; however, a viable replacement did not enter service with American forces in substantial numbers until late 1944. Manufactured largely from stamped parts and popularly known as the 'Grease Gun', the M3 and the later M3A1 were influenced by the success of the German MP 40 and the British Sten series. Like the Thompson, the M3 fired an 11.4mm (0.45in) round. Other US submachine guns included the Reising Model 55, which also utilized an 11.4mm (0.45in) cartridge.

Meanwhile, the Imperial Japanese Army deployed only one submachine gun in substantial numbers during the entire Pacific War, the Type 100. Fed by a prominent 30-round clip, the Type 100 fired the notoriously underpowered 8mm (0.314in) round, and its rate of fire was inferior to Allied models, particularly early in the war.

The British Sten Mk II was easily recognized with its side-loading feature and stamped metal stock. The Sten was constructed of only 47 components, and more than two million examples of the weapon were manufactured during the war. It fired a 9mm (0.35in) cartridge from a 32-round magazine that could accept captured German ammunition. Although its firepower was highly valued, the Sten developed a reputation for jamming with repeated use.

Late-war Assault Rifles

Weight

▶ **SKS**
▶ **AVT-40**
▶ **Gewehr 43**
▶ **FG 42**
▶ **MP 43**

Perhaps no other infantry-weapon concept of World War II developed with such far-reaching impact as the German idea of the assault rifle, an individual soldier's weapon capable of both automatic and semiautomatic fire. When the Maschinenpistole 43 entered service in 1943, it did so under something of a misnomer. The MP 43 was essentially the same weapon as the Sturmgewehr 44, arguably the world's first operational assault weapon, and the MP designation had been assigned to conceal its development from Hitler, who initially opposed the project. Gas-operated, the MP 43 fired a 7.92mm (0.312in) cartridge from a 30-round magazine. Meanwhile, the semiautomatic Gewehr 43 entered service the same year. Firing an 8mm (0.314in) cartridge from a 10-round detachable box magazine, it was based on the Soviet SVT-40.

Early in the war, German arms manufacturers were tasked with the development of an airborne rifle capable of both automatic and semiautomatic modes. By 1943, the *Fallschirmjägergewehr 42*, or FG 42, was in production. Intended to function as an assault rifle, it fired a 7.92mm (0.312in) cartridge from a 10- or 20-round box magazine and was produced in limited numbers.

To complement the semi-automatic SVT-40 rifle, the fully automatic AVT-40 was issued to some Red Army units as early as 1940. The AVT-40 fired the same 7.62mm (0.3in) round via a gas-operated short-stroke system, but the limited capacity of its 10-round box magazine was considered a liability by its users. Late in the war, the SKS semiautomatic carbine was introduced for Soviet armoured troops and others operating in confined spaces. The SKS was considerably shorter than standard rifles at 1021mm (40.2in) and fired the 7.62mm (0.3in) cartridge from a 10-round box magazine. It did not reach the front in quantity until 1945.

SKS
3.85kg
(8.5lb)

AVT-40
3.9kg
(8.6lb)

SKS Weight: 3.85kg (8.5lb)

AVT-40 Weight: 3.9kg (8.6lb)

Gewehr 43
4.1kg
(9lb)

FG-42
4.53kg
(10lb)

MP 43
5.1kg
(11.2lb)

Weight
A crucial
element in
the overall
effectiveness of
combat arms,
weight was
minimized
by weapons
designers
whenever
possible. Lighter
materials and
smaller
specifications
for some
purpose-designed
weapons
contributed to
progressive
improvements
in the weight of
late-war rifles.

Gewehr 43 Weight: 4.1kg (9lb)

FG 42 Weight: 4.53kg (10lb)

MP 43 Weight: 5.1kg (11.2lb)

Small Arms   195

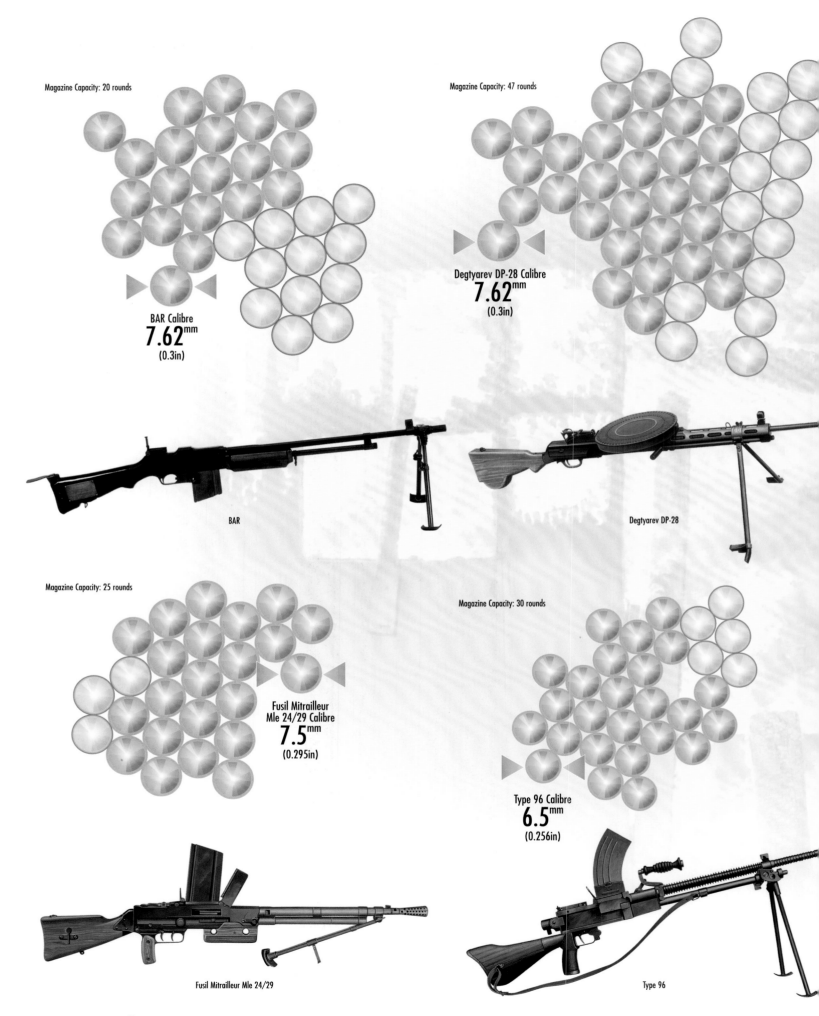

Magazine Capacity: 20 rounds

BAR Calibre
7.62mm
(0.3in)

BAR

Magazine Capacity: 47 rounds

Degtyarev DP-28 Calibre
7.62mm
(0.3in)

Degtyarev DP-28

Magazine Capacity: 25 rounds

Fusil Mitrailleur
Mle 24/29 Calibre
7.5mm
(0.295in)

Fusil Mitrailleur Mle 24/29

Magazine Capacity: 30 rounds

Type 96 Calibre
6.5mm
(0.256in)

Type 96

Calibre

Although most light infantry-support machine guns of World War II were comparable in firepower, the Japanese Type 96 fired a smaller round and lacked the punch of contemporary Allied weapons.

Bren Mk II Calibre

7.7mm
(0.303in)

Bren Mk II

KEY

◯ Rounds available in magazine.

◯ Rounds fired in a three-second burst.

◯ Rounds fired after loading second magazine.

Squad-support Light Machine Guns

Three-second-burst Weight of Fire, Calibre and Magazine Capacity

▶ **Browning Automatic Rifle**
▶ **Degtyarev DP-28**
▶ **Bren Mk II**
▶ **Fusil Mitrailleur Mle 24/29**
▶ **Type 96**

The Bren Mk II was the standard light infantry-support weapon of its type for British and Commonwealth troops during World War II, and every member of a British infantry squad was expected to know how to operate the Bren. The Japanese Type 96 light machine gun (LMG) incorporated elements of the French Hotchkiss and the Czech ZB vz.26. Designed by Kijiro Nambu (1869–1949), the weapon fired a light 6.5mm (0.256in) cartridge from a 30-round top-loading box magazine. Intended to correct repeated jamming, oiling the rounds only made the issue worse. In sharp contrast, the standard-issue Soviet LMG of World War II, the Degtyarev DP-28, was robust and reliable, withstanding field tests that subjected it to incredible abuse. The DP-28 fired a 7.62mm (0.3in) cartridge from a 47-round pan magazine.

The Browning Automatic Rifle (BAR), a World War I-vintage weapon, offered semiautomatic fire support at the squad level for US forces. The BAR fired a 7.62mm (0.3in) round from a 20-round box clip and was distinctive with its somewhat superfluous bipod. Utilized throughout World War II, the BAR was known for its heavy weight of 8.8kg (19.4lb). The Fusil Mitrailleur Mle 24/29 served as the standard French light machine gun for more than 40 years. Developed in the 1920s, it fired a 7.5mm (0.295in) cartridge from a 25-round box magazine.

ABOVE: The British Bren Mk II light machine gun was adapted from a Czechoslovakian design and issued to the British Army in 1941 with basic improvements to the initial Bren that had entered service four years earlier. The Bren fired a 7.7mm (0.303in) cartridge from detachable top-feed magazines of 20, 30 or 100 rounds at a rate of approximately 500 rounds per minute.

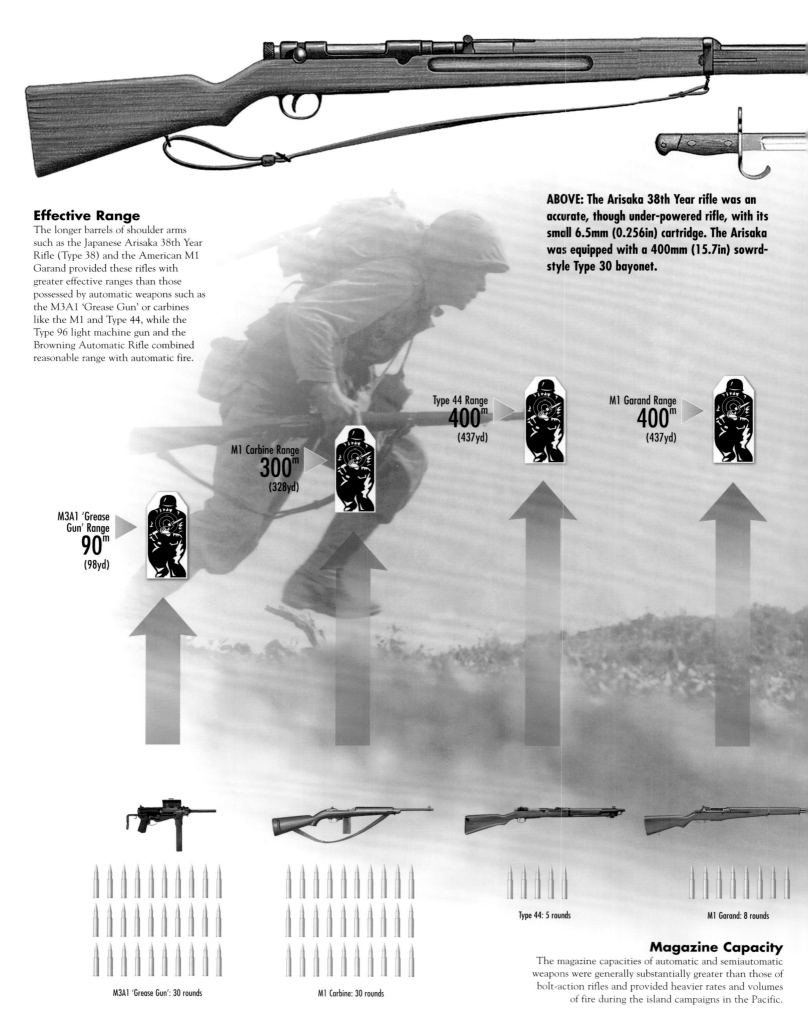

Effective Range

The longer barrels of shoulder arms such as the Japanese Arisaka 38th Year Rifle (Type 38) and the American M1 Garand provided these rifles with greater effective ranges than those possessed by automatic weapons such as the M3A1 'Grease Gun' or carbines like the M1 and Type 44, while the Type 96 light machine gun and the Browning Automatic Rifle combined reasonable range with automatic fire.

ABOVE: The Arisaka 38th Year rifle was an accurate, though under-powered rifle, with its small 6.5mm (0.256in) cartridge. The Arisaka was equipped with a 400mm (15.7in) sowrd-style Type 30 bayonet.

Type 44 Range
400ᵐ
(437yd)

M1 Garand Range
400ᵐ
(437yd)

M1 Carbine Range
300ᵐ
(328yd)

M3A1 'Grease Gun' Range
90ᵐ
(98yd)

M3A1 'Grease Gun': 30 rounds

M1 Carbine: 30 rounds

Type 44: 5 rounds

M1 Garand: 8 rounds

Magazine Capacity

The magazine capacities of automatic and semiautomatic weapons were generally substantially greater than those of bolt-action rifles and provided heavier rates and volumes of fire during the island campaigns in the Pacific.

BAR Range
1500ᵐ
(1640yd)

Battle for Okinawa

Effective Range and Magazine Capacity

▶ **M3A1 'Grease Gun'**
▶ **M1 Carbine**
▶ **Type 44**
▶ **M1 Garand**
▶ **Arisaka 38th Year Rifle**
▶ **Type 96**
▶ **Browning Automatic Rifle**

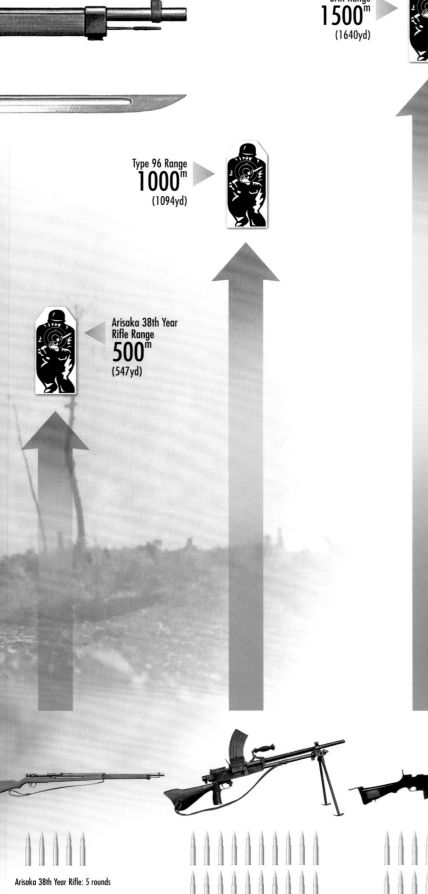

Type 96 Range
1000ᵐ
(1094yd)

Arisaka 38th Year
Rifle Range
500ᵐ
(547yd)

Arisaka 38th Year Rifle: 5 rounds

Type 96: 30 rounds

BAR: 20 rounds

In the spring of 1945, American troops invaded the island of Okinawa, Japanese home territory rather than conquered land. In the prolonged battle for control of the island, US Marines and Army troops relied on the substantial firepower of automatic and semiautomatic weapons during close-in fighting to subdue a well-hidden enemy bent on death rather than surrender.

The M1 Garand semiautomatic rifle was the standard-issue weapon of the US forces, and with its eight-round en bloc clip it provided a head-to-head edge over the bolt-action Arisaka Type 38, which carried only five rounds in its internal magazine. However, the availability of the fully automatic 'Grease Gun', the M3 and M3A1, gave the individual American soldier a tremendous advantage over Japanese forces that fielded few submachine guns. The M3 carried up to 30 rounds in a detachable box magazine and the improved M3A1 was equipped with a built-in loading tool and a detachable stock.

The 6.5mm (0.256in) Japanese Type 96 light machine gun was patterned after early French Hotchkiss models and was essentially obsolescent by 1945. It had originally been introduced as a replacement for the Type 11, which was inefficiently fed by an ammunition hopper rather than the top-loading box magazine of the Type 96. The World War I-vintage Browning Automatic Rifle (BAR) carried a 20-round clip but was a comparatively heavy weapon.

The small American M1 Carbine was vastly superior to the Japanese Type 44, also known as the Cavalry Rifle. The M1 Carbine carried up to 30 rounds; the Type 44 just five. On Okinawa, the M1 Carbine proved capable in the hands of soldiers traversing rugged, undulating terrain and facing a stubborn enemy.

Personnel

The manpower of the 1944 infantry squad varied, with the Germans fielding 10 soldiers and the American squad consisting of 12. Each was designated as a cohesive unit commanded by a junior officer who directed its tactical deployment.

Weapons

The German infantry squad packed a strong punch with the fine MG 34 machine gun providing automatic fire support while the squad leader carried the excellent MP 40 submachine gun.

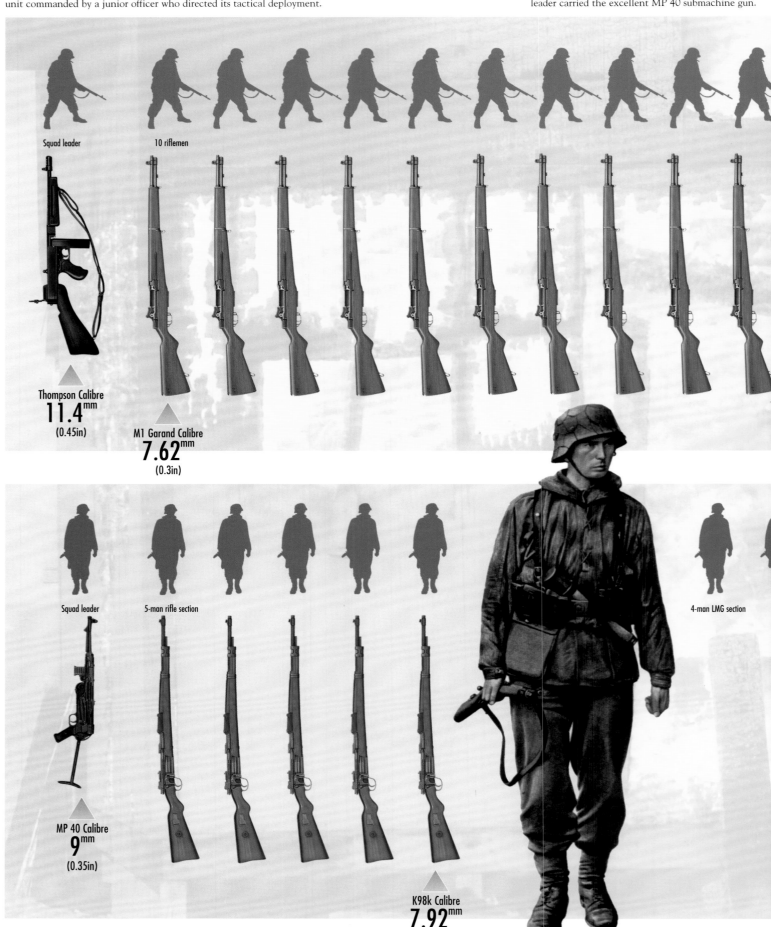

Squad leader

10 riflemen

Thompson Calibre
11.4mm
(0.45in)

M1 Garand Calibre
7.62mm
(0.3in)

Squad leader

5-man rifle section

4-man LMG section

MP 40 Calibre
9mm
(0.35in)

K98k Calibre
7.92mm
(0.312in)

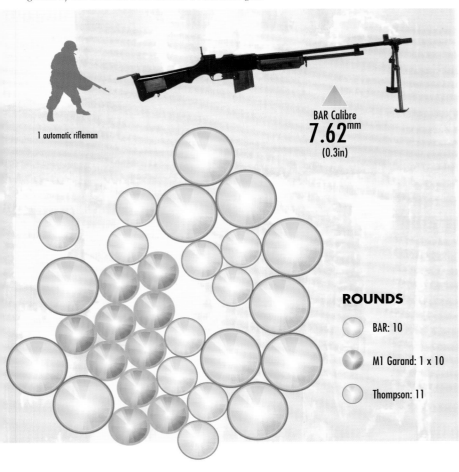

1 automatic rifleman

BAR Calibre
7.62mm
(0.3in)

ROUNDS
BAR: 10

M1 Garand: 1 x 10

Thompson: 11

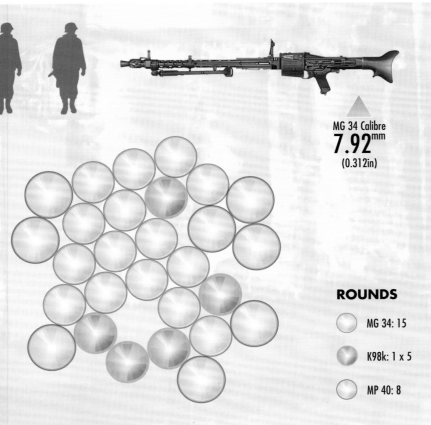

MG 34 Calibre
7.92mm
(0.312in)

ROUNDS
MG 34: 15

K98k: 1 x 5

MP 40: 8

Infantry Squads Compared: 1944

One-second Burst Weight of Fire, Personnel and Weapons

▶ **US Army Infantry Squad**
▶ **German Infantry Squad**

The introduction of automatic weapons to the infantry squad brought a new dimension to tactical warfare, and often the outcome of an encounter between small units of opposing armies was determined by concealment, weapons positioning and the element of surprise.

By 1944, the German infantry squad had been modified from its original structure of 13 infantrymen to a more manageable number of 10. The change was based on combat experience during the Polish Campaign of 1939. While the reduced number of available infantrymen had a negative impact on the firepower of the squad, the addition of the MG 34 machine gun, with a rate of fire of up to 900 rounds per minute, compensated well. In addition, the squad leader was armed with the outstanding MP 40 submachine gun, capable of a substantial rate of fire in its own right. The German infantryman was armed with the standard Mauser Karabiner 98k rifle, a quality bolt-action weapon that served throughout the war.

Conversely, the US Army infantry squad of 1944 placed emphasis on the individual rifleman, whose primary weapon was the semiautomatic M1 Garand rifle, the first semiautomatic rifle to become standard issue in any army. The M1 entered service in 1936, and its eight-round en bloc clip provided a superior rate of fire to the five-round stripper clip of the K98k.

American squad leaders carried the popular Thompson submachine gun, which had been developed towards the end of World War I as a possible means of breaking the stalemate of trench warfare. Instead, the Thompson became notable during the Prohibition Era of the 1920s in America before its adoption by the military in 1938. The Browning Automatic Rifle (BAR) was also a weapon of World War I and could be classified as a light machine gun with a 20-round clip. Although its performance did not approach that of the MG 34, the BAR was fired by a single soldier, while the MG 34 required a crew of four.

Heavy Machine Guns 1

Rate of Fire (Rounds per Second)

▶ **MG 42**
▶ **MG 34**
▶ **Vickers Mk 1**
▶ **Browning M2**
▶ **DShK 1938**

An outstanding precision weapon, the *Maschinengewehr* 34, or MG 34, was adopted by the *Wehrmacht* in 1935 as its standard light machine gun and excelled in both offensive and defensive deployment. The MG 34 was based on the Solothurn 30, an earlier Rheinmetall design that had been in service with the Swiss Army. Heinrich Vollmer (1885–1961) of Mauser modified that weapon and his improvements to the firing system produced an impressive rate of fire of up to 900 rounds per minute.

Even so, the MG 34 was costly to produce, and as World War II progressed a more economical weapon was sought. Utilizing similar production techniques to those of the MP 38 submachine gun, German factories produced the MG 42, perhaps the most outstanding weapon of its kind to serve during the war. Assembled with numerous stamped parts, the MG 42 fired at an astonishing rate of 1200 rounds per minute.

The British Vickers heavy machine gun traced its origin to pre-World War I days and the designs of American-born inventor Hiram Maxim (1840–1916). While even its appearance recalled an earlier generation of weapons and the British had made plans to replace it, the Vickers Mk I remained in service throughout the war and even into the 1960s. Another apparent throwback was the Soviet DShK 1938, modified from an earlier 1920s model to accept a belt feed. Often mounted on a two-wheeled carriage and fitted with a shield, the DShK 1938 fired its 12.7mm (0.5in) ammunition at up to 550 rounds per minute.

When the 12.7mm (0.5in) Browning M2 was converted to an air-cooled configuration in 1933, the barrel tended to overheat rapidly. This setback was corrected with the installation of a thicker barrel, and the resulting model was designated the M2HB. Lighter than the water-cooled version, the M2HB fired up to 635 rounds per minute.

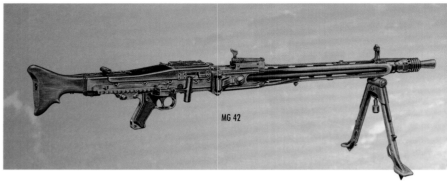

MG 42

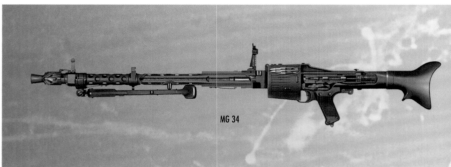

MG 34

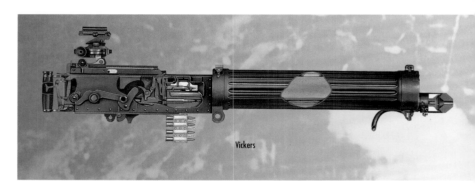

Vickers

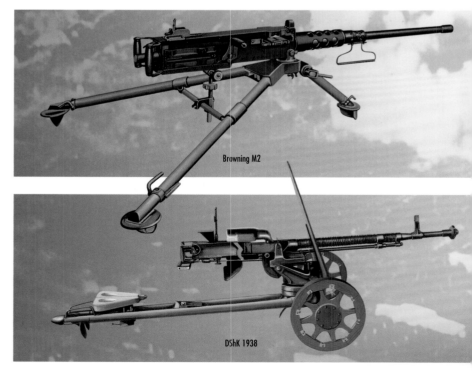

Browning M2

DShK 1938

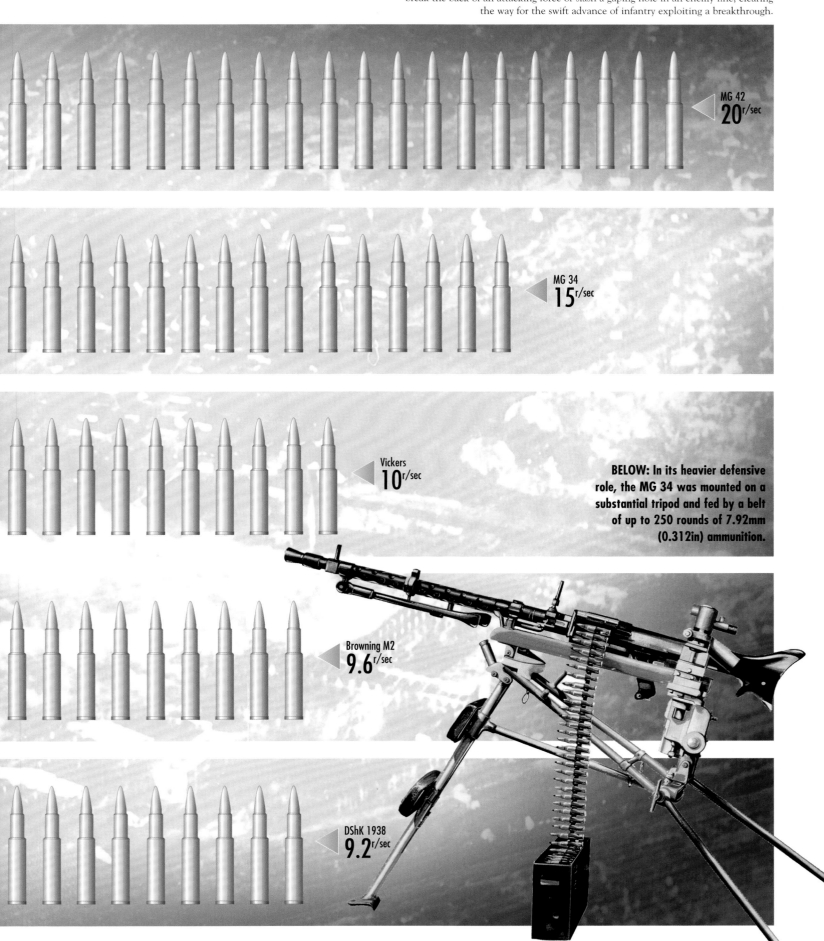

Rate of Fire (rounds per second)

Concentrated machine-gun fire was devastating to enemy troops and potentially could break the back of an attacking force or slash a gaping hole in an enemy line, clearing the way for the swift advance of infantry exploiting a breakthrough.

MG 42
20 r/sec

MG 34
15 r/sec

Vickers
10 r/sec

BELOW: In its heavier defensive role, the MG 34 was mounted on a substantial tripod and fed by a belt of up to 250 rounds of 7.92mm (0.312in) ammunition.

Browning M2
9.6 r/sec

DShK 1938
9.2 r/sec

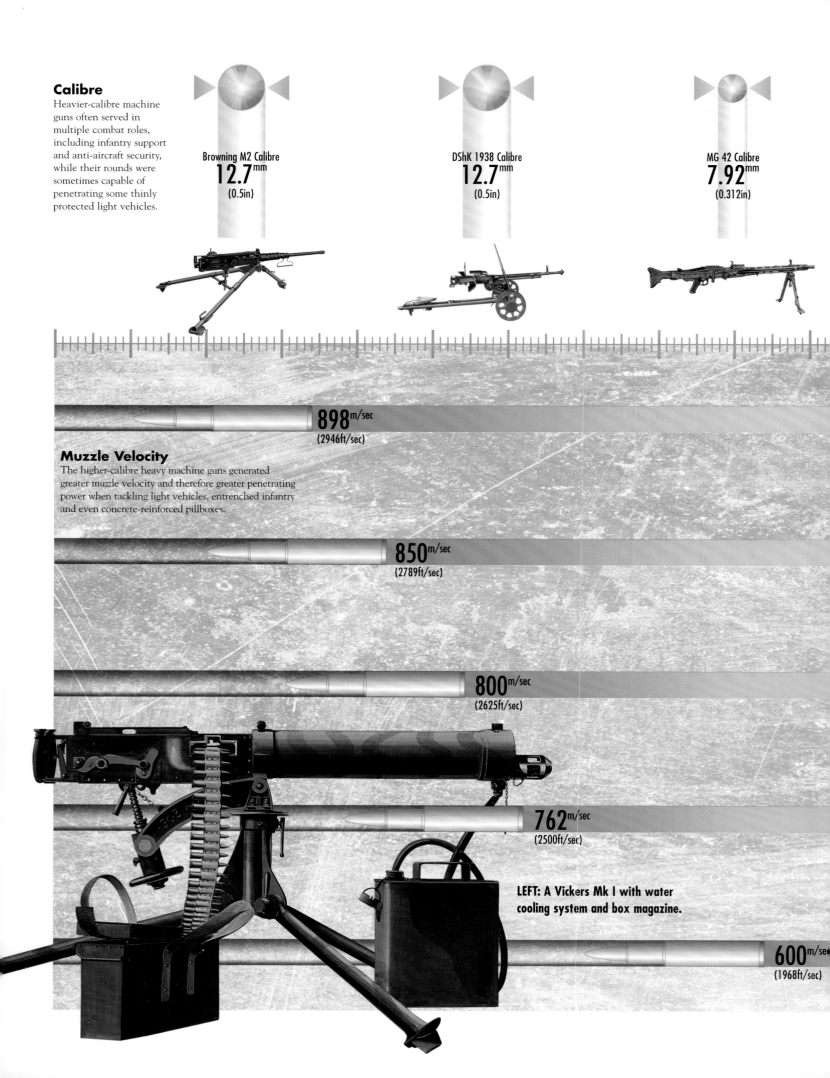

Calibre

Heavier-calibre machine guns often served in multiple combat roles, including infantry support and anti-aircraft security, while their rounds were sometimes capable of penetrating some thinly protected light vehicles.

Browning M2 Calibre
12.7mm
(0.5in)

DShK 1938 Calibre
12.7mm
(0.5in)

MG 42 Calibre
7.92mm
(0.312in)

898m/sec
(2946ft/sec)

Muzzle Velocity

The higher-calibre heavy machine guns generated greater muzzle velocity and therefore greater penetrating power when tackling light vehicles, entrenched infantry and even concrete-reinforced pillboxes.

850m/sec
(2789ft/sec)

800m/sec
(2625ft/sec)

762m/sec
(2500ft/sec)

LEFT: A Vickers Mk I with water cooling system and box magazine.

600m/sec
(1968ft/sec)

MG 34 Calibre
7.92^{mm}
(0.312in)

Vickers Calibre
7.7^{mm}
(0.303in)

Heavy Machine Guns 2

Calibre and Muzzle Velocity

► **MG 42**
► **MG 34**
► **Vickers Mk 1**
► **Browning M2**
► **DShK 1938**

Browning M2

DShK 1938

MG 42

MG 34

Vickers

The German MG 34 was a rugged and reliable infantry-support weapon that entered production in 1934 but was available in too small numbers to fully retire its predecessor, the MG 13, when World War II broke out. Even so, it gained the grudging respect of Allied soldiers and proved dominant on the battlefield with its impressive rate of fire and ease of maintenance and operation in combat conditions. Its barrels could be changed rapidly by disengaging a latch, sliding the receiver out of the way and inserting the new barrel into the weapon. Another advantage was its double-crescent trigger that basically allowed the operator to choose semiautomatic or automatic mode.

The MG 42, meanwhile, provided German infantry units with a decided firepower advantage with a rate of fire that topped 1500 rounds per minute, significantly above that of contemporary Allied machine guns. Perhaps its most impressive attribute was its stellar battlefield performance despite its mass-production assembly. The MG 42 was also transported with relative ease due to a favourable weight of 11.5kg (25lb). Its greatest drawback in the field may well have been the entourage of six soldiers that served the weapon.

The Vickers Mk I also required a crew of six for optimal performance; however, its weight of 18kg (39.6lb) meant that transporting the weapon presented something of a challenge, while the Browning M2 and Soviet DShK 1938 were heavier 12.7mm (0.5in) weapons that weighed 38.5kg (84.9lb) and 35.5kg (78.3lb) respectively. Variants of the M2 were not only used in infantry support but also served aboard aircraft and on armoured vehicles as anti-personnel and anti-aircraft weapons. The DShK 1938 served as the primary machine gun of the Red Army throughout World War II, and its wheeled carriage facilitated rapid deployment on the open terrain of the Russian steppes.

Machine Guns on Iwo Jima

Effective Range

▶ **Browning M1919**
▶ **Type 92**
▶ **Browning M2**
▶ **Type 3**
▶ **Type 1**

For more than a month in early 1945, US Marines and Japanese troops fought and died for control of a craggy, sulphur-stained Pacific island called Iwo Jima. Shaped roughly like a pork chop, Iwo Jima had been turned into a fortress by the defending Japanese, who had honeycombed the island with tunnels, concealed gun emplacements, pillboxes and machine-gun nests.

Within these reinforced positions, the Japanese placed their standard infantry-support machine guns, the Types 1, 3 and 92. A licence-built version of the French Hotchkiss Model 1914, the Type 3 was distinctive, with its tripod mount and prominent cooling rings. Since the 1930s, the Imperial Japanese Army had been receiving the Type 92 – an improved version of the Type 3 – which became Japan's standard infantry heavy machine gun during World War II.

Nicknamed the 'Woodpecker' by Allied soldiers for its staccato firing sound, the Type 92 was prone to jamming, and an attempt to rectify the situation by oiling its 30-round 7.7mm (0.303in) cartridge strips failed miserably. In 1941, the Type 1, a scaled-down version of the Type 92, entered service firing the same ammunition but offering a much lighter platform at 31kg (68lb) compared with the Type 92's 55kg (121lb).

A pair of Browning machine guns, the M1919 and the M2, proved superior in performance to their Japanese counterparts during the arduous US trek across the Pacific. The M1919 was a 7.62mm (0.3in) air-cooled weapon that weighed only 14kg (31lb) and was fired primarily from a tripod. Fed by a 250-round belt, the weapon could fire up to 600 rounds per minute. The M2 gained lasting fame as a 12.7mm (0.5in) machine gun that was heavier than any infantry machine gun fielded by the Japanese. Early versions of the M2 were water-cooled, but later models were air-cooled and fired up to 575 rounds per minute.

Effective Range

The effective range of infantry-support machine guns established a perimeter of concentrated fire that protected vulnerable positions, such as those held by American Marines at Iwo Jima. Often, the advantage of concealment gave the range of the Japanese guns an even greater edge in defensive combat.

Browning M1919
2000ᵐ
(2187yd)

Type 92
2000ᵐ
(2187yd)

Browning M1919

Type 92

Browning M2
1800m
(1968yd)

Type 3
1500m
(1640yd)

Type 1
1400m
(1531yd)

ABOVE: US Marines man a captured Japanese Type 92 heavy machine gun during fighting for the island of Iwo Jima, March 1945.

Browning M2

Type 3

Type 1

Anti-tank Rifles

Effective Range and Armour Penetration

▶ **PTRD-41**

▶ **PTRS-41**

▶ **Type 97**

▶ **Panzerbüchse 39**

▶ **Granatbüchse 39**

▶ **Boys Mk I**

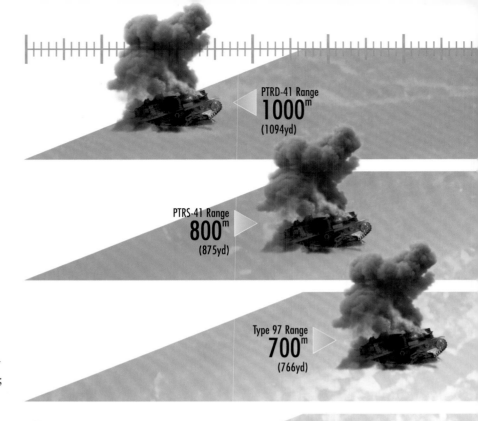

PTRD-41 Range
1000ᵐ
(1094yd)

PTRS-41 Range
800ᵐ
(875yd)

Type 97 Range
700ᵐ
(766yd)

Among the earliest methods of dealing with enemy armour, the anti-tank rifle had largely become obsolete by the outbreak of World War II; however, several models remained in service and were produced in large numbers. The Soviet PTRD-41 and its follow-on the PTRS-41 were man-portable weapons at 17.24kg (38lb) and 20.3kg (44.8lb) and fired a 14.5mm (0.57in) projectile. The recoil from both was substantial, and they fell into disfavour with Soviet troops although more than 1.5 million were produced. The PTRS-41 had a semiautomatic mode.

In contrast, the Japanese Type 97 anti-tank rifle was much heavier at 59kg (130lb) and fired a 20mm (0.79in) round from a seven-round clip, producing a tremendous recoil that made the weapon highly inaccurate. The British Boys anti-tank rifle was outmoded soon after its introduction in 1937. The 16kg (35.3lb) bolt-action weapon was steadied with a bipod and fired a 13.97mm (0.55in) cartridge. The German Panzerbüchse 39 fired a relatively small 7.92mm (0.312in) cartridge whose performance was improved with the introduction of tungsten-core ammunition. An improved anti-tank rifle, the Granatbüchse 39, was easier to transport and capable of firing three types of grenade against infantry and armoured targets.

Effective Range

The effective ranges of World War II-era anti-tank rifles varied substantially, influenced heavily by barrel length and calibre. Most such weapons required the operators to move within a few hundred metres of the target to have any real hope of disabling a tank.

BELOW: The Universal Carrier was a mainstay of Commonwealth forces throughout the war, and this example was placed in service with the Soviet Red Army through Lend-Lease. It mounts the Boys anti-tank rifle and the standard British light machine gun of the war, the Bren.

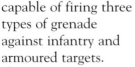

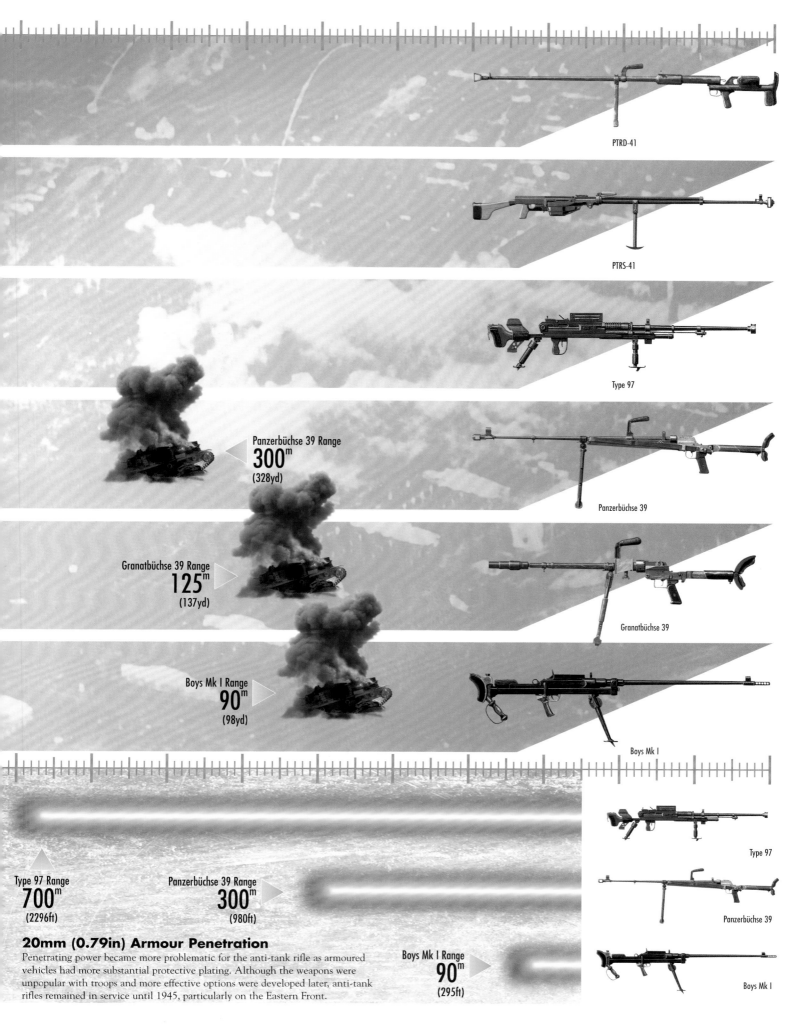

PTRD-41

PTRS-41

Type 97

Panzerbüchse 39 Range
300^m
(328yd)

Panzerbüchse 39

Granatbüchse 39 Range
125^m
(137yd)

Granatbüchse 39

Boys Mk I Range
90^m
(98yd)

Boys Mk I

Type 97 Range
700^m
(2296ft)

Panzerbüchse 39 Range
300^m
(980ft)

20mm (0.79in) Armour Penetration

Penetrating power became more problematic for the anti-tank rifle as armoured vehicles had more substantial protective plating. Although the weapons were unpopular with troops and more effective options were developed later, anti-tank rifles remained in service until 1945, particularly on the Eastern Front.

Boys Mk I Range
90^m
(295ft)

Type 97

Panzerbüchse 39

Boys Mk I

Anti-tank Weapons

Effective Range and Calibre

▶ **Panzerfaust 30**
▶ **RPzB Panzerschreck**
▶ **PIAT**
▶ **M9 Bazooka**

The proliferation of tanks and armoured vehicles on the battlefield led to a generation of anti-tank weapons capable of destroying or disabling the heaviest armour. Early anti-tank rifles fired high-calibre shells that were effective against tanks during the interwar years. However, these were rendered obsolete as the thickness and slope of armour protection were enhanced during the 1930s and 1940s. To provide infantrymen with a fighting chance, designers developed effective shoulder-fired anti-tank weapons.

In 1943, the US Army introduced the M1 Bazooka, a hollow tube that fired a rocket-propelled 60mm (2.36in) high-explosive (HE) warhead, one of the world's first HEAT (High-Explosive Anti-Tank) rounds. By 1944, the M9 version had been introduced with a reinforced launch tube, metal rather than wooden grips, and an improved M6A3 rocket capable of penetrating 102mm (4in) of armour. For ease of transport, the Bazooka could be broken down into two parts.

German industry produced large numbers of anti-tank weapons during the war, particularly as enemy armour approached the frontiers of the Reich later in the conflict. Patterned after a captured M1 Bazooka, the RPzB Panzerschreck fired an 88mm (3.5in) HE rocket, and more than 300,000 were made from 1943. The most numerous of German anti-tank weapons was the Panzerfaust, relatively inexpensive to produce and highly effective against Allied armour. It was operated by a single soldier and launched a 2.9kg (6.4lb) hollow-charge round containing 0.8kg (1.8lb) of high explosive. More than six million were produced from 1943, and relatively little training was needed to fire the weapon.

The British PIAT (Projector, Infantry, Anti-Tank) operated like a spigot mortar, using a cocked spring to launch an 89mm (3.51in) bomb capped with 1.1kg (2.4lb) of high explosive. Typically served by two soldiers, the weapon involved a tube, a trigger apparatus and a spring, which was notoriously difficult to cock. Around 115,000 PIATs were produced during the war.

Calibre

As armour protection steadily increased during the war, the firepower and penetrating ability of anti-tank weapons did likewise, often employing innovative rocket power to launch to considerable distances hollow-charge warheads or bombs tipped with high explosive. Such weapons were most effective against more thinly armoured areas rather than a tank's substantial frontal protection.

Effective Range

Although the Panzerfaust required its operator to move perilously close to the armoured target, other anti-tank weapons were effective from appreciable ranges, assisted by rocket power or, in the case of the British PIAT, a heavy spring that operated in similar fashion to a spigot mortar to hurl its high-explosive bomb.

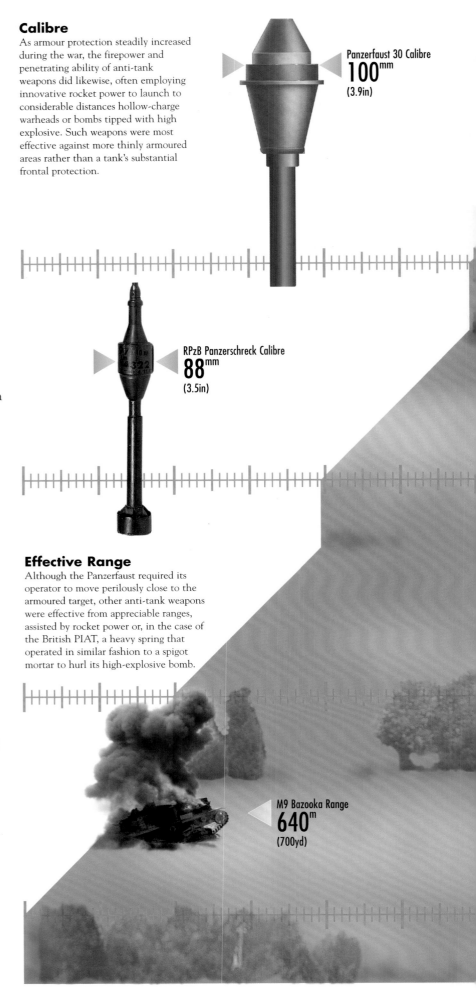

Panzerfaust 30 Calibre
100mm
(3.9in)

RPzB Panzerschreck Calibre
88mm
(3.5in)

M9 Bazooka Range
640m
(700yd)

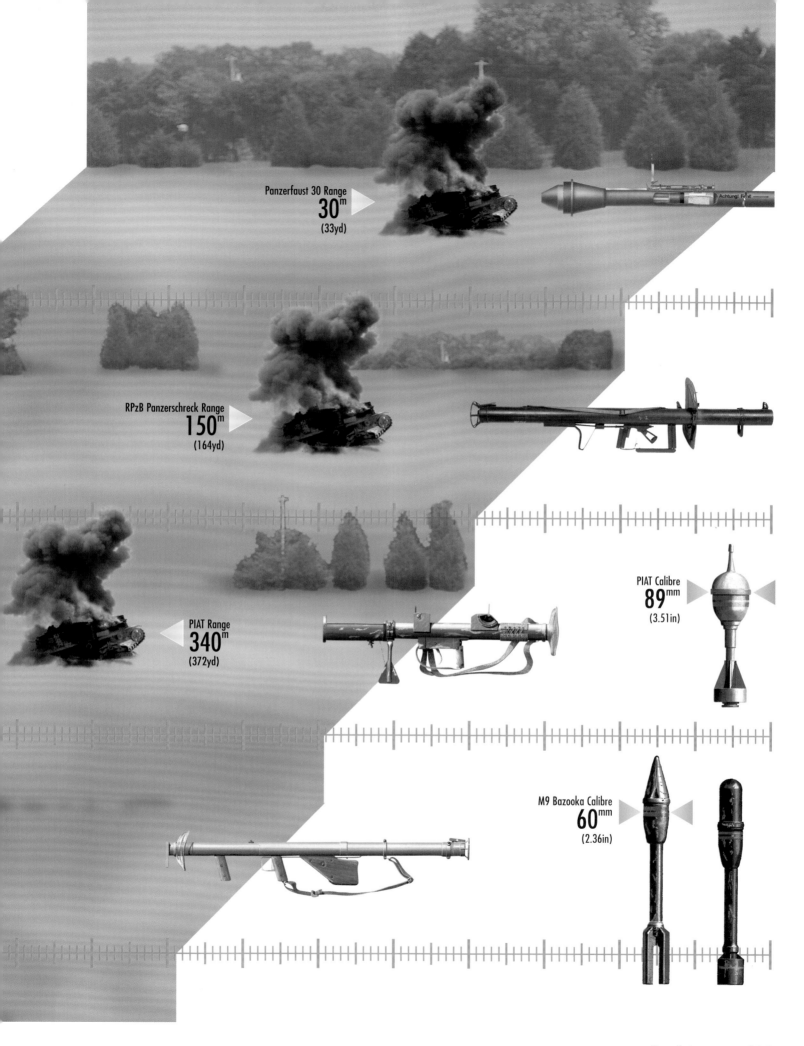

Panzerfaust 30 Range
30^m
(33yd)

RPzB Panzerschreck Range
150^m
(164yd)

PIAT Range
340^m
(372yd)

PIAT Calibre
89^{mm}
(3.51in)

M9 Bazooka Calibre
60^{mm}
(2.36in)

Grenades

Range, Armour Penetration and Weight

▶ **M9A1 Rifle Grenade**
▶ **Panzerwurfmine**
▶ **Eihandgranate 39**
▶ **Mills Bomb**

Grenades, rifle-launched or hand-thrown, were often the most effective weapons carried by the ordinary World War II infantryman. Packing a destructive explosive charge, the grenade was utilized against infantry strongpoints, pillboxes, machine-gun nests and even armoured vehicles.

Among the most recognizable grenades of the war was the standard-issue British Mills Bomb, developed by William Mills (1856–1932) and first produced in 1915. The Mills Bomb was a fragmentation grenade that was secured with a pin and resembled a small pineapple. Originally, the explosive detonated with a seven-second delay, subsequently reduced to four seconds. Across a series of modifications that included a rifle-grenade variant, more than 70 million Mills Bombs were manufactured into the 1980s, and the grenade remained standard issue with the British Army until 1972. Its explosive element was a combination of TNT, barium nitrate and wax.

The German Model 39 Eihandgranate ('egg hand grenade') entered service in 1939. It was fashioned with a smooth sheet-metal body, and its fuse assembly was screwed into the top, its colour indicating the time interval to detonation. The typical delay was four seconds, but the Type 39 was particularly adaptable for use in booby traps. Rigged to explode immediately upon a certain action such as the opening of a door, it caused many casualties among unwary Allied soldiers.

The Panzewurfmine was purpose-built for the the *Wehrmacht* as an anti-tank weapon. It was stabilized in flight by fins and a canvas apron resembling a small parachute, and the idea was for the soldier to hurl the grenade from a relatively short distance, allowing it to fully deploy in flight so that the hollow-charge warhead, similar to that of the more widely known Panzerfaust, made contact with the armoured target as closely to the optimum 90-degree angle as possible. Although the grenade proved disappointing in combat, two versions, long and short, each with 500g (1.1lb) warheads, were produced.

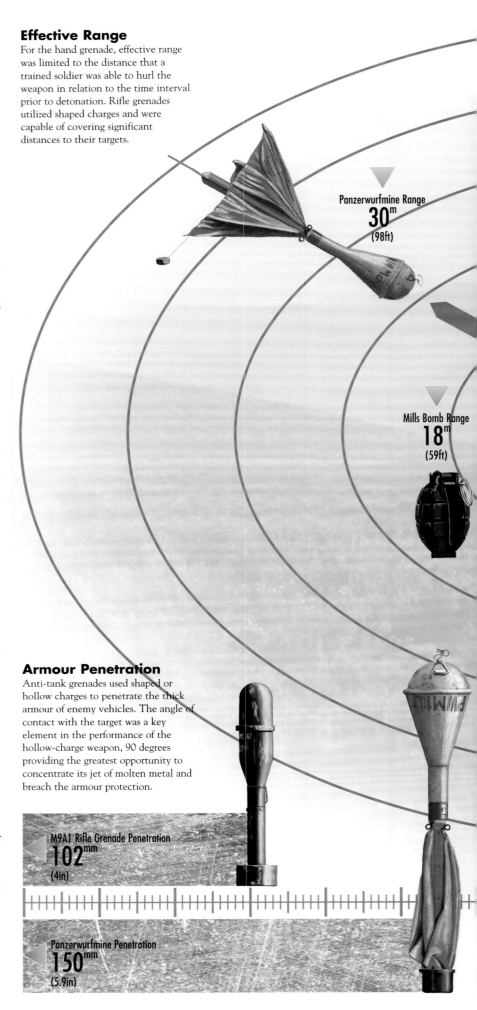

Effective Range
For the hand grenade, effective range was limited to the distance that a trained soldier was able to hurl the weapon in relation to the time interval prior to detonation. Rifle grenades utilized shaped charges and were capable of covering significant distances to their targets.

Panzerwurfmine Range
30ᵐ
(98ft)

Mills Bomb Range
18ᵐ
(59ft)

Armour Penetration
Anti-tank grenades used shaped or hollow charges to penetrate the thick armour of enemy vehicles. The angle of contact with the target was a key element in the performance of the hollow-charge weapon, 90 degrees providing the greatest opportunity to concentrate its jet of molten metal and breach the armour protection.

M9A1 Rifle Grenade Penetration
102ᵐᵐ
(4in)

Panzerwurfmine Penetration
150ᵐᵐ
(5.9in)

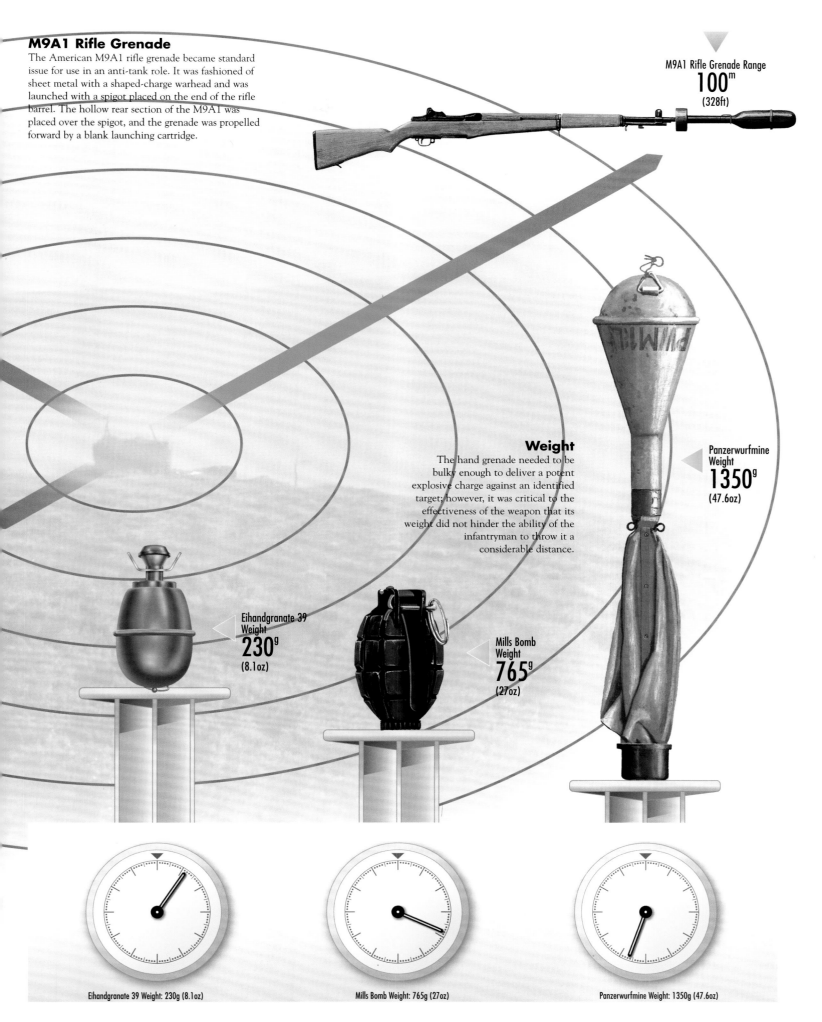

M9A1 Rifle Grenade

The American M9A1 rifle grenade became standard issue for use in an anti-tank role. It was fashioned of sheet metal with a shaped-charge warhead and was launched with a spigot placed on the end of the rifle barrel. The hollow rear section of the M9A1 was placed over the spigot, and the grenade was propelled forward by a blank launching cartridge.

M9A1 Rifle Grenade Range
100^m
(328ft)

Weight

The hand grenade needed to be bulky enough to deliver a potent explosive charge against an identified target; however, it was critical to the effectiveness of the weapon that its weight did not hinder the ability of the infantryman to throw it a considerable distance.

Panzerwurfmine
Weight
1350^g
(47.6oz)

Eihandgranate 39
Weight
230^g
(8.1oz)

Mills Bomb
Weight
765^g
(27oz)

Eihandgranate 39 Weight: 230g (8.1oz)

Mills Bomb Weight: 765g (27oz)

Panzerwurfmine Weight: 1350g (47.6oz)

Effective Range

Spewing a mixture of fuel and powerful propellant, the flamethrower was notable for an effective range that often required the operator to move dangerously close to his intended target. The soldier carrying the prominent apparatus was then exposed to retaliatory fire.

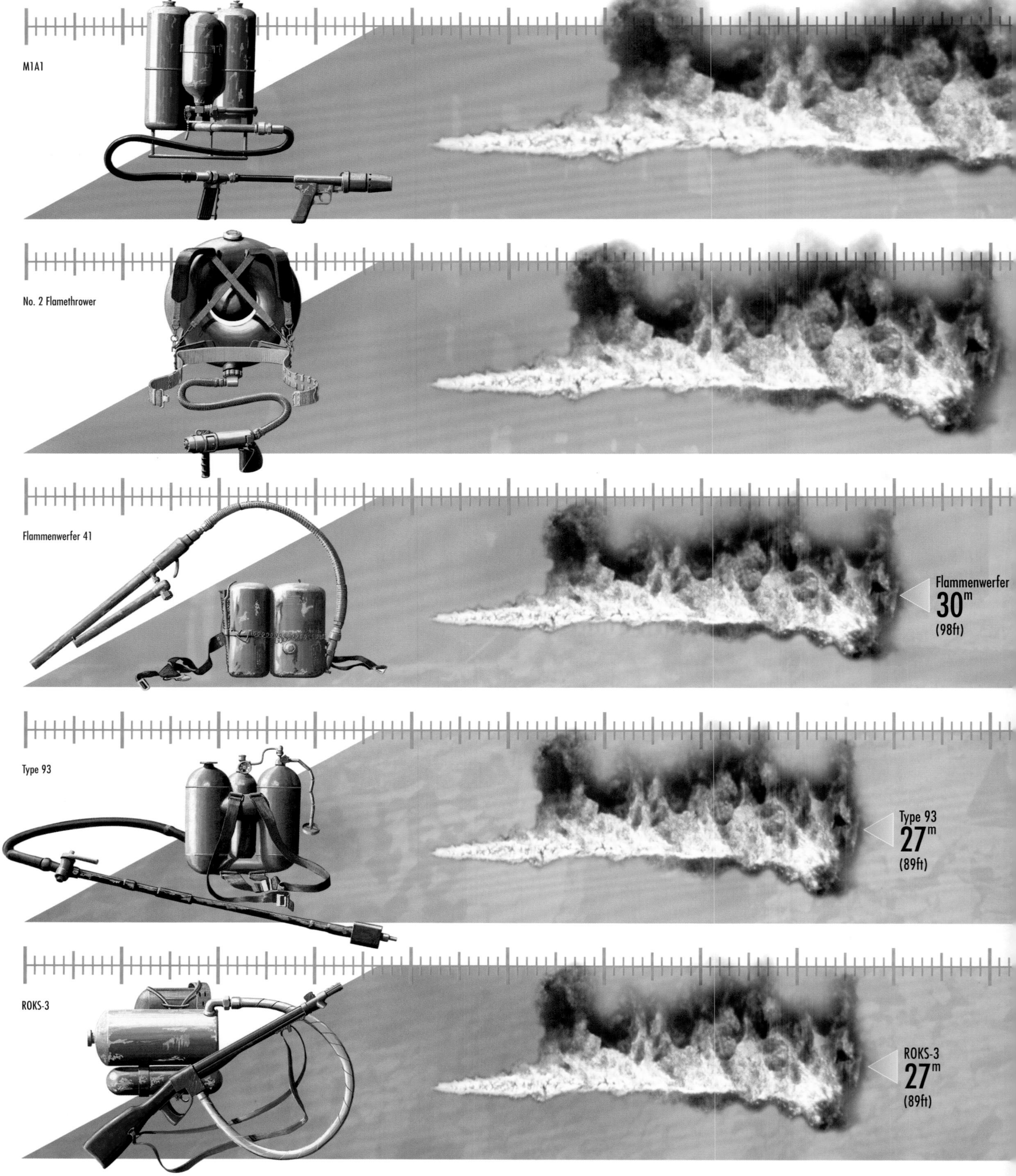

M1A1

No. 2 Flamethrower

Flammenwerfer 41

Flammenwerfer
30m
(98ft)

Type 93

Type 93
27m
(89ft)

ROKS-3

ROKS-3
27m
(89ft)

Flamethrowers

Effective Range

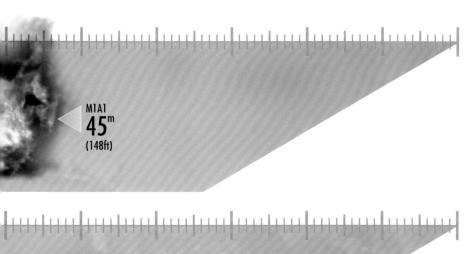

M1A1
45ᵐ
(148ft)

No. 2 Flamethrower
36ᵐ
(118ft)

▶ **M1A1**
▶ **No. 2 Flamethrower**
▶ **Flammenwerfer 41**
▶ **Type 93**
▶ **ROKS-3**

The flamethrower was one of the most-feared ground weapons of the war, both by those who faced it in battle and by those who carried the tanks of flammable liquids into combat. Nevertheless, it was cruelly effective in reducing enemy strongpoints, particularly those reinforced with concrete and steel, as well as in neutralizing concentrations of enemy troops in confined areas.

The Germans used the flamethrower with telling effect on the Eastern Front, finding it effective at reducing stubborn pockets of Soviet defenders in the rubble and sewers of Stalingrad. Meanwhile, the American M1 and M1A1 were developed from 1940 forward, with the first combat deployment of the M1 against a Japanese fortification resulting in a dismal failure. The Soviet ROKS-3 was recognizable by its rectangular box-like fuel tank and heavy muzzle. Its flame was ignited by pulling the trigger, which then fired a cartridge in a revolving cylinder. The Type 93 flamethrower entered service with the Imperial Japanese Army in 1933 and was deployed on the Asian continent, where it was prone to ignition failure during cold temperatures.

BELOW: US Marines use an M1A1 flamethrower to flush out Japanese defenders during the fighting for the island of Okinawa, 1945

Special Ops Weapons

Effective Range and Magazine Capacity

▶ **Liberator M1942**
▶ **Welrod Silent Pistol**
▶ **Hudson M3A1 with Silencer**
▶ **Sten Mk II 'Silent Sten'**
▶ **De Lisle Carbine**

Covert operations in Nazi-occupied Europe posed tremendous risks for those agents who undertook them. Activities ranged from sabotage to disruption of communications, ambush and assassination attempts against prominent political and military figures. Such endeavours required specialized weapons, easily concealed and sometimes equipped with silencers.

Among the more unusual special operations weapons were a pair of pistols, the American Liberator M1942 and the British Welrod. The Liberator was cheaply constructed of stamped components expressly for distribution to resistance fighters. The Welrod was designed by the covert Special Operations Executive (SOE) with assassination in mind, housing an integral silencer with a 9mm (0.35in) or 8.1mm (0.32in) chambered round.

Three weapons were equipped with silencers for special operations work – the British Sten Mk II and De Lisle Carbine and the US-made Hudson M3A1. The 'Silent Sten' entered service in 1942 and was widely used by both SOE agents and resistance operatives. It silencer reduced the Sten's report effectively until 10 shots had been fired. After that, carbon build-up made the 9mm (0.35in) weapon substantially louder.

The De Lisle Carbine was based on the Mk III SMLE rifle, its receiver modified to accept the 11.4mm (0.45in) round. A single-shot bolt-action weapon, the De Lisle was intended for assassination at a distance. Only 129 were made and placed in service primarily with British Commandos. The American Hudson M3A1 was a modification of the M3 submachine gun. At the request of the Office of Strategic Services (OSS), a silencer was developed. Although the weapon fired at 45 rounds per minute, low muzzle velocity resulted in weak knockdown capability, while its silencer was less effective than the British Sten's.

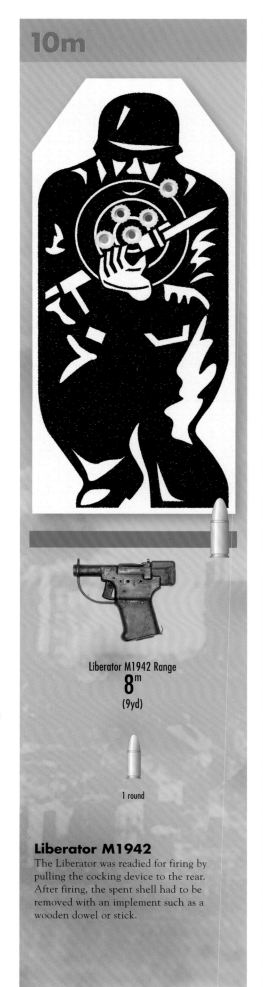

10m

Liberator M1942 Range
8ᵐ
(9yd)

1 round

Liberator M1942
The Liberator was readied for firing by pulling the cocking device to the rear. After firing, the spent shell had to be removed with an implement such as a wooden dowel or stick.

20m

Welrod Silent Pistol Range
20ᵐ
(22yd)

8 rounds

Welrod Silent Pistol
The Welrod held a six- or eight-round magazine; however, chambering a second round was cumbersome and it was unlikely that a follow-up shot could be delivered. Reloading was accomplished only by removing the entire grip, and chambering the second round involved twisting a cap at the rear of the barrel, pulling backwards and then pushing forwards.

50m

75m

100m

Effective Range

Special-operations weapons were developed with relative ranges in mind. It was reasoned that assassinations or self-defence efforts would generally only happen at short range, while a single-shot rifle would possibly allow an agent to maintain concealment.

Hudson M3A1 with Silencer Range
50ᵐ
(55yd)

Sten Mk II 'Silent Sten' Range
70ᵐ
(77yd)

De Lisle Carbine Range
250ᵐ
(273yd)

7 rounds

30 rounds

32 rounds

Magazine Capacity

Magazine capacity was somewhat irrelevant in special-operations pistols. At close quarters, the agent was likely to only fire a single shot, even though a magazine might carry multiple rounds. Rifles were often single shot, while automatic weapons could sustain fire for longer periods and over wider areas.

Glossary

Ack-Ack: A primarily British term for anti-aircraft fire, which evolved from the use of the word 'Ack' for the letter 'A' in the British phonetic alphabet.

Air Superiority: A situation whereby enemy air forces can only operate at a significant disadvantage. This may be a local and temporary situation or may be a more widespread advantage.

Allies: Term describing the cooperative military and political alliance that opposed the Axis in World War II and was headed principally by the United States, Great Britain, and the Soviet Union.

Anti-aircraft Artillery: Artillery weapons with related equipment, such as searchlights or radar, utilized by units on the ground to engage and shoot down enemy aircraft.

Anti-Submarine: Any vessel, aircraft or weapons system intended primarily for use against enemy submarines. Also, the missions carried out by these platforms, which can include detection and tracking without making an attack.

Armoured Fighting Vehicle (AFV): A heavily armoured combat vehicle designed to directly engage the enemy with a powerful weapon; i.e., a tank.

Arsenal: A storage facility for ordnance and ordnance stores.

Artillery: Heavy support weapons, normally firing in a high ballistic arc. Artillery may be of the gun (tube) type or launch rockets. Some guided-missile launchers are considered to be artillery weapons.

Automatic, Fully Automatic: A weapon that will continue to load and fire as long as the trigger is held and ammunition is available, using the energy of firing each round to load the next.

Axis: In 1936, Benito Mussolini used the term to describe Germany, Italy, and their allies as a pact around which the events of the world would turn.

Ballistic Missile: A missile that follows a ballistic arc. Ballistic missiles are unpowered for much of their flight, relying on velocity gained while their motor is running.

Ballistics: A body of science connected with the behaviour of projectiles. **Internal Ballistics** is concerned with conditions inside the weapon as it is fired; **External Ballistics** is concerned with the projectile in free flight; **Terminal Ballistics** deals with the behaviour of the projectile once it has struck the target.

Barrage: A heavy curtain of artillery fire placed in front of friendly troops to screen and protect them.

Battery: The primary artillery unit, often consisting of three to six cannon of like calibre.

Blitzkrieg: Literally translated as 'lightning war', this describes the coordinated German offensive use of tactical air power and concentrated armoured thrusts supported by fast-moving infantry.

Bolt-Action: A bolt-action weapon may be a single-shot design, loaded directly into the chamber, or fed from a magazine. Either way, the spent case is not ejected until the bolt is manually worked. This makes it easy to collect spent cartridge cases but does not allow rapid shooting.

Calibre: The diameter of the bore of a gun, or the diameter of a projectile.

Cannon: Traditionally, a smoothbore artillery piece used for more or less direct fire.

Concealment: Concealment is any obstacle or object that will obscure sight but provides little protection from a bullet or shell fragment to anyone concealed behind it.

Convoy System: The procedure of grouping Allied merchant ships for voyages across the Atlantic. The system provided for easier protection by screening vessels and for mutual support.

Displacement: The water that is forced to move by an object floating or submerged in it.

Elevation: The angle between the axis of an artillery piece and the horizontal plane.

Field Artillery: Artillery weapons that are light and mobile enough to be utilised under the often fluid conditions of the battlefield.

Flak: The abbreviation for the German word 'fliegerabwehrkanone', meaning anti-aircraft gun; a generalised term meaning antiaircraft gunfire.

Gun: An artillery cannon with a long barrel that fires on a flatter trajectory than a howitzer; a general term for a type of rifle, revolver or pistol firing a projectile.

Gun Howitzer: An artillery weapon with a long barrel capable of firing at extreme high or low angles.

Hard Point: A station on the wing or fuselage of an aircraft where munitions or fuel tanks can be carried.

Heer: The German Army of World War II.

High Explosive (HE): A warhead intended to cause damage by exploding. This results in blast damage and secondary fragmentation from objects destroyed in the explosion.

Howitzer: An artillery cannon capable of firing at a high angle of trajectory to provide plunging fire against targets.

Incendiary: A weapon designed to cause damage by burning at high temperatures.

Kriegsmarine: The German Navy of World War II.

Landing Craft: Vehicles for delivering personnel and equipment to beaches and to provide logistical and fire support. Their designations included: LCA: Landing Craft, Assault; LCI: Landing Craft, Infantry; LCI (L): Landing Craft, Infantry Large; LCM: Landing Craft, Mechanized; LCP: Landing Craft, Personnel; LCS: Landing Craft, Support; LCS (S): Landing Craft Support Small; LCT: Landing Craft, Tank;

LCV: Landing Craft, Vehicle;
LCVP: Landing Craft, Vehicle, Personnel;
LSM: Landing Ship, Medium;
LST: Landing Ship, Tank;
LSV: Landing Ship, Vehicle;
LVT: Landing Vehicle, Tracked.

Lend-Lease: US program of supplying Great Britain and later the Soviet Union with war materiel from 1941 to 1945.

Logistics: The provision of supplies, ammunition and equipment in support of combat units.

Luftwaffe: The German Air Force of World War II.

Magazine: A compartment for the storage of ordnance and weaponry.

Munitions: A general term for bombs, rockets, missiles, shells and other weapons.

Muzzle Brake: A device by which some of the muzzle gases generated by firing a weapon are redirected in a direction that counteracts recoil and the tendency of the muzzle to rise. A muzzle brake makes a powerful weapon much more controllable.

Muzzle Velocity: The speed of a projectile the moment it leaves the muzzle of a gun. Higher muzzle velocity increases the speed and penetrating power of the projectile.

Ordnance: Military weapons collectively, along with the ammunition and equipment to keep them in good repair.

PaK: Abbreviation of the German word 'panzerabwehrkanone', meaning anti-tank gun.

Panzer: German term for a tank or armoured vehicle.

Payload: The part of a bomb, missile or rocket that carries out the task assigned to it. Payloads can be destructive, such as explosives or incendiary materials, or can be non-lethal, such as smoke or propaganda leaflets.

Projectile: A fired object, such as an artillery shell.

RADAR: Radio Detection and Ranging; i.e., a method of detecting distant objects and determining their position, velocity, or other characteristics by analysis of very high frequency radio waves reflected from their surfaces.

RAF: British Royal Air Force.

Range: The horizontal distance from a weapon to its target or to the point where its projectile strikes the target or the ground.

Red Army: The armed forces of the Soviet Union.

Rifling: Spiral grooves cut into the barrel of a weapon to spin the bullet as it passes. A spun bullet is gyroscopically stabilized and therefore much more accurate than otherwise. Any longarm which possesses a rifled barrel is technically a 'rifle'.

Rocket: A device propelled by the expulsion of gases at high velocity produced by internal combustion and carrying an explosive warhead.

Self-propelled: Capable of movement via employment of a contained propulsion system.

Semi-automatic: Also referred to as 'self-loading', a semi-automatic weapon uses the energy of firing a round to eject the spent case and chamber the next. This may not always be desirable for a sniper, as spent cases may land outside his cover or attract attention as they reflect light. The internal workings of the weapon can also disrupt the aim point.

Shell: The projectile that carries a warhead or payload to the target.

Shrapnel: High velocity metal fragments dispersed by an exploding projectile.

Small Arms: Firearms light enough to be carried by infantry soldiers. The term is sometimes also loosely applied to support weapons such as man-portable mortars and machine guns.

Smoothbore: A non-rifled weapon such as a musket or shotgun, which fires a ball or group of pellets without imparting spin stabilization. Smoothbore weapons are inherently inaccurate and generally unsuitable for sniping, though a long barrel can somewhat compensate.

Sniper: The leader and main shooter of a sniper team, or a graduate of a formal sniper-training school. Also, a military marksman trained to observe and shoot from a concealed position. In popular usage, any person who uses a rifle from a concealed position.

Support Weapons: Relatively light weapons intended to support infantry from fairly close range. Support weapons include grenade launchers, machine guns and anti-tank weapons.

Suppressing Fire: High-intensity fire from small arms or support weapons aimed at the general area of the target. Suppressing fire is mainly intended to force the enemy to seek cover instead of shooting back, though it can cause casualties.

Suppressor: A device designed to reduce the noise of a weapon being fired by trapping some of the muzzle gases. It is not possible to completely 'silence' a weapon; there will always be some sound upon firing. A more popular term is 'silencer'.

Tube Artillery: Traditional gun and howitzer systems, firing a heavy shell. Conventionally, howitzers have a short barrel and fire in a high arc, while guns have a longer barrel, higher muzzle velocity and fire in a flatter arc.

Trajectory: The path followed by a bullet in flight, which will be a ballistic arc caused by the interaction of the projectile's muzzle energy, gravity and air resistance.

Warhead: The destructive payload of a weapon such as a missile or rocket.

Wehrmacht: The German armed forces, but particularly used to refer to the army.

Index